Environmental Policy Convergence in Europe

Has globalisation led to a convergence in policy-making across nations and, if so, what are the causal mechanisms? This book analyses the extent to which the environmental policies of nation states have converged over the last thirty years and whether this convergence has led to a strengthening or weakening of environmental standards (a race to the top, or a race to the bottom). It also analyses the factors that account for these developments. Based on a unique empirical data set, the study covers the development of a wide range of environmental policies in twenty-four OECD countries, including EU member states as well as Norway, Switzerland, Japan, Mexico and the USA, with particular emphasis on the impact of institutional and economic interlinkages among these countries.

KATHARINA HOLZINGER is Chair of International Relations and Conflict Management at the University of Konstanz.

CHRISTOPH KNILL is Chair of Comparative Public Policy and Administration at the University of Konstanz.

BAS ARTS is Chair of the Forest and Nature Conservation Policy Group at Wageningen University and research centre.

Environmental Policy Convergence in Europe

The Impact of International
Institutions and Trade

Edited by

KATHARINA HOLZINGER, CHRISTOPH KNILL

AND BAS ARTS

CAMBRIDGE
UNIVERSITY PRESS

CAMBRIDGE UNIVERSITY PRESS
Cambridge, New York, Melbourne, Madrid, Cape Town, Singapore, São Paulo,
Delhi

Cambridge University Press
The Edinburgh Building, Cambridge CB2 8RU, UK

Published in the United States of America by Cambridge University Press,
New York

www.cambridge.org
Information on this title: www.cambridge.org/9780521888813

© Cambridge University Press 2008

First published 2008

Printed in the United Kingdom at the University Press, Cambridge

A catalogue record for this publication is available from the British Library

Library of Congress Cataloging-in-Publication Data

Environmental policy convergence in Europe : the impact of international
institutions and trade / edited by Katharina Holzinger, Christoph Knill and
Bas Arts.
    p. cm.
    Includes bibliographical references and index.
1. Environmental policy–Economic aspects–Europe. 2. Environmental
protection–Economic aspects–Europe. 3. International cooperation.
4. Europe–Environmental conditions. I. Holzinger, Katharina. II. Knill,
Christoph. III. Arts, Bas.

    HC240.9.E5E623 2008
    333.7094–dc22

                                                          2008007228

ISBN 978-0-521-88881-3 hardback

Contents

Figures

Tables

Contributors

KATHARINA HOLZINGER is Professor of International Relations and Conflict Management in the Department of Politics and Management at the University of Konstanz, Germany.

CHRISTOPH KNILL is Professor of Political Science and Public Administration in the Department of Politics and Management at the University of Konstanz, Germany.

BAS ARTS is Professor of Forest and Nature Conservation at the University of Wageningen, the Netherlands.

STEPHAN HEICHEL is Research Associate in the Department of Politics and Management at the University of Konstanz, Germany.

HELGE JÖRGENS is Research Associate in the German Advisory Council on the Environment and the Environment Research Group at the Free University of Berlin, Germany.

JELMER KAMSTRA is Researcher in the Centre for International Development Issues at Radboud University Nijmegen, the Netherlands.

DUNCAN LIEFFERINK is Senior Researcher in the Department of Political Sciences of the Environment at Radboul University, Nijmegen, the Netherlands.

JEROEN OOIJEVAAR is a researcher at 101 Research, a consultancy in Voorburg, the Netherlands.

JESSICA PAPE   is Research Associate in the Department of Politics and Management at the University of Konstanz, Germany.

THOMAS SOMMERER   is Research Associate in the Department of Politics and Management at the University of Konstanz, Germany.

SIETSKE VEENMAN   is Researcher in the Department of Political Sciences of the Environment at Radboud University Nijmegen, the Netherlands.

Preface

This book is the result of a collaborative European research project. After first ideas to organise a joint project on the convergence of environmental policies had been put forward at a 'tapas' bar in Barcelona in autumn 2000, seven political scientists at five universities participated in the common endeavour: Christoph Knill (University of Jena, and later on, Konstanz, coordination), Katharina Holzinger (Max Planck Institute for Research on Collective Goods Bonn, and later on, University of Konstanz), Martin Jänicke and Helge Jörgens (Free University Berlin), Bas Arts (University of Wageningen) and Duncan Liefferink (University of Nijmegen) and Andrea Lenschow (University of Salzburg and later on, Osnabrück). In a series of very inspiring, enjoyable and sometimes exciting meetings – one of them took place on 11 September 2001 – this group developed a joint research design and a proposal under the Fifth Framework Programme of the European Commission.

Under this programme, our research was supported by the RTD programme 'Improving the human research potential and the socio-economic knowledge base', contract no. HPSE-CT-2002-00103. Funds were provided from January 2003 to June 2006. This way the initial group could be complemented by a full dozen senior and junior researchers: Stephan Heichel, Jessica Pape, Maren Riepe, Jale Tosun and Natascha Warta in Konstanz, Thomas Sommerer and Tobias Meier in Hamburg, Per-Olof Busch in Berlin, Johan Albrecht, Jelmer Kamstra, Jeroen Ooijevaar and Sietske Veenman in Nijmegen, and Dieter Pesendorfer in Salzburg. Some of them joined us for the full period of time, others stayed only for a while to carry out certain tasks.

The book presents only part of the research that was under-taken for this project. It presents the results of the quantitative study providing answers to the questions of how much, in which direction and for which reasons environmental policies in the developed world have converged over the last thirty years. However, the project entails also a second study that strives to analyse the causal processes of policy convergence more deeply. To this end, case studies on the development of five environmental policies in four countries have been carried out. These case studies will appear in a separate book. Two further volumes that emerged in the context of this project have already been published: a special issue 'Cross-national policy con-vergence. Causes, concepts and empirical findings' of the *Journal of European Public Policy*, edited by Christoph Knill in 2005, and a special issue 'Transfer, Diffusion und Konvergenz von Politiken' of *Politische Vierteljahresschrift*, edited by Katharina Holzinger, Christoph Knill and Helge Jörgens in 2007.

The editors would like to thank the European Commission and all universities and other organisations that supported the project directly or indirectly. We are indebted to the above-mentioned members of the project, who spent considerable effort and time in order to make the project a success. It was great fun to work with them all. Moreover, we are grateful to a great number of subcon-tractors in twenty-four countries who helped collecting the data on environmental policies we needed. Without them, their knowledge on national environmental policies, and their native language skills, we would not have been able to pursue our research question. Finally, we would like to thank Helen Förster for her excellent assistance in editing the final book manuscript.

Abbreviations

CEE	Central and Eastern Europe
CP	Communicative potential
EFTA	European Free Trade Association
ENC	Encompassingness
EU	European Union
GATT	General Agreement on Tariffs and Trade
GDP	Gross Domestic Product
IUCN	The World Conservation Union
NAFTA	North American Free Trade Agreement
NEPI	New Environmental Policy Instruments
NGO	Non-governmental organisation
NO	Non-obligatory policies
NT	Non-trade-related policies
OB	Obligatory policies
OECD	Organisation for Economic Cooperation and Development
OP	Obligatory potential
OSCE	Organisation for Security and Cooperation in Europe
TEU	Treaty on European Union
TR	Trade-related policies
UK	United Kingdom
UN	United Nations
UNEP	United Nations Environmental Programme
US	United States
WTO	World Trade Organisation

1 Introduction

KATHARINA HOLZINGER, CHRISTOPH KNILL
AND BAS ARTS

One of the key issues of globalisation research in the social sciences
is the question of whether globalisation leads to the convergence of
political institutions, policies, the legal order and societal structures
(Guillén 2001: 235). Is the world becoming ever more similar as a
result of globalisation and Europeanisation as the 'world society
approach' (Meyer et al. 1997) implies? Does the strong growth of
economic and institutional interlinkages between nation states
lead to increasingly similar policy measures across countries? Or is
the search for convergence emerging from the domestic impact
of globalisation and European integration 'an impossible quest'
(Dimitrova and Steunenberg 2000: 201), because domestic responses
to global or European challenges are strongly influenced by existing
domestic structures and institutions (see, for example, Cowles,
Caporaso and Risse 2001; Héritier et al. 2001; Knill 2001)?

Although there has been an intensified and renewed debate on
the convergence and divergence of national policies in recent years,
we still have a limited understanding of the phenomenon of policy
convergence. What explains the adoption of similar policies across
countries over time? If it exists, is convergence of policies driven by
economic processes or by emerging structures of global governance,
that is, the rise of regional and global political institutions? Under
which conditions can we expect domestic policies to converge or
to diverge further apart? Why do countries converge on some policy
measures, but not on others? In the literature, many factors have
been suggested in order to account for the mixed empirical evidence
of both convergence and divergence. However, there is still a lack
of systematic theoretical and empirical investigations about their
actual explanatory relevance. There are few quantitative studies

which investigate the convergence of policies in a certain domain over a large number of countries and an extended period of time and which combine this approach with causal analysis.

Against this background, the purpose of this book is twofold. In empirical terms, we address two important research questions for which the existing literature so far provides no systematic answers: (1) To what extent can we observe a convergence of environmental policies across countries? (2) In which direction do environmental protection levels develop; that is, does convergence coincide with an environmental race to the top or a race to the bottom? In theoretical terms, our central focus is on the role that international factors play in this development. More specifically, we investigate if and to what extent the observed patterns can be traced to growing institutional and economic interlinkages among nation states. What role is played by international cooperation, transnational communication and regulatory competition between states with regard to the convergence and direction of environmental policies and standards?

We chose environmental policy as the empirical subject for several reasons. First, there is a large amount of – partly conflicting – theoretical literature for this policy domain, analysing policy diffusion or policy convergence and predicting races to the bottom or, alternatively, to the top of the regulatory level. Second, there is some empirical evidence of a global spread of certain policies. However, we still lack systematic investigations on a larger scale. Third, environmental policy is, on the one hand, an important, complex and interesting policy field that deserves thorough analysis; on the other hand, environmental policies are measurable and thus amenable to systematic and quantitative comparison.

In view of the theoretical questions addressed, the focus of this study is far from being restricted to environmental policy, but has important implications and linkages to many areas which in recent years have become booming research industries. This holds first and foremost for research on the domestic impact of globalisation and Europeanisation. In both areas the question of whether growing institutional and economic interlinkages at the global and supranational level make a difference for the formulation and implementation of domestic policies is at the centre of many studies. Notwithstanding an ever growing number of studies in this field, we still have a limited understanding with regard to the causal driving forces behind global and European influences as well as the conditions and consequences of their effects. The underlying study contributes to this debate in varying ways. On the one hand, we investigate and compare systematically the specific impact of three potential causes of global and European impacts on national policy-making, namely the role of regulatory cooperation at the level of international organisations and the European Union (EU), the integration of states into transnational communication networks, and regulatory competition as a consequence of the growing integration of global and supranational economies. On the other hand, we provide a thorough analysis of the consequences of these developments. Do they lead to the convergence of policies and, if yes, at which regulatory level?

The focus of this book, however, goes beyond issues of globalisation and Europeanisation. It is analytically and theoretically closely linked to the research literature on policy diffusion, policy transfer and policy convergence. The starting point of studies in these fields is the question of which factors are most crucial in driving the cross-national spread of policies or their growing similarity across countries. To what extent are such developments caused by international or domestic factors? To what extent are such developments simply the result of independent but parallel problem pressures with which states are confronted? On the basis of the underlying study, we are able to make important contributions to these questions. This holds true not only with regard to the relative impact of different international driving forces, but also their relative impact in comparison to potential domestic factors (which we also include in our explanatory models).

In order to achieve these objectives the underlying study employs a comprehensive and detailed macro-quantitative methodology. This is a precondition not only for giving a broad descriptive view of the development in this field, but also for doing causal analysis.

We therefore analyse the policy development for forty different environmental policy measures in twenty-four member countries of the Organisation for Economic Cooperation and Development (OECD) (including the EU-15 [except Luxembourg], Bulgaria, Hungary, Norway, Poland, Romania, Slovakia and Switzerland as well as Japan, Mexico and the United States) over a period of thirty years (from 1970 to 2000). This way, we are able to make rather precise statements both on the extent to which the environmental policy similarity of the countries under study has increased, and on the extent to which this development coincided with races to the top or races to the bottom.

As the required data were not available from existing sources we collected them by means of an expert survey in all twenty-four countries. On this basis we are able to give a full account of the development of this policy field, that is, to describe and explain the degree of convergence and to describe and explain the direction of convergence.

The analysis is based on two innovative methodological concepts for the measurement of policy convergence. First, we depart from existing approaches which assess the degree of convergence by merely relying on aggregate measures, such as the variation coefficient. Instead, and complementary to existing measurement concepts, we base our assessment of convergence on the systematic comparison of country pairs (pair approach). This way, we are able to make insightful statements for the development of a country pair compared to the whole sample, a possibility that is not available when solely relying on conventional approaches. Second, for the measurement of the direction of convergence, we developed a new concept, namely, the gap approach. It measures the changes of a country's distance from an exemplary model (such as, for instance, the country with the strictest environmental standard during the observation period). As we will show, both the pair and the gap approach offer important departures for advancing our understanding and knowledge of processes of convergence and diffusion.

In our analysis, we find an impressive degree of environmental policy convergence between the countries under investigation. Between 1970 and 2000, the policy similarity of the average country pair increased from 3.5 per cent to 5.6 per cent. At the same time, there is no evidence for often-feared scenarios of races to the bottom. On the contrary, levels of environmental protection steadily became stricter over the years.

When looking at the different effects of international factors on the degree and direction of policy convergence, several findings have to be emphasised. First, it is rather obvious that regulatory cooperation both at the level of international organisations as well as the EU has an important explanatory potential in accounting for the increases in policy similarity and protection levels. Second, and this is probably much less obvious, the mere fact that nation states communicate and exchange information with each other in trans-national networks plays an almost equally important role in explaining the observed developments. Finally, while both cooperative and communicative institutional interlinkages between states are of very high explanatory relevance, we find no support for effects of regulatory competition, neither with regard to the degree nor the direction of convergence. This implies that there is no evidence for races to the bottom as a result of economic integration.

In the following chapters, we develop these findings. Chapter 2 clarifies the underlying concepts of convergence and the links to theoretical discussions on convergence in the broader research context of international relations and comparative politics. The theoretical background of the study is elaborated in chapter 3. Based on the analysis of varying causal factors, we develop hypotheses on the extent to which the main independent variables under study – international harmonisation, transnational communication and regulatory competition – affect the degree and direction of cross-national policy convergence. At the same time, corresponding hypotheses for the impact of varying domestic factors are deduced from existing theories. In chapter 4, we present our research design, the operationalisation of dependent and independent variables and the methods of data collection in closer detail.

On the basis of these theoretical and methodological considerations, the following chapters are dedicated to the presentation of our empirical results. For this purpose, we proceed in three steps. In chapter 5, we provide an aggregate analysis of our empirical findings by relying on conventional approaches to measuring convergence. As we will show, these approaches only allow for the description rather than a thorough causal explanation of our results. We therefore complement this analysis by investigating and explaining the degree of convergence on the basis of the pair approach (chapter 6). In the final step, we account for the observed direction of convergence on the basis of the gap approach (chapter 7). In chapter 8, we summarise our theoretical and empirical findings and discuss the broader research implications of our study.

2 State of the art – conceptualising environmental policy convergence

KATHARINA HOLZINGER, HELGE JÖRGENS
AND CHRISTOPH KNILL

2.1 INTRODUCTION

The study of policy convergence has received considerable attention both in comparative politics and in the field of international studies. Interestingly, both disciplines have approached the subject from opposite starting points and with differing methodologies. Whereas in the field of international studies theoretically derived expectations of an increasing *similarity* of states and political systems driven by economic or ideational forces constituted a dominant thread in the early convergence literature (for a comprehensive overview see Drezner 2001), comparative studies initially focused more on the explanation of empirically observed *differences* between national political systems and programmes (Lundqvist 1974, 1980). Only recently have the two research strands effectively merged into an integrated study of policy convergence that increasingly challenges the traditional boundaries between comparative politics and international relations.

In this chapter we first introduce the concept of policy convergence and explain how it relates to similar concepts like policy transfer, policy diffusion or isomorphism. In a second step we review the existing empirical research on environmental policy convergence both in comparative politics and in international relations. Based on this overview, and drawing more broadly on the general convergence literature, we systematise the major causes of policy convergence that have been identified in these studies. We distinguish between causal mechanisms which translate pressures at the international level into domestic policy change and, possibly, into convergence of domestic policies, and facilitating factors which operate at the level of individual countries or specific policies. By including not only processes at the international level which have been stressed mainly by scholars of international relations, but also country-specific factors which lie at the core of most studies in the field of comparative politics, we attempt to cross the borders of these two disciplines. In the end we develop a heuristic typology which illustrates how the different causal factors and mechanisms may relate to the phenomenon of policy convergence. This typology provides a useful analytical and heuristic tool both for quantitative studies on policy convergence as they are presented in this book and for qualitative case studies which ideally should complement quantitative approaches.

2.2 POLICY CONVERGENCE AND RELATED CONCEPTS

While there is a broad consensus on the definition of policy convergence as 'the tendency of policies to grow more alike, in the form of increasing similarity in structures, processes, and performances' (Drezner 2001: 53; see also Kerr 1983: 3), the empirical and theoretical assessment of policy convergence is generally hampered by the use of different, partially overlapping concepts (Tews 2005a). Policy convergence is often used interchangeably with related notions, such as isomorphism, policy diffusion or policy transfer, a practice that often leads to terminological and eventually even to analytical confusion. Thus, in spite of the general proximity of these concepts, a thorough analysis needs to acknowledge that these concepts stand for analytically distinct fields of study. In the following we will point out the differences between the concepts of policy diffusion, transfer and isomorphism according to four important dimensions: their analytical focus, their empirical focus, their dependent variable and their level of analysis (for an overview, see table 2.1). In doing so, we will demonstrate how they relate to the idea of policy convergence, which stands at the centre of our own analysis in this book.

The study of *policy transfer* emerged in the early 1990s as a sub-field of comparative politics (Dolowitz and Marsh 1996, 2000;

Table 2.1 *Policy convergence and related concepts*

	Policy convergence	Isomorphism	Policy transfer	Policy diffusion
Analytical focus	effects	effects	process	process
Empirical focus	policy characteristics	organisational structures	policy characteristics	policy characteristics
Dependent variable	similarity change	similarity change	transfer content transfer process	adoption pattern

Source: adapted from Knill 2005: 768.

Radaelli 2000; Rose 1991, 1993). Dolowitz and Marsh (2000: 5) define policy transfer as 'the process by which knowledge about policies, administrative arrangements, institutions and ideas in one political system (past or present) is used in the development of policies, administrative arrangements, institutions and ideas in another political system'. The analytical focus of studies of policy transfer therefore is on processes rather than results. Their level of analysis is the individual country – or any other political system – which applies information about the policies of other political units. As policy transfer is not restricted to merely imitating policies of other countries, but can include profound changes in the content of the exchanged policies (Kern, Jörgens and Jänicke 2000; Rose 1991), policy transfer studies, more than the other types of study, place a strong empirical focus on the characteristics of policies and how they change during the transfer process.

Due to its micro-level perspective and due to its concern with the modification of policies during the transfer process, the relation of policy transfer to policy convergence is only an indirect one: policy transfer may, but need not, lead to cross-national policy convergence. Methodologically, the micro-perspective inherent in the concept of policy transfer is mirrored in the predominance of case studies within this field of study. Generally, these case studies concentrate on one or a few countries, describing and analysing in depth the process by which foreign policy experiences are used or even imitated domestically. They focus on the actors and institutions that promote or constrain the adoption of external policies and ask how the specific features of the policy at hand affect its transferability. Their major dependent variables, therefore, are the process and content of individual instances of policy transfer.

Similar to transfer, *policy diffusion* typically refers to processes rather than outcomes (Elkins and Simmons 2005). Essentially, diffusion studies explore how policies, programmes and ideas travel among a large number of political systems. However, while some studies equate diffusion with the more general notion of spread (Eyestone 1977; for a recent example see Marcussen 2005), there is a growing scholarly consensus to restrict the concept of diffusion to those cases where different national adoptions of one and the same policy or programme are directly connected to one another. Diffusion then occurs when a policy decision taken by one government leads other governments to take a similar decision (Simmons and Elkins 2004: 171–2). Policy diffusion, in other words, is the result of multilateral interdependence. This narrower usage is supported by Everett Rogers' (Rogers 2003: 5) seminal definition of diffusion as 'the process by which an innovation is communicated through certain channels over time'. The main focus of policy diffusion studies thus lies on the mechanisms by which policy innovations are communicated among a larger number of countries.

There is, however, a still ongoing dispute among diffusion scholars as to the interpretation of 'communication' and 'interdependence'. For one group of scholars, diffusion includes all conceivable channels of influence between countries, for example (1) the voluntary adoption of policy models that have been communicated in the international system, (2) diffusion processes triggered by legally binding harmonisation requirements defined in international agreements or in supranational regulations and (3) the imposition of policies on other countries through external actors (for recent examples see Meseguer 2005, who distinguishes between horizontal and top-down mechanisms of diffusion, and Radaelli 2005). According to this concept of diffusion, no distinction of different forms of cross-national interlinkages and processes of influence is made. In contrast to this definition and more recently, a second group of scholars suggests a narrower focus of the concept, explicitly restricting diffusion to processes of voluntary policy transfer (Braun and Gilardi 2006; Busch and Jörgens 2005c; Elkins and Simmons 2005; Jörgens 2004; Kern 2000; Tews 2005a). In this view, '(d)iffusion is the spreading of innovations due to communication instead of hierarchy or collective decision-making within international institutions' (Tews 2005b: 65). Consequently, diffusion is conceived as a distinctive group of causal factors that drive international policy convergence rather than a general process that is caused by the operation of varying (voluntary, obligatory and coercive) influence channels. It comprises various mechanisms such as imitation, learning, persuasion, contagion, socialisation or 'taken-for-grantedness' (Braun and Gilardi 2006; Busch, Jörgens and Tews 2005). Diffusion, in this narrower understanding, is only one of several classes of mechanisms that may contribute to cross-national policy convergence. Other possible convergence mechanisms not included within the notion of diffusion are legal harmonisation through international accords, coercive imposition through economic or political conditionality, or similar, but independent, national decision-making.

We are thus confronted with two different conceptions of policy diffusion. On the one hand, the concept describes the process of spreading policies across countries with the possible result of cross-national policy convergence, regardless of the causal factors that are driving this development (e.g., regulatory competition, international harmonisation, imposition). On the other hand, diffusion is conceived as a distinctive causal factor leading to policy convergence by means of voluntary transfer of policy models (in contrast to obliged or imposed forms of transfer). Both conceptions of diffusion are analytically well-grounded and applied in the literature; it is therefore more important to point out their differences than to argue in favour of one or the other approach.

Policy diffusion and policy transfer share the assumption that governments do not learn about policy practices randomly, but rather through common affiliations, negotiations and institutional membership (Simmons and Elkins 2004). Both transfer and diffusion processes hence require that actors are informed about the policy choices of others (Strang and Meyer 1993: 488). Given these conceptual overlaps, diffusion is often equated with policy transfer (Kern 2000; Tews 2002). Notwithstanding these conceptual overlaps, however, analytical differences between diffusion and transfer should not be overlooked. Diffusion and transfer studies differ considerably with regard to their level of analysis and their dependent variable. Diffusion studies usually adopt a macro-level perspective. Their dependent variables are *general patterns* of policy adoption within or across political systems. Analyses of policy transfer, on the other hand, focus on the underlying causes and contents of *singular processes* of bilateral policy exchange. The diffusion literature focuses more on the spatial, cultural and socio-economic reasons for particular adoption patterns rather than on the reasons for individual adoptions as such (Bennett 1991: 221; Jordana and Levi-Faur 2005). Diffusion studies often reveal a rather robust adoption pattern, with the cumulative adoption of a policy innovation over time following an S-shaped curve (Gray 1973).

From these considerations it follows that policy transfer and policy diffusion differ from policy convergence in important ways. First, differences exist with respect to the underlying analytical focus. While diffusion and transfer are concerned with process patterns, convergence studies place particular emphasis on outcomes. Transfer and diffusion thus reflect processes which under certain circumstances might result in policy convergence. This does not imply, however, that the empirical observation of converging policies must necessarily be the result of transfer or diffusion (Drezner

2001). It is well conceivable that policy convergence is the result of similar but relatively isolated domestic events. Second, the concepts differ in their dependent variable. Convergence studies typically seek to explain changes in policy similarity over time. By contrast, transfer studies investigate the content and process of policy transfer as the dependent variable, while the focus of diffusion research is on the explanation of adoption patterns over time (Elkins and Simmons 2005; Gilardi 2005; Jordana and Levi-Faur 2005; Levi-Faur 2005).

The particular focus underlying the analysis of policy convergence places it in close proximity to the concept of *isomorphism* which has been developed in organisation sociology. Isomorphism is defined as a process of homogenisation that 'forces one unit in a population to resemble other units that face the same set of environmental conditions' (DiMaggio and Powell 1991: 66). The central question underlying studies on isomorphism refers to the mechanisms through which organisations become more similar over time. There is thus a broad overlap between studies on policy convergence and isomorphism, with the major difference between the two concepts being on their empirical focus and their level of analysis. The literature on isomorphism concentrates on organisational change and examines variations in similarity of organisational and institutional structures and cultures over time. Studies on policy convergence and diffusion, by contrast, focus on changes in national or state policy characteristics. Policy transfer studies also focus on policy characteristics.

The above considerations underline the need to apply a precise conception of policy convergence that allows for a clear differentiation between convergence and the related concepts of policy transfer, diffusion and isomorphism. We have seen that – notwithstanding certain overlaps – the concepts differ in considerable ways. Having clarified our understanding of policy convergence, the following section summarises existing empirical results with regard to policy convergence in the environmental field.

2.3 ENVIRONMENTAL POLICY CONVERGENCE – EMPIRICAL RESULTS

Having discussed the relationship between policy convergence and other analytical concepts that are often used synonymously in the literature, we are still left with the question by which factors cross-national policy convergence is caused. What are the causal mechanisms behind environmental policy convergence? This question is addressed in the rest of this chapter. In a first step, this section will give an overview of the existing empirical findings on the transfer, diffusion and convergence of environmental policies As we will show, a rich body of diffusion and convergence studies has evolved in the field of environmental policy, turning this policy area into a major subject of convergence studies in general (see also Heichel, Pape and Sommerer 2005). In order to point out the disciplinary origins of the different studies, we broadly differentiate between the sub-fields of comparative politics on the one hand and international studies on the other.

Comparative studies originally focused predominantly on the national determinants of policy choice and policy change. Consequently, their theoretical point of departure was a general assumption of cross-national diversity of environmental policies due to different institutional frameworks, actor constellations, regulatory styles and problem pressures (Kitschelt 1983; Lundqvist 1974). However, comparative studies quickly detected that in spite of widely differing national styles of regulation, advanced industrial countries showed great similarities in deciding which risks required positive state action (agenda setting) and in their successes and failures to actually reduce environmental pollution (policy impacts) (Badaracco 1985; Brickman, Jasanoff and Ilgen 1985; Vogel 1986). While these studies did not directly pose the question of convergence or divergence of national environmental policies, their common finding of 'different styles, similar content' (Knoepfel et al. 1987) was a first step in that direction. In a summary of the findings of this first set of comparative environmental policy analyses Knoepfel et al. (1987: 184) conclude that 'the hypothesis . . . concerning the long-term convergence of policy outputs in environmental regulation must be tested and questioned in a more comprehensive analysis'.

Building on these early findings, a more recent set of comparative studies in the field of environmental politics began to systematically compare the development of domestic capacities for environmental policy-making throughout the entire group of Western industrialised countries. In an empirical assessment of the preconditions of effective environmental policy in OECD countries Jänicke found that besides domestic political, institutional and socio-economic factors, global processes such as policy learning, diffusion and convergence had become independent sources of any country's capacity to address environmental problems (Jänicke 1992: 57, 1996: 28). Especially the creation of basic domestic institutions for environmental protection such as national environmental ministries, environmental protection agencies, general environmental laws or the adoption of environmental protection as a constitutional goal were highly influenced by the actions of international organisations such as the United Nations (UN) and by processes of imitation and learning among related countries. As a consequence, many Western industrialised states responded in a surprisingly homogeneous way to the environmental challenge that had entered the domestic and international policy agendas in the late 1960s and early 1970s (Jörgens 1996). A systematic in-depth comparison by Jänicke and Weidner across thirty industrialised and developing countries confirmed and extended these findings. It reveals a global convergence of governance patterns in environmental policy that covered not only domestic institutions, but also sectoral environmental laws, specific instruments, strategies, actor constellations and even the strengthening of societal capacities (Jänicke and Weidner 1997; Weidner and Jänicke 2002). This convergence did not result from similar but independent reactions to comparable problem pressures, but rather from the increasing number, scope and activity of international environmental regimes and organisations. In addition, information about best practice in environmental protection is increasingly spreading not only among national policy-makers, but also among environmental non-governmental organisations (NGOs), scientific experts and within the business sector (Weidner 2002: 1355–6).

While being increasingly aware of the growing importance of processes of cross-national policy convergence, comparative studies during most of the 1990s still did not search systematically for processes of transfer, diffusion and convergence of environmental policies and their analysis was largely confined to ad hoc explanations. Conscious of these shortcomings, a new generation of studies began to focus explicitly on processes of cross-national diffusion and convergence of environmental policies. On the one hand, these studies were interested in the degree of convergence. On the other hand, they tried to identify the mechanisms that lead to cross-national convergence of environmental policies.

In a systematic analysis of the international diffusion of five selected environmental policy innovations (national environmental ministries, ecolabelling schemes, environmental strategies, CO_2 taxes and soil protection laws) Kern, Jörgens and Jänicke (2000) find strong evidence for the importance of transnational imitation and learning as well as the impact of international institutions on the domestic adoption of environmental policies. However, the extent to which the five environmental policy innovations spread internationally varied considerably. Based on these empirical findings, the authors identify a complex set of explanatory factors including international dynamics as well as the specific domestic political and institutional contexts. In addition, they find that the properties of individual policy innovations and the structure of the underlying environmental problem strongly affect their transferability. The extremely slow spread of soil protection policies shows that low visibility of environmental problems and the lack of technological standard solutions can hamper the spread of regulatory initiatives. Similarly, redistributive policies like environmental taxes are likely to meet with strong domestic resistance and thus proliferate significantly more slowly than environmental ministries or information-based instruments.

These findings are confirmed and broadened by a subsequent comparison of the spread of twenty-two environmental policy innovations across forty-three countries from 1945 to 2000 (Busch and Jörgens 2005a, 2005b). Especially from the early 1970s a considerable extent of policy convergence can be observed throughout the OECD and Central and Eastern Europe (CEE) with strong peaks around the two major UN environmental conferences in 1972 and 1992 (see also Binder 2005: 207). The main driving forces behind this convergence can be divided roughly into three analytically distinct groups of mechanisms operating at the inter- and transnational level: (1) voluntary imitation, rational lesson-drawing, 'scripted' behaviour based on a strong sense of appropriateness, and learning (i.e., diffusion in the narrow sense defined above); (2) compliance with binding European and international law (i.e., legal harmonisation); and (3) political or financial conditionality, for example during the process of EU enlargement (i.e., imposition) (for a distinction of these three groups of mechanisms see Bennett 1991; Busch and Jörgens 2005c; Busch, Jörgens and Tews 2005; Holzinger and Knill 2005b; Howlett 2000; Jörgens 2004; Tews 2005b). However, international driving forces did not affect all policy innovations and all countries alike, but were either enforced or hampered by the properties of individual policy innovations and a wide array of factors at the domestic level. Besides the three groups of international mechanisms, independent responses to pressing environmental problems also played an important role in the observed policy convergence.

In North America scholars have focused repeatedly on the transfer and convergence of environmental policies between Canada and the US. Hoberg and colleagues (Hoberg 1991; Hoberg, Banting and Simeon 1999) identify four types of international influence that promote convergence of Canadian environmental policy with the US: (1) international environmental agreements; (2) economic integration, including trade agreements such as the Canada–US Free Trade Agreement, NAFTA and the World Trade Organisation (WTO); (3) the cross-national transfer of ideas; and (4) cross-border lobbying by environmentalist groups. Focusing on implementation styles rather than policy outputs, Howlett (2000) finds a different pattern of environmental policy convergence between the US and Canada. Based on a comparison of three phases of US and Canadian environmental policy-making, he argues that a form of strong convergence is emerging, 'in which both countries are moving not towards each other but towards a third, common, style, that is associated with the development of self-regulation and voluntary initiatives under the influence of New Public Management ideas and principles' (Howlett 2000: 305). This 'emulation-based convergence' was spurred by general sets of policy ideas which circulated in the international sphere and had profound sectoral effects in both countries.

Besides the international system, the federal system of the US continues to be a major subject of convergence and especially diffusion studies. While some of the most influential work on policy diffusion was conducted in the American states (Berry and Berry 1990; Gray 1973; Mintrom 1997; Mintrom and Vergari 1998; Walker 1969), these studies rarely focused on issues of environmental policy. In a notable exception, Daley and Garand (2005) examine the spread of state programmes for the clean-up of abandoned hazardous waste sites. While the most urgent cases of soil contamination are addressed by the Federal Superfund programme, states are responsible for cleaning up the remaining hazardous waste sites in their jurisdiction. The article finds weak convergence where some states adopted strict programmes similar to the Federal Superfund while others opted for less ambitious programmes relying more strongly on voluntary initiatives. Testing both internal determinants and external diffusion hypotheses, the authors find state wealth, problem pressure and regional diffusion effects to be the most important determinants of strict state programmes. Moreover, they find that vertical diffusion from the federal to the state level has an important effect on state policy choices.

While comparative studies started out looking for cross-national difference and found a surprising amount of similarity, *Europeanisation research* and *international studies* approached the subject of environmental policy convergence exactly the opposite way. Scholars of Europeanisation quickly detected that the powerful economic as well as political homogenising pressures within the EU do not necessarily lead to uniform action at the level of member states, but often produce a quite heterogeneous patchwork of institutions, instruments and policy styles (Héritier and Knill 2001). In a comparative assessment of environmental policies in ten EU member states, Jordan and Liefferink (2004, 2005) examine 'how far the EU has succeeded in encouraging the content, structure and style of national environmental policies to converge'. They find that, in spite of the enormous importance that the EU has acquired over the last decades in the field of environmental policy, only limited convergence of national environmental policies in the EU member states has occurred. The study shows that convergence is strongest with regard to the setting of individual environmental standards, a fact that is explained by the EU's ability to issue binding environmental legislation. The study also finds that 'some structural developments were shared by several member states, notably regarding the roles of national environmental ministries, national parliaments and NGOs' as a result of learning processes within the EU decision-making bodies. By contrast, however, 'national decision-making procedures, coordination mechanisms and political traditions . . . have remained essentially the same in spite of EU membership' (Jordan and Liefferink 2005: 111).

In a similar study on the effects of European environmental and transport policies on national administrative styles and structures in the United Kingdom (UK) and Germany, Knill (2001) finds a varied pattern of change which includes elements of convergence towards a European model as well as divergence and domestic persistence. While a certain degree of Europeanisation of national administrations can be observed, deeply entrenched institutional traditions at the domestic level stand in the way of a more far-reaching convergence. Paradoxically, the impact of EU policies on national administrations grows and cross-national convergence increases as the degree of legal obligation of European policies declines. Ultimately, a European steering mode based on competition or communication proves superior to a 'coercive' approach as regards its impact on administrative convergence in EU member states (Knill and Lenschow 2005).

At the level of policy instruments Jordan *et al.* (2002) examine the spread of new environmental policy instruments (NEPIs – namely voluntary agreements and market-based instruments like eco taxes or tradable permits) in four EU member states and by the EU itself. In spite of a general increase in the use of voluntary and market-based instruments, the authors find little convergence with regard to the specific way these instruments are applied and implemented in the different national contexts and at the EU level. As in other Europeanisation studies, domestic institutional constraints are found to partially neutralise the international diffusion effects as 'states (and the EU) usually alter NEPIs transferred from elsewhere in order to ensure that they fit in with wider national (and supranational) institutional features and regulatory styles' (Jordan *et al.* 2002: 156).

In the field of *international studies*, the theoretically derived expectation of cross-national environmental policy convergence was most pronounced. However, the most widespread of these hypotheses, the prediction of a global race-to-the-bottom regarding environmental, consumer or worker protection, has repeatedly been challenged on empirical grounds. In his study on the relationship between trade policies and protective consumer and environmental regulation Vogel (1995, 1997) refutes the race-to-the-bottom hypothesis by showing that 'competition from nations with weaker environmental regulations has not prevented richer, greener nations from strengthening their own regulatory standards' (Vogel 1997: 556). On the contrary, he finds substantial evidence that nations are increasingly adopting the stricter standards of their richer and greener trading partners. In a similar vein, but from an institutionalist perspective, Botcheva and

Martin (2001) use the example of the Montreal Protocol on the Protection of the Ozone Layer to illustrate their theoretically derived hypothesis that the threat of significant negative environmental externalities, combined with strong international institutions which formulate clear environmental protection goals, provide transparency and secure compliance, will provide a strong incentive for countries to converge in their efforts to save the ozone layer. Both studies point towards a significant degree of environmental policy convergence at a high level of environmental protection.

In a large-scale empirical analysis Frank, Hironaka and Schofers (2000) examine the global proliferation of five characteristic features of modern environmentalism – the creation of national parks, the establishment of national branches of international environmental associations, membership in intergovernmental environmental organisations, environmental impact assessment laws and the creation of national environmental ministries – over the twentieth century. Testing both for domestic and international factors they find that for all five measures the top-down international explanation provides a stronger explanation of the observable environmental policy convergence than the bottom-up domestic alternative. The authors interpret these findings as a sign of an ongoing redefinition of the constitutive idea of the modern 'nation state' to include environmental protection as one of its basic responsibilities. Especially countries with strong ties to world society prove to be receptive to this emerging global norm. In a similar vein, Meyer et al. (1997) describe the creation of a world environmental regime based predominantly on discourse, science and societal association. Contrary to the predominant approaches in international relations, nation states are not seen as constitutive elements of this world environmental regime. By contrast, the authors show that the regime evolved long before nation states entered the global environmental arena. Rather than shaping this global regime, nation states' attitudes towards environmental issues themselves are to a certain extent shaped by this global discourse. 'Most nation states had no central organised structures (such as ministries) dealing with the environment until late in the process. This reflects, in a sense, a top-down history, in which the rise of universalistic discourse and organisation rather belatedly construct nation states' aims and responsibilities more than the bottom-up political processes of power and interest that are mentioned more often' (Meyer *et al.* 1997: 645). While this study does not explicitly measure or explain environmental policy convergence, it describes a wider process of worldwide societal and governmental homogenisation with regard to the relationship of human society to nature.

2.4 CAUSES OF CROSS-NATIONAL POLICY CONVERGENCE

As has been shown in the previous section, the literature on environmental policy convergence and its related concepts offers a broad range of causal factors to explain changes in the similarity of policies across countries. At a very general level, these factors can be grouped into two categories: (1) causal mechanisms triggering the convergent policy changes across countries and (2) facilitating factors which affect the effectiveness of these mechanisms. The factors relevant in these two categories are summarised in table 2.2 and will be discussed in more detail in the following sections.

Table 2.2 *Causal mechanisms and facilitating factors of cross-national policy convergence*

Causal mechanisms	Independent problem-solving
	Imposition
	International harmonisation
	Regulatory competition
	Transnational communication
Facilitating factors	Cultural similarity
	Socio-economic similarity (income)
	Pre-existing policy similarity

2.4.1 Causal mechanisms

With respect to causal mechanisms, both the general literature on policy convergence and respective studies in the field of environmental policy emphasise rather similar aspects which refer basically to five central factors (cf. Bennett 1991; DiMaggio and Powell 1991; Dolowitz and Marsh 2000; Drezner 2001; Hoberg 2001; Holzinger and Knill 2004, 2005b).

First, cross-national policy convergence might simply be the result of similar, but *independent responses* of different countries to the same contextual factors. The major contextual factor in our field of research is parallel environmental problem pressure. Policy convergence then is caused by similar policy problems which countries react to independently (Bennett 1991: 231).

Second, emphasis is placed on the *harmonisation* of national policies through international or supranational law. Countries are obliged to comply with international rules on which they have deliberately agreed in multilateral negotiations.

Third, some studies emphasise convergence effects stemming from the *imposition* of policies. Imposition refers to constellations where countries or international organisations force other countries to adopt certain policies by exploiting asymmetries in political or economic power.

Fourth, *regulatory competition* emerging from the increasing economic integration of European and global markets has been identified as one important factor that drives the mutual adjustment of policies across countries.

Finally, cross-national policy convergence can be the result of *transnational communication*. Under this heading, several mechanisms are summarised which all have in common that they predominantly rest on communication and information exchange among countries (see Holzinger and Knill 2005b). They include lesson-drawing (where countries deliberately seek to learn from successful problem-solving activities in other countries), joint problem-solving activities within transnational elite networks or

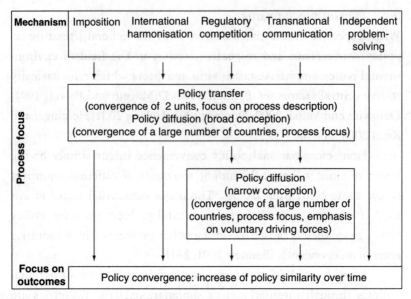

Figure 2.1 Causal mechanisms and the notions of policy transfer, diffusion and convergence

epistemic communities, the promotion of policy models by international organisations with the objective of accelerating and facilitating cross-national policy transfer, the emergence of widely accepted international norms of appropriate behaviour as well as the emulation of policy models.

In the latter case, one could certainly argue that communication is also of relevance with regard to the other mechanisms of imposition, international harmonisation or regulatory competition. In these cases, however, communication and information exchange are basically a background condition for the operation of the mechanisms rather than the central factor actually triggering convergence.

Figure 2.1 provides an overview of how the different causal mechanisms are linked to the concepts of convergence, diffusion and transfer discussed in section 2.2 above. As becomes apparent, not all causal mechanisms that might yield convergence are also relevant in bringing about transfer or diffusion. This holds true especially for independent problem-solving. Moreover, the figure illustrates the distinction between different concepts of policy diffusion. In contrast to the broad understanding of diffusion (which includes policy spreads triggered by imposition, harmonisation, regulatory competition as well as transnational communication), the narrow conception restricts the phenomenon of diffusion to non-obligatory and non-coercive driving forces (regulatory competition and transnational communication).

2.4.2 Facilitating factors

What are potential facilitating factors that affect the degree of cross-national policy convergence? The first group of factors in that respect refers to characteristics, or more precisely, the similarity of the countries under investigation. It is argued that cultural similarity plays an important role in facilitating cross-national policy transfer. In their search for relevant policy models, decision-makers are expected to look to the experiences of those countries with which they share an especially close set of cultural ties (Lenschow, Liefferink and Veenman 2005; Strang and Meyer 1993). Moreover, similarity in socio-economic structures and the level of income has been identified as a factor that facilitates the transfer of policies across countries (see, for instance, on environmental policy, Jänicke 1998). Finally, the pre-existing policy similarity has been identified as a factor that influences the likelihood of convergence.

2.5 CONCLUSION

The overview of the state of the art with respect to the notion of policy convergence and related notions, empirical research on environmental policy convergence, and the causal mechanisms discussed in the convergence literature shows that there are still a number of research deficits.

First of all, empirical research on environmental policy convergence lacks studies comparing the development of the environmental policies in large numbers of countries and for extended periods of time. There are no quantitative studies of environmental policy convergence which are based on an encompassing data set of environmental policies. Thus, at the descriptive level we know that there has been diffusion of many policy innovations; however, we have only limited information as to what extent the environmental policies of many countries have in fact become more similar over time.

Second, there are no large-n studies of environmental policy convergence that analyse not only the degree of convergence, but also the direction of the convergence movement, that is, do countries move towards stricter environmental policies or do they lower their levels of protection? This is an important question, as theories of regulatory competition predict that under the conditions of a globalised economy there will be a race-to-the-bottom of environmental policies.

Third, in the environmental field there are so far no studies relying on a differentiated approach to the measurement of convergence. There are various conceptions of convergence, reaching from the simple idea that convergence is the decrease of variation over time to a notion of convergence that focuses on the catching-up of laggard countries. Moreover, there are no attempts to systematically measure the similarity of such complex things as environmental policy measures. While diffusion studies are only concerned with the adoption of a policy measure, like a policy against acid rain, the similarity of such a policy itself is not taken into account. For the study of convergence not only the presence of a policy but also its precise form is of interest. Which instruments are applied? At which level is a limit value set? Finally, in measuring convergence we should not restrict ourselves to metrical indicators, as this is easiest to deal with in statistical models.

Fourth, at the explanatory level, there is a lack of studies of environmental policy convergence that test and compare the effects of several causal factors of policy convergence in multivariate statistical models and that are based in the many theories of policy convergence put forward in the literature. Here it is important to test not only those factors where data are easily available (such as gross national product, trade openness, environmental expenditure or environmental quality data), but to test those explanatory factors which seem to be most promising at the theoretical level, even if one has to collect the data and build new data sets beforehand.

Fifth, and with reference to the separation of the comparative and international studies of policy convergence, there is a lack of studies that take into account both international and domestic factors potentially explaining policy convergence.

Sixth, we need studies of environmental policy convergence that systematically analyse the variance in the similarity increase of different types of policies (such as different environmental media, trade-related versus non-trade-related policies) and of different dimensions of a policy (the instruments applied or the setting of limit values).

In view of these deficits this book aims at bringing together the two traditions of comparative and international studies of environmental policy transfer, diffusion and convergence. We focus on environmental policy *convergence* as this allows us to grasp all dimensions of environmental policy change. As figure 2.1 shows, convergence is the most encompassing perspective. Focusing on transfer, diffusion or isomorphism would lead us to neglect important aspects of environmental policy change.

In a large-n study we measure and explain the convergence of forty environmental policies in twenty-four mostly European countries over a period of thirty years. We do not restrict ourselves to measuring the extent and direction of policy convergence but we aim at explaining the increase in policy similarity by a whole bundle of potential driving factors of homogenisation of policies.

Our main research interest is in analysing three international causal mechanisms driving policy convergence: international harmonisation, transnational communication and regulatory competition (see figure 2.1). We do not take into account the mechanism of imposition because this does not play a significant role in environmental policy in Europe. Although some authors see the Eastern enlargement of the EU as a process of imposition or conditionality we prefer to classify the accession to the EU as part of the mechanism of international harmonisation (cf. chapter 3). Domestic factors that may influence processes of environmental policy convergence are controlled for. This way we grasp the mechanism of similar but independent responses to the same contextual factors, such as environmental problem pressure or political demand for environmental protection.

The three causal mechanisms we intend to analyse correspond to three theories predicting policy convergence: theories of international cooperation, theories of cross-national policy learning and the theory of regulatory competition. All of these theories have a micro-foundation: national governments are the main actors bringing about policy change. With this background the data to be explained in our study are *policy output* data rather than policy outcome data. We are interested in changes in the actual policies adopted by government, not in changes of the environmental quality. Changes in environmental quality may be brought about by many factors not related to theories of cross-national policy convergence, such as implementation deficits or increase in behaviour damaging the environment.

Finally, we apply a careful and multifold approach to the measurement of convergence. First, we collect data on several dimensions of a policy (the adoption, the instrument used and the exact setting of values) in order to grasp the similarity of policies and policy repertoires as deeply as possible. Second, we develop two innovative conceptions of convergence measurement:

(1) The pair approach: In this concept we measure the degree of convergence on the basis of a comparison of all country pairs for each policy, an approach that avoids a number of methodological problems of classical measurement of sigma-convergence.

(2) The gap approach: In this concept we measure the direction of convergence by analysing the changes in distance of countries to the environmental front-runner country for a given policy.

Both approaches together allow us to provide a differentiated picture of the degree and direction of environmental policy convergence in Europe and its causes. This way we are able to provide a new contribution to the explanation of environmental policy convergence in Europe.

3 Theoretical framework: causal factors and convergence expectations

KATHARINA HOLZINGER AND
CHRISTOPH KNILL

3.1 INTRODUCTION

As has been shown in the previous chapter, the study of cross-national policy convergence is a highly popular research area in political science. Notwithstanding these far-reaching research efforts, it is generally acknowledged that we still have a limited understanding of the causes and conditions of policy convergence.

It is the objective of this chapter to develop the theory further by a systematic discussion of the causal factors of policy convergence and by the formulation of general theoretical expectations on policy convergence for each factor. We proceed in the following steps. First, we briefly present the central aspects we distinguish for the assessment of policy convergence. In a second step, we identify and compare different causal factors of cross-national policy convergence. Having elaborated on the major causes of policy convergence, however, we still know little about the conditions under which these factors actually lead to convergence. This is the objective of the third part of our analysis, in which we develop theoretical expectations for the different aspects of cross-national policy convergence. These hypotheses form the background for the empirical study of environmental policy convergence in Europe presented in the following chapters. Specifications of these expectations in the form of testable hypotheses that relate to the different empirical models used in this study will be presented in the respective chapters (6 and 7).

3.2 HOW TO CONCEPTUALISE POLICY CONVERGENCE?

For the purpose of the underlying study, we define policy convergence

> as any increase in the similarity between one or more
> characteristics of a certain policy (e.g. policy objectives, policy
> instruments, policy settings) across a given set of political
> jurisdictions (supranational institutions, states, regions, local
> authorities) over a given period of time. Policy convergence thus
> describes the end result of a process of policy change over time
> towards some common point, regardless of the causal processes.
>
> (Knill 2005: 768)

This definition of policy convergence still leaves a broad range of options of how to empirically assess and evaluate similarity changes (Heichel, Pape and Sommerer 2005). In this book, we distinguish various aspects, including not only the degree, but also the direction and scope of convergence.

3.2.1 Degree of convergence

With respect to the degree of convergence, we first of all have to clarify the criteria on the basis of which we judge whether policies across countries are similar or not. In this context, a general distinction can be drawn between the similarity of policy outputs (the policies adopted by a government) and policy outcomes (the actual effects of a policy in terms of goal achievement). While studies on both dimensions can be found in the literature, we concentrate in the following analysis on policy outputs, as policy outcomes are only indirectly related to the causal mechanisms of convergence. They are usually affected by many intervening variables. The adoption of a programme is thus a poor predictor of its implementation.

For the measurement of similarity change, we start from the concept of sigma-convergence. According to this concept, the degree of convergence increases with the extent to which the policies of different countries have become more similar to each other over time. Thus, convergence degree is the decrease of standard deviation from time t_1 to t_2.

In addition to sigma-convergence, various concepts to assess the degree of cross-national policy convergence are applied in the literature. The concept of beta-convergence measures the extent to which laggard countries catch up with leader countries over time, implying, for instance, that the former strengthen their regulatory standards more quickly and fundamentally than the latter. By contrast, gamma-convergence is measured by changes of country rankings with respect to a certain policy. According to this approach, convergence increases with the degree of mobility, i.e., the extent to which country ranks change over time (Heichel, Pape and Sommerer 2005: 831–3).[1]

The concepts of sigma-, beta- and gamma-convergence imply different definitions and hence reference points for assessing changes in policy similarity over time (Knill 2005: 769). As will be shown in chapter 5, it is therefore hardly surprising that we arrive at partially different assessments with regard to the degree of convergence, depending on the concrete concept applied.

In addition to the above-mentioned approaches, we develop a new and more sophisticated measurement concept based on the comparison of country pairs in chapter 6. The *pair approach* allows us to measure sigma-convergence not only for metrical, but also for nominal data. Moreover, the pair approach allows for analysing the extent to which individual country pairs converge to the whole group or sub-groups of the countries under investigation.

3.2.2 Direction of convergence

In contrast to the degree of convergence, convergence direction indicates the extent to which similarity changes coincide with an upward or downward shift of the mean from time t_1 to t_2. Convergence at

---

[1] The concepts of sigma-, beta-, and gamma-convergence are presented in more detail in chapter 4.

the top or bottom presupposes therefore both a decrease of standard deviation and a shift of the mean (Botcheva and Martin 2001: 4).

The direction of convergence is usually related to the extent of state intervention or to the strictness of a regulation. Lax standards or laissez-faire policies are identified with the 'bottom', strict standards or interventionist policies with the 'top' (Drezner 2001: 59–64). The direction of convergence can best be measured whenever the policies under consideration come in degrees, which can be associated with a normative judgement on the quality of a policy. Typical examples are the levels of environmental and consumer protection or labour standards. However, it is not always easy to identify what the top and the bottom are in a policy, because there may be different value judgements. For example, in media regulation there are competing goals of restricting harmful content on the one hand and freedom of information on the other hand. However, when policy instruments are compared it seems not to make much sense to speak of directions of convergence. Instruments simply exist or not. Still the presence of a certain instrument can be considered 'the top', whereas its absence equates with 'the bottom'. Moreover, although in rare cases, a certain instrument can be assumed to provide stricter (or less strict) regulation than another one. Therefore, the analysis of direction of convergence will not only include those environmental policies from the sample used in the empirical study for which metrical data are available (standards), but also those which only produce nominal ones (instruments) (see chapter 7).

In this study, we apply a newly developed conception of so-called delta-convergence for the measurement of the direction of convergence. According to this *gap approach*, we measure convergence by looking at the distance (delta) of the countries' policies to a certain model, e.g., the best performing country, the least performing country, or the mean country (for details on delta-convergence see chapters 4 and 7). According to this conception, for instance, a race-to-the-top would be indicated by the reduction of countries' distances to the top performer over time. As shown in table 3.1, the comparison

Table 3.1 *Potential configurations of convergence aspects*

Standard deviation	Regulatory mean	Interpretation
No change	No change	Persistence of diversity and level of regulation
	Upward or downward shift	Persistence of diversity, but common movement into the same direction
Decrease	No change	Less diversity, but persistence of level of regulation
	Upward or downward shift	Less diversity at the top or bottom
Increase	No change	More diversity, but persistence of level of regulation
	Upward or downward shift	More diversity, but common movement into the same direction

Source: adapted from Holzinger and Knill 2005c: 777.

between the policies in time t_1 and t_2 for a number of countries can yield different interpretations, depending on the underlying conception of convergence.

3.2.3 Scope of convergence

For the development of hypotheses on the degree and direction of convergence only those sub-groups of countries and policies are of theoretical interest that can be expected to be actually affected by a certain mechanism of convergence. For example, if we talk about international harmonisation we would not expect any convergence effects on countries which are not members of the international institutions in which harmonisation efforts take place. Hence, our statements about convergence degrees or directions are not related to all countries and policies under investigation, but only to the affected sub-groups. It is important to emphasise that convergence within sub-groups affected by a certain mechanism can, but need not, result in convergence for the whole sample of countries and policies under investigation.

To grasp the potential effects of certain mechanisms on *all* countries and policies under investigation, we rely on a further aspect, namely the *scope of convergence*. The scope of convergence increases with the number of countries and policies that are actually affected by a certain convergence mechanism, with the reference point being the total number of countries and policies under investigation. There is no straightforward relationship between degree and scope of convergence. Although it might often be the case that an increase in the number of converging countries actually reduces the variation among all countries, there are conceivable constellations in which the opposite might be the case (cf. chapter 5 for empirical results of the variation analysis). For example, a sub-group of countries might converge towards a point far away from the other countries.

In view of the research questions underlying this study, we distinguish sub-groups of obligatory and non-obligatory policies; i.e., policies for which legally binding requirements at the international or supranational level are existent or absent. Moreover, we differentiate between policy items that are more or less likely to be affected by international trade (trade-related versus non-trade-related policies). These distinctions are based on several hypotheses which will be developed in more detail in the following sections. With regard to countries, it is of particular interest to distinguish sub-groups according to their potential affectedness by the far-reaching harmonisation activities of the EU. Our country sample allows for a differentiation between founding members of the EU, countries participating in the different enlargement rounds, accession candidates, non-members closely associated with the EU (Norway and Switzerland), and non-members without particular association (Japan, Mexico and the US). Table 3.2 gives an overview of different indicators of policy convergence.

3.2.4 Convergence on different policy dimensions

In the literature, we generally find a broad list of policy dimensions on which convergence might occur, including, for instance, policy

Table 3.2 *Aspects of policy convergence*

Aspects	Research question	Reference point	Operationalisation
Convergence degree	How much similarity increase over time?	Sub-group of countries and policies affected by a certain mechanism	Decrease in standard deviation over time; sophisticated sigma-convergence based on paired comparison
Convergence direction	In what direction (upward or downward shift of the regulatory mean)?	Sub-group of countries and policies affected by a certain mechanism	Mean change; delta-convergence distance to best or least performers
Convergence scope	How many and which countries and policies are converging?	All countries and policies under investigation	Number of countries and policies

Source: Holzinger and Knill 2005c: 778.

output or content, policy style or process as well as policy outcomes (Bennett 1991: 418). Another, more encompassing differentiation is suggested by Dolowitz and Marsh (1996: 349–50), including 'policy goals, structure and content; policy instruments or administrative techniques; institutions; ideology; ideas, attitudes and concepts'. With regard to these dimensions, further differentiations have been applied. For instance, for the category of policy output – which is the particular focus of the underlying investigation – Hall (1993) distinguishes between policy paradigms, policy instruments and policy settings.

For the purpose of this study, we compare convergence effects on three different policy dimensions, namely, the extent to which countries have developed a specific policy or not with regard to a certain problem (*policy presence*), the *policy instruments* applied (e.g., command-and-control regulation versus policies based on economic incentives) as well as the *settings* of these instruments (i.e., levels of environmental standards). We expect significant differences in the degree of convergence across the different dimensions, as they imply different requirements with regard to the classification as 'similar' or 'dissimilar policy'.

For the dimension of policy presence, similarity is already given as soon as the countries in question adopt a political programme in response to a specific problem, regardless of the concrete instruments or instrument settings defined in the programme. It is obvious that convergence with regard to the dimension of policy presence can hence occur rather easily. The only condition is that countries respond politically to a certain problem; notwithstanding a potentially high level of variance across national responses (e.g., the application of command-and-control regulation versus self-regulation). By contrast, convergence on policy instruments requires not only that countries have enacted a certain policy, but also that they apply the same instruments within that programme. The similarity requirement is even more demanding when it comes to the dimension of settings, implying that countries have adopted policies that are based on similar instruments and their similar 'tuning' (in terms of similar standard levels or tax rates). These considerations lead to the following hypothesis:

H 1   Policy dimension hypothesis
The degree of policy convergence varies across different policy dimensions. It will be highest for the dimension of policy presence and lowest for the dimension of policy settings, regardless of the policy type.

At first glance, this expectation seems to be in contradiction with Hall (1993), who argues that policy change is most likely for policy settings but becomes increasingly difficult when it comes to policy instruments and paradigms. Changes in settings are considered rather unproblematic, as they can be achieved within existing instruments and paradigms. In a similar way, instrumental changes are considered to be more likely than paradigm changes, as the latter imply the departure from dominant and institutionally strongly entrenched ideas of how to perceive and resolve certain political problems.

This partial contradiction with our hypothesis can be resolved, however, when we examine more closely the dependent variables underlying Hall's study and our own investigation. Hall is concerned with the explanation of domestic policy change rather than cross-national policy convergence. The fact that domestic policy settings might be adjusted rather quickly and smoothly does not imply that different countries easily switch to similar settings. Given the 'high degrees of freedom' with respect to this policy dimension, i.e., the *de facto* infinite number of possible levels of regulation, convergence constitutes a rather demanding development, not least because it also requires that countries have adopted a respective policy and similar instruments in the first place. Moreover, the category of 'paradigm' does not exist in our three dimensions.

3.3 WHAT CAUSES POLICY CONVERGENCE?

The literature provides us with many potential factors that might lead to cross-national policy convergence (see Bennett 1991; DiMaggio and Powell 1991; Dolowitz and Marsh 2000; Drezner 2001; Hoberg 2001). Moreover, suggestions on causal factors can be found not only in studies explicitly concerned with policy convergence, but also in the literature on policy transfer, diffusion and isomorphism that is closely related to the study of convergence. Transfer and diffusion are processes that might result in convergence. Thus, the factors triggering these processes can be interpreted as potential causes of convergence. The same holds true for the mechanisms driving isomorphism – a concept that differs from convergence only with respect to its empirical focus on organisational structures (see chapter 2). Notwithstanding the broad variety of convergence causes emphasised in the literature, these factors basically refer to five distinct convergence mechanisms (Holzinger and Knill 2005a) that are presented in the following section.

3.3.1 Overview of causal factors

First, emphasis is placed on the harmonisation of national policies through international or supranational law. Countries are obliged to comply with international rules on which they have deliberately agreed in multilateral negotiations. Second, several studies emphasise convergence effects stemming from the imposition of policies. Imposition refers to constellations in which countries or international organisations force other countries to adopt certain policies by exploiting asymmetries in political or economic power. Third, cross-national policy convergence can be caused by communication and information exchange in transnational networks. Fourth, regulatory competition emerging from the increasing economic integration of European and global markets has been identified as one important factor that drives the mutual adjustment of policies across countries. Finally, cross-national policy convergence might simply be the result of similar, but independent, responses of different countries to parallel problem pressure (e.g., ageing of societies); i.e., policy convergence is caused by similar policy problems that countries are reacting to (Bennett 1991: 231).

As we are predominantly interested in the convergence effects caused by institutional and economic interlinkages among countries, we concentrate in the following on those mechanisms that are actually relevant in the context of our study, namely, international harmonisation, transnational communication and regulatory competition. This is not to deny the significance of other variables that are associated with convergence effects triggered by similar constellations of domestic policy problems. However, these variables will be considered as complementary rather than primary sources of explanation.

Moreover, and in contrast to the above-mentioned classification, we do not consider effects of imposition as a convergence mechanism in its own right. This can basically be traced to the fact that effects of imposition are hardly relevant for the sample of policies and countries under investigation in this book. On the one hand, constellations of a unilateral imposition of a policy on a country by another country or 'direct coercive transfer' (Dolowitz and Marsh 1996: 347) play no role in the context of our study. Such constellations, which might occur after a war, for example, are generally very rare and do not lead to far-reaching convergence, as they will hardly ever involve many countries.[2]

On the other hand, the second imposition scenario, namely conditionality exerted by international institutions, also applies only to a limited extent to our cases. First, conditionality is based on the exchange of policies for loans. For instance, it is argued that the spread of neo-liberal monetary and trade policies to Third World countries was driven by such conditionalities. Governments pressed by international financial institutions switched to liberal trade regimes (cf. Dolowitz and Marsh 1996: 347; Meseguer Yebra 2003). However, a comparable scenario of environmental policy convergence driven by financial and economic pressures through international institutions does not apply to our cases under investigation. A second form of conditionality, which is indeed potentially relevant for some of our countries under study, is the exchange of policy adjustments for membership in international institutions. It has been argued that the EU accession of CEE countries has been governed by this principle (Schimmelfennig and Sedelmeier 2004; Tews 2002). CEE countries willing to join the EU had to

---

[2] According to Bennett 'convergence by penetration' arises when states are forced to conform to actions taken elsewhere by external actors (1991: 227). His main examples are multinational businesses that exert pressure on governments to harmonise policies concerning products (1991: 228). However, as multinational firms can surely not *force* governments and as they have no *political* power, we subsume this kind of pressure for international cooperation under convergence through regulatory competition. Another example is voluntary international agreements, for instance at the level of the OECD and the Council of Europe (Bennett 1991: 228). In our view, these fall under the mechanism of transnational communication (promotion of policy models) rather than reflecting convergence through imposition.

comply with the *acquis communautaire* and with the so-called Copenhagen criteria.

In line with this argument, we hence often find a distinction between harmonisation and imposition in the literature (cf. Bennett 1991; Dolowitz and Marsh 1996, 2000). This distinction is typically based on the extent to which international cooperation rests upon symmetric or asymmetric power relations between the involved states. However, we consider this differentiation to be unhelpful, as it is difficult to draw a clear analytical boundary between international negotiations characterised by symmetric or asymmetric relations of power. In negotiations at the international or European level, it will almost always be the case that some states are more influential than others. How can we judge whether the power constellations imply a voluntary or an imposed agreement from the perspective of individual countries? Why do scholars generally speak of conditionality with respect to the recent Eastern enlargement of the EU, but not with respect to earlier enlargement rounds, although in these cases also, accession was contingent upon the domestic adoption of the *acquis communautaire*?

In view of the fundamental analytical difficulties in drawing a distinction between harmonisation and imposition, we take the existence of international or supranational policies to which member countries or accession countries (by way of membership anticipation) adjust, as the decisive analytical starting point – regardless of the extent to which the adoption of these policies has been characterised by symmetric or asymmetric power relations between the involved countries. We therefore consider potential conditionality effects in the context of EU enlargement under the heading of (pre-accession) harmonisation rather than imposition.

The hypotheses on policy convergence we will formulate in section 4 are hence based on the distinction of the mechanisms of international harmonisation, transnational communication and regulatory competition. As summarised in table 3.3, each mechanism combines an incentive and a corresponding response, i.e., the

Table 3.3 *Mechanisms of policy convergence*

Mechanism	Incentive	Response
International harmonisation	Legal obligation through international law	Compliance
Transnational communication		
Lesson-drawing	Problem pressure	Transfer of model found elsewhere
Transnational problem-solving	Parallel problem pressure	Adoption of commonly developed model
Emulation	Desire for conformity	Copying of widely used model
International policy promotion	Legitimacy pressure	Adoption of recommended model
Regulatory competition	Competitive pressure	Mutual adjustment
Other factors		
Parallel problem pressure Political demand	Parallel domestic constellation	Independent similar response

Source: adapted from Holzinger and Knill 2005c: 780.

behaviour actually leading to convergence. The causal mechanism leads to convergence, if the response actually occurs.

3.3.2 International harmonisation

The mechanism of international harmonisation leads to cross-national convergence if the involved countries comply with uniform legal obligations defined in international or supranational law. Harmonisation refers to a specific outcome of international cooperation, namely to constellations in which national governments are legally required to adopt similar policies and programmes as part of their obligations as members of international institutions.

International harmonisation and more generally international cooperation presuppose the existence of interdependencies or externalities which push governments to resolve common problems through cooperation within international institutions, hence sacrificing some independence for the good of the community (Drezner 2001: 60; Hoberg 2001: 127). Once established, institutional arrangements will constrain and shape the domestic policy choices, even as they are constantly challenged and reformed by their member states. This way, international institutions are not only the object of state choice, but at the same time consequential for subsequent governmental activities (Martin and Simmons 1998: 743).

3.3.3 Transnational communication

Under the term 'transnational communication' we summarise a number of different but related mechanisms, including lesson-drawing, transnational problem-solving, emulation and the transnational promotion of policy models. They have in common that their operation is *purely* based on communication among countries. By contrast, the other mechanisms presuppose legal obligation (harmonisation) or competitive pressure (regulatory competition). Communication might also play a role in these cases; however, it is not the main factor accounting for convergence effects. So far, in the literature no established heading for these different, but closely related, mechanisms exists. One could certainly argue that each of the mechanisms summarised under transnational communication can be considered as a mechanism in its own right. However, they share an important characteristic that crucially distinguishes them from all other causal mechanisms: namely, they presuppose nothing but information exchange and communication with other countries.

Lesson-drawing The mechanism of lesson-drawing refers to constellations of policy transfer in which governments rationally utilise available experience elsewhere in order to solve domestic problems. According to Rose, who introduced the concept, lesson-drawing is based on a voluntaristic process whereby government A learns from government B's solution to a common problem what to do ('positive lessons') or what not to do ('negative lessons'). The government is modelled as a rational actor who poses the question: 'Under what circumstances and to what extent would a programme now in effect elsewhere also work here?' (Rose 1991: 4). The creation of new programmes, however, need not be based on the mere copying of other policies, but can take many different forms, ranging from hybrids of transferred and domestically developed components to completely new models. Rose also emphasises that drawing a lesson does not require policy change: a programme elsewhere may be evaluated negatively or there may be no way to transfer it (Rose 1991: 22). Therefore, lesson-drawing is not the same as policy convergence.

A closely related concept is presented by Meseguer Yebra (2003) who applies the concept of Bayesian learning to policy learning. Bayesian learning is a mode of rational, experience-based learning. Governments are modelled as perfectly rational learners. They update their beliefs on the consequences of policies with all available information about policy outcomes in the past and elsewhere. They choose the policy that is expected to yield the best results (Meseguer Yebra 2003). Bayesian learning is a formal mechanism, but the notion of learning in this concept is very similar to Rose's concept of lesson-drawing. However, in Meseguer Yebra's approach, governments will converge in their policy choices if they are exposed to the same information. This implies that there is a 'best solution' – given a certain state of information. However, only if governments are not perfectly rational and do not collect all available information, may divergence occur.

Transnational problem-solving Similar to lesson-drawing, transnational problem-solving assumes processes of rational learning. In the latter case, however, convergence is not the result of bilateral transfer. Rather, it is driven by the joint development of common problem perceptions and solutions to similar domestic problems and their subsequent adoption at the domestic level. Transnational problem-solving typically occurs within transnational elite networks or epistemic communities, defined as networks of policy experts who share common principled beliefs over ends, causal beliefs over means and common standards of accruing and testing new knowledge (Haas 1992: 3). Common educational and normative backgrounds typically facilitate joint development of common policy models in such constellations (DiMaggio and Powell 1991: 73).

It is easily conceivable that transnational problem-solving in elite networks can prepare the ground for subsequent activities of international harmonisation. This holds true especially for problems characterised by strong interdependencies. At the same time, however, it is emphasised that international institutions play an important role in forging and promulgating transnational epistemic communities (Elkins and Simmons 2005). In other words, regular negotiations and discussions on problems subject to harmonisation provide the ground for joint problem-solving in related areas that do not necessarily require a joint solution through international law. This argument is supported by the findings of Kern (2000: 144) who shows that international institutions play an important role in accelerating and facilitating cross-national policy transfer. They constitute important channels for multilateral communication and policy diffusion. Kern shows that – compared to policy exchange resting on bilateral and horizontal communication between countries – policy models spread much broader and faster if these countries are members of the same international institution.

Emulation of policies Policy convergence through emulation is driven by the mere desire for conformity with other countries rather than the search for effective solutions to given problems. Consequently, emulation usually implies the simple copying of policies adopted elsewhere. Which factors account for this search for conformity? In the literature, various aspects are mentioned.

First, it is argued that emulation is a function of the number of countries that have already adopted a certain policy. As argued in herding theories, it can be optimal for a country to follow the behaviour of others even without using further information than the sheer number of followers. The fact that many others apply a certain policy serves as information that this might be the best thing to do (Levi-Faur 2002). In theories of population ecology, a different rationale is emphasised: emulation is the result of the socially embedded behaviour of actors (Baum and Oliver 1992; Meyer and Rowan 1977). The most widespread solution to a problem becomes the obvious way of dealing with it whereas other possible solutions are no longer considered.

Second, emulation can be driven by the striving of organisations to increase their social legitimacy by embracing forms and practices that are valued within the broader social and institutional environment (DiMaggio and Powell 1991: 70). States might sometimes copy mimetically the policies of other states simply to legitimate conclusions already reached (Bennett 1991: 223).

Third, a psychologically based rationale for emulation is the desire of actors 'not to be left behind', a mechanism that has been transferred to the behaviour of state actors within the international system (Finnemore 1996; Meyer et al. 1997; Tews 2002). In the theory of DiMaggio and Powell 'mimetic isomorphism' occurs especially when an innovation is poorly understood and when its consequences are still unclear (1991: 69). The fear of being left behind might be a result of uncertainty, but might also be a motive in itself.

Fourth, there are rational motivations. Bennett observes that emulation might be a consequence of time pressures: 'the more urgency that is perceived, the more likely will be the imitation of solutions without lengthy analysis and investigation' (1991: 223). Moreover, compared with more demanding forms of learning, the costs of information are probably much lower for simple imitation (Tews 2002: 180).

International policy promotion   Countries might not only be inspired to adopt a certain policy because of rational learning or their desire for conformity. They can also be motivated to do so because of legitimacy pressures emerging from the promotion of policy models by international institutions.[3] In contrast to the mechanism of transnational problem-solving, policy convergence is not the result of joint problem-solving efforts of countries represented in transnational networks, but is driven by the active role of international institutions that are promoting the spread of distinctive policy approaches they consider particularly promising.

Cross-national policy transfer is stimulated by non-binding international agreements or propositions on broad goals and standards that national policies should aim to achieve, institutionalised peer review and identification of best practice (benchmarking) as well as the construction of league tables ranking national policies in terms of performance to previously agreed criteria (Humphreys 2002: 54; Tews 2002: 174). International institutions, such as the EU, the OECD or the World Bank, but also NGOs and transnational interest organisations (Keck and Sikkink 1998), play a highly active role in this process. In constantly searching for new policy ideas, disseminating best practice and evaluating domestic policy performance, they function as mediators of cross-national policy transfer, urging national governments to adopt successful policy models (Kern, Jörgens and Jänicke 2000: 10). Countries that deviate from recommended policy models or rank low in international league tables face pressure to legitimate their policy approaches in light of 'international scrutiny'.

In many instances, promotion activities by international institutions originate from the activities of individual states seeking to convince other countries to copy their policy models. Countries

---

[3] Policy promotion need not be restricted to the activities of international institutions, but can also be pursued by individual countries, i.e., on a bilateral basis. One example is the Dutch activities to promote the National Environmental Policy Plan during the 1990s (Liefferink 1999).

which have developed innovative policy concepts generally have a strong interest to establish their approach as an international solution in order to minimise costs of institutional and economic adjustment to potentially diverging internationally promoted policy models. This pattern of leaders using international institutions as leverage when trying to drag along the laggards has not only been observed in the EU (Andersen and Liefferink 1997; Héritier, Knill and Mingers 1996), but also at the level of the OECD and other international institutions (Jänicke 1998: 334; Wallace 1995: 267).

3.3.4 Regulatory competition

While the mechanism of international harmonisation is based on domestic compliance with legal obligations, regulatory competition is expected to lead to cross-national convergence, as countries facing competitive pressure mutually adjust their policies. Regulatory competition presupposes economic integration among countries. Especially with the increasing integration of European and global markets and the abolition of national trade barriers, the international mobility of goods, workers and capital puts competitive pressure on the nation states to redesign domestic market regulations in order to avoid regulatory burdens restricting the competitiveness of domestic industries. The pressure arises from (potential) threats of economic actors to shift their activities elsewhere, inducing governments to lower their regulatory standards.

This way, regulatory competition among governments may lead to a race-to-the-bottom in policies, implying policy convergence (Drezner 2001: 57–9; Hoberg 2001: 127; Simmons and Elkins 2004). Theoretical work, however, suggests that there are a number of conditions that may drive policy in both directions (Holzinger 2002, 2003; Kern, Jörgens and Jänicke 2000; Scharpf 1997; Vogel 1995), including, for example, the type of policy concerned (product or process standards), or the presence of interests other than business in national politics.

3.3.5 Other factors

It is the central objective of this study to analyse the extent to which international economic and institutional interlinkages among countries lead to similarity increases in their environmental policies. In focusing on the three causal mechanisms described above, however, we do not imply that other convergence causes might not be relevant. We therefore discuss other explanatory factors of convergence mentioned in the literature. This way, we are able to make a more comprehensive judgement about the relative explanatory power of the international convergence causes in which we are primarily interested.

The factors addressed in the following are closely related to the fact that convergence of policies between several countries can arise as a result of similar but independent responses of political actors to parallel problem pressures. Just as individuals open their umbrellas simultaneously during a rainstorm, governments may decide to change their policies in the presence of tax evasion, environmental pressures, such as air pollution, or an ageing population.[4] As Bennett notes, the analyst of policy convergence 'must avoid the pitfall of inferring from transnational similarity of public policy that a transnational explanation must be at work' (1991: 231).

In the context of environmental policy parallel problem pressure relates to two factors. First, the presence of certain environmental problems might trigger some governmental response to combat these problems. Second, the same is true for the presence of political demand for environmental policy exerted by green movements, green parties or the general public. Both factors are correlated to some degree, as it is unlikely (although conceivable) that an environmental movement will develop when there are no environmental problems. However, the presence of environmental problems

---

[4] This phenomenon has also been discussed under the names of functional, technocratic or technological determinism (Bennett 1988: 417; Rose 1991: 9), clustering (Simmons and Elkins 2004), spurious diffusion (Gilardi and Braun 2005; Gilardi 2005), or parallel domestic pressures (Hoberg 2001: 127).

does not necessarily imply the existence of an environmental movement. Thus, both factors have to be taken into account for the analysis of convergence.

First, similar policy responses can be the result of similar environmental pressures different countries are confronted with. Environmental problem pressure can be generally assumed to increase with population density and can thus be approximated by this indicator. Other indicators are the levels of certain emissions or environmental quality factors. One prominent indicator in this respect is CO_2 emissions, since they arise from a whole range of activities damaging the environment. Second, it is argued that similar policy responses are driven by similarity in political demand. In this context, the number and influence of environmental organisations and the existence and influence of green parties can be seen as the most important factors.

In addition to the above-mentioned indicator, two variables have to be emphasised that affect both environmental pressure and demand for environmental policies. On the one hand, the cultural similarity among countries (e.g., in terms of legal traditions, historical heritage, language, religion or geographical proximity) plays an important role in this respect. It not only facilitates the transfer and emulation of policies, hence leading to increases in cross-national policy similarity over time, but also implies that the political process of defining and addressing environmental problems is characterised by similar patterns. In a similar way, it can be argued that the extent to which countries already pursue rather similar policies and regulatory approaches (i.e., the pre-existing similarity) plays an important role in rendering cross-national policy transfer more or less difficult.

On the other hand, an important indicator affecting both environmental pressure and political demand is the level of income in a country. The so-called 'Environmental Kuznets Curve' (Panayotou 1993; Stern and Common 2001) indicates that the level of environmental pollution grows with the GDP up to a certain point, but then decreases again.[5] The usual explanation for this shape points at two factors. First, economic structure is assumed to account for the level and structure of environmental problems: the more industrialised a country is the more environmental pollution problems will be present. More industrialised countries are usually richer than rural societies (Panayotou 1993; Syrquin 1988). Second, the richer a country is the higher is the political demand for environmental protection. Environmental policy is a luxury good and thus demand for it grows with the level of income (Beckerman 1992; Boyce 2004). Thus, similar income levels should imply similar environmental policies.

3.4 WHEN DOES POLICY CONVERGENCE OCCUR?
Having identified the causal mechanisms of policy convergence, it is the objective of this section to develop theoretical expectations about the conditions of their operation. We aim at further specifying the mechanisms in order to develop testable hypotheses with respect to degree, direction and scope of cross-national policy convergence for each mechanism. To answer these questions, a point of reference is needed. As a reference point, we assume a situation where no mechanism is at work and where the policies of the countries under consideration are characterised by diversity.

Although we are aware of the fact that countries might be exposed to several mechanisms of convergence and that these mechanisms might interact (cf. Holzinger and Knill 2005a), the following considerations are based on the analysis of the isolated effects of different mechanisms. Our primary interest is to theoretically investigate the effects and operation of individual convergence mechanisms.

3.4.1 International harmonisation
The scope of cross-national convergence triggered by international harmonisation is affected by two factors. First, as convergence effects

---

[5] The Kuznets curve is an inverse U-shaped curve.

are restricted to those countries that are actually committed to international agreements or supranational regulations, the scope of convergence through harmonisation increases with the number of countries that are members of the respective international institution or regime with the power to enact legally binding rules. Second, the number of policies affected through harmonisation increases with the number of areas covered by the legislation of the international organisation in question.

With regard to the extent to which international harmonisation triggers cross-national convergence, two factors can be identified. First, the degree of convergence varies with the legal specification of international law. Specification is particularly high, if international law requires the total or minimum harmonisation of national standards. Convergence effects are less pronounced, by contrast, if legal rules are defined in a less rigid way, leaving member states broad leeway for selecting appropriate instruments to comply with international policy objectives. In this respect, varying discretion levels are conceivable, ranging from differentiated regulatory requirements, the prescription of broad objectives rather than detailed substantive or procedural regulations, to mutual recognition and opting-out clauses.

Second, the degree of similarity will increase with the extent to which compliance with legal obligation can actually be enforced. International institutions reveal important differences in terms of their enforcement powers (see Abbott and Snidal 1998). The EU can be characterised as an institution in which such powers are comparatively well developed, given the direct effect and the supremacy of European law, the influential role of the European Court of Justice in the enforcement of Community law, the – albeit restricted – monitoring activities of the European Commission as well as the opportunity financially to sanction non-compliant member states (see Zürn and Joerges 2005). Against this background, the converging effects of European legislation can be expected to be higher than those of intergovernmental organisations or international regimes, where enforcement powers are less developed.

To what extent does convergence through international harmonisation coincide with upward or downward shifts of the regulatory mean? The answer to this question basically depends on factors such as decision rules, interest constellations and the distribution of power between the involved actors (typically national governments and international organisations), which shape the negotiations at the level of international institutions. Theoretical modelling generally predicts an outcome which reflects a compromise, hence lying somewhere between countries favouring extreme positions of either rather strict or weak regulations, with a strong tilt towards the preferences of the more powerful states (Drezner 2001: 61; for the EU: Holzinger 1994: 465–8; Tsebelis 2002: chapter 11). With regard to environmental policy, several factors favour the view that harmonisation implies an overall increase in the strictness of regulatory levels; i.e., a compromise that is closer to the strictest rather than weakest regulatory level found in the member states of the international institution in question.

First, it has been argued by several authors (Holzinger 2003; Scharpf 1997; Vogel 1995) that in certain constellations those countries preferring stricter levels of environmental regulation are more influential in international negotiations, implying that international harmonisation takes place at the top rather than the bottom level. This argument has been developed in particular for the case of product standards. In this case, all member states (regardless of their preference for strict or weak standards) share a common interest in international harmonisation in order to avoid market segmentation as a result of different national product requirements (Holzinger 2002: 69). While all countries share a common interest in harmonisation, those states with a preference for strict standards are in a stronger position to put through their preferences in international negotiations. On the one hand, the trade regimes of the EU (Art. 30 TEU) and the WTO – for reasons of health and safety protection – allow high-regulating countries to ban the import of products that are not in line with the strict domestic standards. As all countries share an interest in international harmonisation, high-regulating countries are therefore in certain cases able unilaterally to impose their strict standards as the international rule. Based on this argument, we should expect that – at least for product standards – international harmonisation implies an upward shift of the regulatory mean.

Second, especially for harmonisation at the level of the EU, additional structural features of the policy-making process might favour an upward shift for other policy types (production standards and non-trade-related policies) for which the above-mentioned interest constellation favouring harmonisation at the top does not apply. The fact that we observe European harmonisation at the top rather than the bottom of existing member state regulations also in these areas (cf. Knill 2003: 73–88) has been explained by particular dynamics emerging from a regulatory contest in influencing EU policies between the member states (Héritier, Knill and Mingers 1996).

These dynamics emerge from the interest of national governments to minimise institutional costs of adjusting domestic regulatory arrangements to EU policy requirements. Especially high-regulating countries with a rather comprehensively and consistently developed regulatory framework of environmental policies and instruments might face considerable problems of adjustment, if European policies reflect regulatory approaches and instruments that depart from domestic arrangements. As a result, these countries have a strong incentive to promote their own concepts at the European level. In so doing, the most promising way is to rely on the strategy of the 'first move', i.e., to try to shape European policy developments early on, during the stages of problem-definition and agenda-setting. This requires that member states have to win the support of the EU Commission, which has the formal monopoly to initiate policies at the EU level. The Commission, in turn, is generally interested in strengthening and extending supranational policy competencies. As a consequence, only those domestic initiatives that fit with these objectives of the Commission have a chance of succeeding. This specific interaction of national and supranational interests favours the development of innovative and ambitious policies at the EU level, hence driving EU harmonisation more towards the top rather than the bottom of domestic regulation levels (Knill 2003: 131–4).

Third, even if we assume that the final agreement only lies in the middle between high-regulating and low-regulating countries, there is still a high probability that the mean of national regulatory levels becomes stricter. This can be traced to the fact that by far the largest part of environmental standards follows the principle of minimum rather than total harmonisation. In the case of minimum harmonisation, it is still possible for countries with a preference for higher regulatory levels to enact standards beyond the minimum level specified in international agreements.[6] In contrast to total harmonisation, deviations to the top are therefore still possible, while countries with lower standards are obliged to raise their standards at least to the international minimum level. Given the dominance of minimum harmonisation, we thus predict that international environmental policy cooperation is likely to result in shifting the regulatory mean upward. This expectation rests on the assumption that not all high-regulating countries will lower their standards towards the minimum level.

H 2   Harmonisation hypotheses

H 2.1   Degree of convergence

The degree of convergence through harmonisation increases with the obligatory potential of international or supranational institutions (as expressed by the specification of international legal requirements and the capacities of the organisation to enforce the national transposition as well as compliance with these legal obligations).

---

[6] In the EU, for instance, this possibility is regulated in Article 95 TEU (Knill 2003: 127).

H 2.2   Direction of convergence
International harmonisation leads to stricter levels of regulation in the member countries. These effects are more pronounced for the EU than for other international organisations.

In summary, it is therefore likely that the international harmonisation of environmental standards coincides with an overall increase in the strictness of domestic regulatory levels. In this context, we expect that the effects of strengthening of EU harmonisation are more pronounced than upward shifts resulting from harmonisation activities of other international regimes. This expectation is based on the fact that the structural dynamics emerging from a regulatory contest between the member states in order to influence the respective policy developments constitute a specific feature of the EU political system.

3.4.2 Transnational communication

With respect to the number of countries and policies potentially affected by transnational communication, only a few restrictions apply, given the rather undemanding precondition of information about policy choices of other countries. It is therefore impossible to identify factors that restrict the scope of convergence through transnational communication for certain policies or countries.

The fact that transnational communication might potentially affect all countries and policies under investigation does not imply, however, that this mechanism produces cross-national policy convergence in each constellation. Rather, its operation varies with several factors. First, research on emulation emphasises that the probability of adoption increases with the number of countries that have already switched to a certain policy model (Bikhchandani, Hirshleifer and Welch 1992; Levi-Faur 2002). In other words, the degree of pre-existing policy similarity across countries crucially affects the likelihood of future similarity changes through emulation.

Second, as argued in the literature on lesson-drawing, the degree of convergence varies with the extent to which countries share cultural linkages. In their search for relevant policy models, decision-makers are expected to look at the experiences of those countries with which they share an especially close set of cultural ties (Strang and Meyer 1993). Especially in constellations characterised by high uncertainty about the consequences of policy choices, decision-makers are likely to imitate the practices of nations with which they share linguistic, religious, historical or other cultural linkages (Friedkin 1993; Simmons and Elkins 2004).

Third, as information and knowledge exchange between states is the essential requirement for most transnational communication mechanisms to become effective (Simmons and Elkins 2004), the degree of convergence will be particularly high among those countries that are strongly interlinked in varying transnational networks. Of particular importance in this respect is common membership in international institutions that play an important role in increasing the interaction density between their members, hence intensifying transnational information exchange (Kern 2000: 267).

To what extent does convergence through transnational communication lead to shifts in the level of domestic regulations? One could certainly argue that the fact that states adopt a certain innovation or copy policy concepts successfully applied in other countries need not automatically imply that this results in an increase in regulatory levels. However, as with international harmonisation, there are several theoretical arguments that let us expect that the effects of transnational communication also imply an increase in the strictness of domestic levels of regulation.

First, it has been emphasised that in processes of policy-learning, the involved actors rely on 'cognitive heuristics'. Rather than relying on all available information on policy developments and respective effects from abroad, national governments pursue a more selective approach, focusing on specific 'reference models'. A first pattern that can be observed is the concentration on countries or international organisations which enjoy high experience and reputation with respect to their problem-solving capacity in a certain policy area

(Dobbin, Garrett and Simmons 2003; Rose 1991). This focus on 'miracle models' (Meseguer Yebra 2003; Simmons and Elkins 2004) has also been reported for the role of environmental pioneer countries (Andersen and Liefferink 1997). Rather than looking at 'best countries', a second heuristic is to search for 'best policies', i.e., national governments explore successfully applied models that fit most with their specific problem constellation, implying an orientation towards similar countries, for example in terms of cultural similarity (Brune and Garrett 2000; Rose 1991; Simmons and Elkins 2004). Both patterns imply that governments adjust their policies to pioneer models or countries that either generally or at least related to a certain cultural space enjoy a high degree of reputation in terms of their problem-solving capacity. This orientation can hence hardly be expected to coincide with a lowering of regulatory standards, but will typically imply an increase in the strictness and comprehensiveness of environmental regulation.

Second, upward shifts of regulatory levels are triggered by the communicative influence of international organisations. This holds true in particular with regard to their role in the promotion of policy models based on the dissemination and evaluation of what they consider as 'best practice'. This competition of ideas can generally be expected to result in an overall strengthening of regulatory concepts. Since international organisations will in general promote the most progressive national approach, benchmarks will be set at the level of the highest-regulating country. Hence, an upward shift of the mean will be the likely result.

H 3   Communication hypotheses

H 3.1   Degree of convergence
The degree of convergence through transnational communication increases with the communicative potential of the institution in question (as expressed by the interaction density and breadth among its member states).

H 3.2   Direction of convergence
Transnational communication leads to stricter levels of regulation in the involved countries.

3.4.3 Regulatory competition

A number of conditions can be derived from theories of regulatory competition (Holzinger 2003; Scharpf 1997; Vogel 1995), which affect our convergence aspects. To begin with, these theories point to various factors that restrict the scope of potentially converging countries and policies. On the one hand, potential convergence effects of regulatory competition presuppose economic integration between market economies. Even in constellations of high economic integration, no competitive pressures will emerge in and between non-market economies. This scenario applies in particular to the CEE countries before 1990. On the other hand, a qualification applies to the policies for which convergence effects are predicted. Adjustments will be most pronounced for trade-related policies, such as product or process standards. No convergence is expected for policies which are subject to low competitive pressures from international markets. This holds true for all policies that are not directly related to products or to production processes, such as nature or bird protection policies. It holds also true if trade-related policies are concerned, but the effects of the regulation on production costs are low. In this case they do not affect competition between industries in different countries.

In general, theories of regulatory competition predict that countries adjust policy instruments and regulatory standards in order to cope with competitive pressures emerging from international economic integration. The more exposed a country is to competitive pressures following from high economic integration (emerging from its dependence on trade of goods, capital and services with other countries) the more likely it is that its policies will converge to other states with international exposure. In other words, the degree of convergence depends on the level of competitive pressures to which countries are exposed.

There is an ongoing debate in the literature on the direction of convergence caused by regulatory competition. Often a distinction is made between product and production process standards (Holzinger 2003; Scharpf 1997). In the case of process standards, we find a widely shared expectation that policy convergence will occur at the lowest common denominator; states will gravitate towards the policies of the most laissez-faire country (Drezner 2001). If the regulation of production processes implies an increase in the costs of production, potentially endangering the international competitiveness of an industry, regulatory competition will generally exert downward pressures on economic regulations (Scharpf 1997: 524). It is assumed that governments are ready to lower environmental standards in the face of lobbying and exit threats exerted by the respective industry.

Expectations are less homogeneous for product standards. While industries in both low-regulating and high-regulating countries have a common interest in harmonisation of product standards to avoid market segmentation, the level of harmonisation can hardly be predicted without the examination of additional factors. Most important in this context is the extent to which high-regulating countries are able to enforce stricter standards. If it is possible to erect exceptional trade barriers, as for example for health or environmental reasons under EU and WTO rules, convergence at a high level of regulation is to be expected. If such exceptional trade barriers cannot be justified, by contrast, competitive pressure will induce governments to lower their standards (Holzinger 2003: 196; Scharpf 1997; Vogel 1995).

As such exceptional trade barriers can usually be justified in the environmental sector (see above) we expect that a downward shift of the regulatory level will only occur in the case of process standards. Based on the arguments presented above and in the previous sections, we hypothesise that regulatory competition will lead to an upward shift of environmental regulation in the case of product standards.

H 4   Regulatory competition hypotheses
H 4.1   Degree of convergence
The degree of convergence increases with the competitive pressures to which countries are exposed (emerging from their dependence on trade of goods, capital and services with other countries).

H 4.2   Direction of convergence
Regulatory competition leads to stricter levels of regulation for product standards, while for process standards a weakening of regulatory standards is expected.

3.4.4 Other factors

Bennett identifies two conditions for parallel problem pressure to lead to the same solution (1988: 419). First, there must be certain intrinsic characteristics of a problem that would inevitably lead to its similar treatment. Second, these characteristics must be universally recognised. The problem with this argument, however, is that the extent to which convergence might be observed is strongly dependent on the definition of 'similar treatment'.

If similarity is defined in a very demanding way, including, for instance, the choice of instruments and regulatory settings, there will rarely be only one solution to a problem (Hoberg 1991; Rose 1991: 9). This is already valid for a relatively simple problem, such as the rainstorm mentioned above. Although many people may open their umbrellas, others may put on a hat, or seek shelter.

If we apply a less demanding definition of similarity, by contrast, there is a higher probability that we observe convergence as a result of parallel problem pressure. For example if the problem is that it starts raining, and the 'similar solution' is that people react to it, we will probably find convergence, as most people will in fact react somehow. Or, if the problem is the ageing of society, and the solution is that the pension schemes are changed, we might also find convergence, as most governments will change pension schemes. This implies, however, still a comparatively low degree of convergence, as the new pension schemes may be very different.

As the bandwidth of possible solutions or reactions to a problem is usually very broad, in the case of parallel problem pressure convergence can be expected only in very general terms (in the sense of mere reaction). A higher degree of convergence can be expected only if some additional conditions are fulfilled, for example, if similarity in environmental pressures and political demand of the affected countries is high. In other words, countries that share a broad number of characteristics are more inclined to independently react to a problem in a similar way (Lenschow, Liefferink and Veenman 2005).

Following our considerations in section 3.3.5 above, we therefore expect that countries are more likely to develop similar environmental policies over time the more they reveal or develop similarities with regard to the following characteristics: population density, emission levels (CO_2 emissions), the existence and influence of green parties, cultural similarity and income levels, as well as existing policies.

This way structural similarity may not only affect the degree of convergence among countries reacting to parallel problem pressures, but will also imply an overall increase in the strictness of regulatory standards. It is highly plausible that an increase in environmental pressures leads to respective adjustments in terms of more comprehensive regulatory approaches and stringent regulatory requirements. At the same time, an increase in political demand should lead to higher levels of protection.

H 5 Hypotheses on other variables

H 5.1 Degree of convergence

The degree of convergence increases with the degree of existing similarities between countries with respect to culture, income levels, demand for environmental protection, problem pressure as well as existing environmental policies.

H 5.2 Direction of convergence

The strictness of environmental regulation increases with the levels of income and environmental problem pressure as well as the demand for environmental protection.

3.5 CONCLUSION

In this chapter, we analysed various causes and factors regarding the scope, degree and direction of cross-national policy convergence.

Starting from the literature on convergence and related concepts, we developed theoretical expectations on the main causal mechanisms suggested by these theories. From these considerations several general conclusions can be drawn.

First, our analysis shows that one should not expect a general increase in the scope and degree of cross-national policy convergence. This is valid not only for the overall picture of the causes of policy convergence, but also for the individual causal mechanisms. Even if the mechanisms have an effect on policy convergence, it is – as a result of their different scope conditions – by no means justified to expect global convergence over all countries, policy areas and policy dimensions. As demonstrated by our analysis, the conditions and effects of convergence vary strongly across the different convergence mechanisms.

Second, we can generally expect an upward shift of the regulatory level of environmental standards. While regulatory competition may lead to a downward shift of the average policy in the case of process standards, the other mechanisms seem to imply a constant move towards stricter environmental policies.

4 Research design, variables and data

STEPHAN HEICHEL, KATHARINA HOLZINGER,
THOMAS SOMMERER, DUNCAN LIEFFERINK,
JESSICA PAPE AND SIETSKE VEENMAN

4.1 INTRODUCTION

This chapter gives an overview of the research design of the project, of the variables under investigation and of the data. Given the central research question underlying this project, convergence of national environmental policies is conceived as the dependent variable. Convergence is observed for twenty-four countries over a period of thirty years. Policy convergence is measured as increasing policy similarity over time. Policy similarity is investigated with respect to three dimensions of policy: presence-of-policy, policy instruments and policy settings. In section 4.2, we specify the operationalisation of and data collection for the dependent variable.

As outlined in chapter 3, the explanatory focus of the project is on three factors as the main independent variables that are expected to account for differences in environmental policy convergence: (1) the degree of interlinkage of countries in international institutions with obligatory potential, (2) the degree of interlinkage of countries in international institutions with communicative potential, and (3) the degree of economic interlinkage, i.e., the extent to which a country is connected with other countries by its trade relations. Moreover, we include further explanatory variables (referred to as 'other variables' in chapter 3). This is due to the fact that there are several other factors that we conceive as potentially having some impact on national environment policies and also on policy convergence, including cultural similarity between countries, pre-existing policy similarity, political demand exerted by green parties or green movements, the

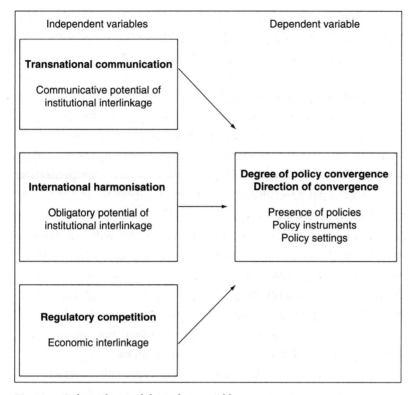

Figure 4.1 Independent and dependent variables

level of income in a country, as well as environmental problem
pressure as a general factor forcing national governments to react
through policy measures. Problem pressure indicators used here
include carbon dioxide emissions and population density. The central
independent and the other variables are introduced in section 4.3
and summarised in figure 4.1.

4.2 DEPENDENT VARIABLE: OPERATIONALISATION
AND DATA COLLECTION

4.2.1 The use of output data

We measure policy convergence by focusing on output rather than
outcome data. We are not interested in the convergence of environmental quality but in the convergence of the regulatory output.

The reason for this choice is that the theories predicting policy convergence have a micro foundation. The theory of regulatory competition assumes that as a result of market forces and industrial lobbying or exit threats, national governments come under pressure to adapt environmental standards and policies. That is, governments are the central actors in this theory. The same is true for policy learning via transnational communication: it is assumed that governments learn from others in international organisations and adapt their policies accordingly. Finally, international harmonisation requires national governments to adjust their policies to the norms agreed upon at the international level. Thus, what counts is what governments (or parliaments, depending on the political system) decide. The theories focus on policy output, not on policy outcomes. Policy output and policy outcome are only very indirectly related. There are many intervening variables affecting the outcomes which are independent of governmental or parliamentary decisions. For example, activities that damage the environment may increase and thus environmental quality degrades more than expected.

Therefore, we use the legal environmental policy output data for the study of convergence. This data type better reflects what is commonly understood as 'environmental policy', namely the 'vast corpus of legislation to restrain citizens and corporations from recklessly fouling the air, land, and water on which they depend for life and health' (Heidenheimer, Heclo and Adams 1990: 309). In that regard, we follow the advice that 'good theories deserve good data' (Baumgartner and Leech 1996) that truly fit the models even if this requires considerable collection efforts.

Policy output data are not systematically compiled by international organisations and thus have to be collected by researchers. Data on policy outcome, instead, can be obtained from existing sources, for example the OECD. Consequently, only a small number of studies employed environmental policy output data in large-n comparative analyses. However, most of these studies remain descriptive (e.g., Binder 2002; Kern, Jörgens and Jänicke 2000; Tews,

Busch and Jörgens 2003), while the rare causal inference analyses have only relied on individual policies (Fredriksson and Millimet 2004; Fredriksson *et al.* 2005; Hironaka 2002). Causal inference studies overwhelmingly employ data on policy outcome, for example emissions or quality data, as proxies for environmental policy.[1]

The data collected for this research project imply at least two important innovations. First, the data are not constrained to single measures but attempt to cover a broad range stretching over all environmental media. Second, environmental limit values are used as metrical data expressing the level and strictness of environmental standards.

4.2.2 Selection of policy items

Policy convergence is assessed by considering forty different environmental policies that were selected according to several criteria. First, they were taken to form a sample covering all environmental media, ranging from air quality protection to general guiding principles, such as sustainability.

Second, the policies cover the whole range of different policy types that are of particular theoretical interest. Hence, to assess the effects of economic interlinkage (regulatory competition), both trade-related policies (product and process standards) and policies that are not subject to competitive pressures are included. To investigate the effects of the obligatory (international harmonisation) and communicative (transnational communication) potential of international institutions, the policy compilation covers not only so-called 'obligatory' policy items for which a legally binding standard at the international level was introduced at some point between 1970 and 2000, but also 'non-obligatory' measures for which no internationally harmonised rules were in force during the observation period.

---

[1] Cf. Bernauer and Koubi 2004; Binder and Neumayer 2005; Crepaz 1995; Fisher and Freudenburg 2004; Jahn 1998, 2000; King and Borchardt 1994; Midlarsky 1998; Murdoch and Sandler 1997; Murdoch, Sandler and Sargent 1997; Neumayer 2001, 2003; Ricken 1995, 1997; Scruggs 1999, 2001, 2003; Shandra *et al.* 2004.

Third, the selection of policies was accomplished with the intention of analysing convergence effects with regard to the three different policy dimensions (presence-of-policy, instruments and settings). This way, we are able to analyse whether convergence varies across the different dimensions. Moreover, the inclusion of setting policies allows us to assess the direction of convergence.

The forty policy items selected are listed in table 4.1. The table indicates their characteristics in terms of the three policy dimensions, trade-relatedness, and the presence of international obligations. Of the forty policies, nineteen belong to the group of obligatory international policies in the year 2000, while for twenty-one policies obligatory international measures did not exist throughout the period. In earlier periods fewer policies were obligatory (see table 4.1). Eleven policies are product-related, fifteen are related to production processes and fourteen are not related to products and production processes. Finally, while all forty policies do indicate presence-of-policy, twenty-eight belong to the instrument type and twenty-one to the setting category (see chapter 6.2.2 for details).

4.2.3 Selection of countries and time period

The goal of this research project is to study convergence of environmental policies in Europe. The sample is therefore primarily composed of European countries. From the pool of all European countries, twenty-one were selected. The European group is complemented by three non-European countries. The overall sample thus includes twenty-four countries.

The core of the sample is constituted by member states of the EU. Of the member states in 2000 fourteen are included.[2] This may look like a lack of variance in the sample with respect to membership. However, the country sample represents all steps in the process of EU enlargements, and therefore over time it includes a sufficient

---

[2] The exception is Luxemburg for which data for some, especially the economic, variables are not available separately.

Table 4.1 *List of environmental policies for the dependent variable*

Policy	Environmental media	Policy type			Trade relatedness of policy			Obligatory policy			
		Setting	Instrument	Policy presence	Product	Process	Non-trade related	1970	1980	1990	2000
1 Sulphur content in gas oil	Air	•	•	•	•				•	•	•
2 Lead in petrol		•	•	•	•				•	•	•
3 Passenger cars NOx emissions		•	•	•	•				•	•	•
4 Passenger cars CO emissions		•	•	•	•			•	•	•	•
5 Passenger cars HC emissions		•	•	•	•			•	•	•	•
6 Large combustion plants SO$_2$ emissions		•	•	•		•				•	•
7 Large combustion plants NOx emissions		•	•	•		•				•	•
8 Large combustion plants dust emissions		•	•	•		•				•	•

Table 4.1 (*cont.*)

Policy	Environ-mental media	Policy type			Trade relatedness of policy			Obligatory policy			
		Setting	Instrument	Policy presence	Product	Process	Non-trade related	1970	1980	1990	2000
9 Coliforms in bathing water	Water	•	•	•			•	•	•	•	•
10 Hazardous substances in detergents			•	•	•					•	•
11 Efficient use of water in industry				•		•					
12 Industrial discharges in surface water lead		•	•	•		•					
13 Industrial discharges in surface water zinc		•	•	•		•					
14 Industrial discharges in surface water copper		•	•	•		•					

						•	•	
				•	•	•	• •	•
•		•						
•		•		• •	•	• •	•	•
•		•		•		•	•	
•		•				•	•	

15 Industrial discharges in surface water chromium

16 Industrial discharges in surface water BOD

Soil

17 Soil protection

18 Contaminated sites policy

Waste

19 Waste recovery target

20 Waste landfill target

21 Glass reuse/ recycling target

22 Paper reuse/ recycling target

23 Promotion of refillable beverage containers

24 Voluntary deposit system beverage containers

Table 4.1 (cont.)

Policy	Environmental media	Policy type			Trade relatedness of policy			Obligatory policy			
		Setting	Instrument	Policy presence	Product	Process	Non-trade related	1970	1980	1990	2000
25 Noise emissions standard from lorries	Noise	•	•	•	•			•	•	•	•
26 Motorway noise emissions		•	•	•			•				
27 Noise level working environment		•	•	•		•		•	•	•	•
28 Electricity from renewable sources	Resources		•	•		•					
29 Recycling construction waste				•		•					
30 Energy efficiency of refrigerators	Climate		•	•	•						•

31	Electricity tax for households		•		•			•	•		
32	Heavy fuel oil levy for industry		•		•	•		•	•		•
33	CO$_2$ emissions from heavy industry				•	•		•	•		
34	Forest protection — Nature		•		•	•	•	•	•		
35	Eco-audit — General					•		•			
36	Environmental impact assessment		•	•	•	•	•	•			
37	Eco-labelling			•			•	•			
38	Precautionary principle: reference in legislation		•	•			•	•			
39	Sustainability: reference in legislation					•		•			
40	Environmental/ sustainable development plan					•		•			

number of non-EU countries. The EU founding members – Belgium, France, Germany, Italy and the Netherlands – form the core group of the sample. Hence in 1970, only five countries out of twenty-four are subject to EU legislation. By 1980, Denmark, Ireland and the UK had become EU members, and by 1990, the Southern enlargement countries, Greece, Portugal and Spain, had joined the EU. At that time, EU members constitute still less than half of the sample (eleven). Former members of the European Free Trade Association (EFTA), Austria, Finland and Sweden, joined the EU in 1995. The group of EU members in 2000 is complemented by two groups of countries from CEE: with Hungary, Poland and Slovakia three countries are included that became EU members in 2004. Finally, Bulgaria and Romania belong to the sample that will probably accede in 2007. Two further countries complete the European group, the EFTA member states Norway and Switzerland.[3]

To control for the EU harmonisation effects and to increase variance regarding several crucial covariates, the sample includes three non-European countries. The US and Japan are countries with a high level of economic development and a high trade volume, while Mexico shows a comparatively low level of economic interlinkage and economic development.

The period of observation reaches from 1970 to the year 2000. This longitudinal perspective ensures that the data on environmental policy are more than a current snap-shot, and that policy changes can be studied in the long term; this is indispensable to each study that aims to analyse processes of convergence. The year 1970 is chosen as a starting point because at that time environmental policies began to develop at the national, as well as at the international, level

---

[3] Several other European countries had to be omitted from our sample. The Czech Republic is not included, as only one successor state of former Czechoslovakia should be part of the sample. This is to avoid an artificial bias towards convergence, because these countries had the same policies until 1990. The same applies to Germany, where only the Western part is included for the period before 1990. For similar reasons, as well as for problems of data accessibility, no country from the former Soviet Union (the Baltics) or former Yugoslavia is part of the sample.

(e.g., with the 1972 UN Conference on the Human Environment in Stockholm). The observation period ends in 2000, the last year for which data were available for all variables when data collection started in 2003.

Basically, there are two extreme strategies for analysing convergence: first, one can take only two points of measurement, and second, one can use a time series design. Taking only two points in time (1970, 2000) does not allow us to see intermediate developments. Many policy changes are likely to have happened in between. Time series design is not adequate either, because of low variance over time: environmental policy is not expected to change on a yearly base – the process of domestic policy-making takes its time, as does the influence that comes from the international level. As it is rarely the case that several changes occur within a decade, an intermediate strategy is employed: policy convergence is measured for each decade separately. The research design is therefore based on the measurement of policy similarity at four points in time: 1970, 1980, 1990 and 2000. This way most policy changes are covered.

4.2.4 Data collection and processing

The dependent variable describes the evolution of forty environmental policy items in twenty-four countries over thirty years. This vast amount of data was collected with the help of expert surveys. This way, a comprehensive database was compiled, offering unique opportunities for studying patterns of environmental policy convergence between the countries involved. In the following, we discuss the measures taken to ensure data validity and reliability during data collection and data processing.

Expert surveys The necessary output data could not be compiled from existing sources. The ECOLEX database on environmental law, developed by the World Conservation Union, the UN Food and Agriculture Organisation and the UN Environment Programme comes closest to our requirements, but even here 'historical' information on early environmental legislation is often lacking. To obtain this information, it proved necessary to access the original laws, decrees and ordinances.

In so doing, we relied on expert surveys. Expert surveys are generally seen to have several crucial advantages over alternative approaches. Precisely because they reflect the judgements of experts, they acquire a certain weight and legitimacy. Furthermore, as expert judgements are reasonably comprehensive, they permit the collection of comparable and standardised data. Despite these advantages, however, problems of validity and reliability of the data may occur. For instance, the same question may be interpreted in different ways by different experts. Measurement errors could occur for example when experts overlook legislation. However, as we asked the experts for facts (introduction of laws, use of instruments, setting of limit values etc.) and not for opinions or attitudes, most of the problems regarding the validity and the reliability of data that are common to social science surveys did not apply here.

An important step in guaranteeing the quality of data was to make a careful selection of experts to carry out the work. First, in order to address adequately the wide variety of questions in the survey, the experts had to have a comprehensive overview of environmental policy development from 1970 to 2000. Second, the group of experts should be as homogeneous as possible, so as to ensure the comparability of data (Frankfort-Nachmias and Nachmias 1996). In order to meet both criteria, we limited our selection to academics with a background in political science or law and preferably working at research institutes or universities.

The design of the questionnaire and the manual The questionnaire had a standardised set up so as to limit the room for interpretation to a minimum (see table A4.1 in the annex for an example). At the same time, open questions ('remarks section') were included to allow for the description of item-specific characteristics. This facilitated the checking of data comparability. The questionnaire was accompanied by a detailed manual, presenting general instructions and definitions as well as background information on each individual policy item to ensure the validity and reliability of the data (see below).

As set out above, the selection of policies addressed by the project covered one or more of the three dimensions: presence-of-policy, policy instrument and setting. The first type – 'presence-of-policy' questions – asked for the mere existence of certain environmental policies in 1970, 1980, 1990 and 2000 and, if they existed, the year of their introduction.

The second type – 'policy instrument' questions – addressed the kinds of instruments used to tackle environmental problems as well as their application over time. Experts were asked to select one 'dominant' instrument type from the following list:

(1) obligatory standard, prohibition or ban
(2) technological prescription
(3) tax or levy
(4) subsidy or tax reduction
(5) liability scheme(s)
(6) planning instrument
(7) public investment
(8) data collection / monitoring programmes
(9) information based instrument
(10) voluntary instrument
(11) other instruments[4]

Since in practice almost always mixes of instruments are used to address a given problem, this implied that experts assessed the role of different instrument types before selecting the 'dominant' one. In order to prevent an arbitrary interpretation of what is 'dominant' and due to problems the pre-testers encountered with this question,

---

[4] The last instrument type served only as a residual category in case an expert felt unable to assign the national instrument to one of the existing types. For the rare cases where this occurred we were usually able to subsume the national policy instrument under one of the existing categories after consulting the expert.

it was specified in the accompanying manual that if there was an instrument mix including an 'obligatory standard, prohibition or ban', this instrument should be counted as dominant. This instruction rests on the argument that obligatory instruments tend to dominate over other instruments in the mix, because other instruments like subsidies or information rights are then usually designed to support this obligation. Although this induced a certain bias towards the 'obligatory' type of instruments, this procedure ensured that experts interpreted the question in a consistent way and that results would be comparable. In addition, experts were requested to indicate the exact name of the instrument and briefly explain its function (e.g., gasoline tax reduction for lead-free petrol as an instrument to regulate lead emissions from vehicles). This was to be accompanied by the name of the legislation containing the regulation in order to facilitate cross-checking by the project team.

The third type of questions related to environmental policy settings. Here experts were asked to provide numerical values of limit values, emission standards, quantified goals or tax rates. In addition, the experts were requested to indicate the unit of measurement. Finally, each policy item in the questionnaire contained a section for further remarks and one for references. The remarks section enabled experts to describe in more detail particular characteristics of the policy in question. This enhanced validity as it enabled the research team to retrace the decisions taken by the expert in problematic cases. The reference section improved reliability by enabling the project team to verify the information.

The aim to receive adequate, complete, precise and comparable data was further served by providing an extensive manual to accompany the questionnaire. In the first part of the manual definitions of basic terms and instructions were given that allowed for a consistent interpretation of the questions. The second part contained sections on every policy item covered by the questionnaire, clarifying technical terms used and defining very precisely which information we were looking for (see table A4.2 in the annex for an example).

Before the questionnaires were sent out, two experts were asked to carry out a pre-test. Pre-testing is the only way to evaluate in advance whether a questionnaire causes problems for interviewers or respondents (Graesser *et al.* 2000: 459; Presser 2004; 109). The comments of the two pre-testers led to substantial improvements of both the questionnaire and the manual.

Experts were asked to keep in touch with the research team during the entire process of filling in the questionnaire. If further specifications of questions turned out to be necessary, these were immediately communicated to all other experts. This further reduced the risk of inconsistencies and increased the validity of the data.

Data processing After the questionnaire had been received back from the experts, two further steps were undertaken to increase the validity and reliability of the data. First, the material provided by the experts was systematically cross-checked. For this purpose, we relied on data available from other databases, for instance, the OECD, the European Environment Agency, as well as from ECOLEX and other relevant scientific literature, including an existing data set compiled by one of the project partners (Busch and Jörgens 2005a). Moreover, a random sample of six questions for detailed cross-checking was selected for each country, which took into account the variety of questions asked (presence-of-policy, instruments, settings). All checks were carried out in order to see whether the information given by the experts was reliable.

Second, the data set was 'cleaned' by clarifying and correcting remaining inconsistencies and errors. Three basic types of inconsistencies emerged:

(1) Different units of measurement. In the large majority of cases this only entailed the recalculation of settings into a single unit, e.g. mg/m^3. In a few cases, however, differences were not due only to the application of different measurement units as such, but also to the use of different measurement procedures. Emissions,

for instance, were measured at different heights or at different distances from the source. If possible, transformation tables were created. Where this was not possible, which was the exception rather than the rule, this constituted a missing value in the data set. In those cases, of course, the existence of a limit value was still recorded to avoid unnecessary loss of data.[5]

(2) Differentiated standards. For a limited number of items, it turned out that standards in some or all countries were even more differentiated than anticipated in the questionnaire and manual, for example different limit values for different industrial (sub-) sectors, for different sizes of plants, for old and new plants, for different regions. In those cases, as a rule, we chose the environmentally strictest values in place. For example, for noise levels around streets, we took the values applying at night in the highest protection zones.

(3) Different interpretations of policy instruments in use. In a few cases, the precise character of policy instruments in use turned out to be difficult to determine for experts, leading to inconsistent interpretations. In relation to taxes on water extraction, for instance, it proved impossible in most countries to distinguish between a tax meant for regulatory purposes (i.e., as an incentive to change behaviour) and a tax only intended for covering administrative costs, or a combination of both. Therefore, it was decided that all taxes/fees/charges given in questionnaires should count as a tax.

The phase of data processing was completed with the compilation of a raw data set in SPSS statistical software. Presence of a policy for each point of measurement was coded as '1' (yes) or '0' (no). Policy instrument data were re-coded on a scale ranging from '1' ('obligatory standard, prohibition or ban') to '10' ('voluntary instrument'). Data on settings were included as numerical values. The final result was

---

[5] In the case of air pollution from passenger cars, emission standards were based on different test cycles and harmonisation was not possible in the case of CO emissions. In order not to lose data and guarantee comparability, two sub-groups were constructed, with limits expressed as g/km and volume per cent, respectively.

one complete set containing the entire information for the sample countries from 1970 to 2000, as well as four separate data blocs for 1970, 1980, 1990 and 2000.

4.2.5 Types of convergence

It is essential to any study of convergence to address the question of how convergence can actually be measured. The theoretical contributions by Bennett (1991: 296ff.), Seeliger (1996: 288) and Unger and Waarden (1995: 3) have convincingly demonstrated that convergence means, by definition, the increase of policy similarity. From the literature, different operationalisations of this basic definition of convergence can be deduced which refer to different ideas of similarity (see Heichel, Pape and Sommerer 2005).

Sigma-convergence as 'growing together' The most basic way of assessing policy convergence is to analyse the extent to which the policies of countries have become more similar over time (sigma-convergence). Following this approach, convergence occurs if there is a decrease in variation of policies among the countries under consideration. This concept is named after the algebraic notation for variance, sigma (Sala-i-Martin 1996: 1326ff.). In its traditional form, a decreasing coefficient of variance, the normalised standard deviation, also known as dispersion index, indicates convergence. However, many other ways to operationalise sigma-convergence are applied (see Heichel, Pape and Sommerer 2005). This approach to convergence is used in studies on tax revenue and governmental expenditure or on tax rates as well as on trade policy. As the most important approach to convergence, sigma-convergence will be analysed in depth in chapters 5 and 6.

Beta-convergence as 'catching up' A second approach to investigating similarities across countries, often used in economics, is the study of beta-convergence. It occurs when poor economies grow faster than rich ones and it is named after the growth coefficient, beta

(Sala-i-Martin 1996: 1326ff.) An example of an adequate transformation from economics to the context of analysing policy laggards and policy frontrunners in immigration policy shows the valuable contribution of this logic to policy analysis (Holzer and Schneider 2002: 64). Here, beta-convergence occurs when the degree and speed of tightening asylum regulations in formerly liberal countries is higher than in formerly restrictive ones. For environmental policy, beta-convergence occurs when countries with lax environmental regulations tighten their regulations faster than those applying strict regulation from the beginning. This concept will be applied to the assessment of convergence of environmental policies in chapter 5.

Gamma-convergence as 'mobility' A recent variant of convergence research is gamma-convergence. It was developed in response to beta-convergence, which has been criticised for not sufficiently capturing aspects of cross-country dynamics (Boyle and McCarthy 1999). For the analysis of gamma-convergence, country rankings for different points in time are compared to assess the mobility of countries. If countries in the first ranks fall behind or countries in the last ranks catch up over time, convergence occurs. Policy change is analysed by simple measures of association, like the Kendall index of rank concordance (Boyle and McCarthy 1999). A low degree of similarity between rankings indicates high mobility of countries over time. The concept of gamma-convergence adds an additional perspective to the study of policy convergence as it may occur where other approaches do not detect changes. Country rankings, for example, may change without a significant decrease of cross-country variation or without an approximation towards an exemplary policy model. Although the study of gamma-convergence is not very common yet, it represents nonetheless a promising tool for policy studies, as the idea of comparing ordinal classifications is also compatible with a qualitative research design. In addition to changes in growth rates, gamma-convergence will be studied in chapter 5.

Delta-convergence as 'minimising distance to an exemplary model'
Many studies on convergence analyse different aspects than those sketched above. What they have in common is an approach to convergence based on the decreasing distance of policies towards an exemplary model, for example a model promoted by an international organisation or a frontrunner country. Based on the algebraic notation of 'distance', delta, this concept can be called delta-convergence. Empirically, gamma- and delta-convergence often occur simultaneously. If countries reach total similarity relative to a policy model, variance between them is obviously reduced. However, if delta-convergence is not complete, policies may approach the model by parallel moves without becoming more similar. By the reference to an exemplary policy model that may be the strictest, the laxest, or the mean level of environmental regulation, delta-convergence adds aspects of the direction of convergence to the analysis. It will be applied in depth to environmental policy convergence in chapter 7.

Depending on the type of convergence investigated, empirical results might be interpreted very differently. Evidence of sigma-convergence, for instance, does not necessarily mean that there is also gamma-convergence. Moreover, evidence of beta-convergence does not imply that there must also be sigma-convergence: the fact that laggard countries change more fundamentally than leader countries is not a sufficient condition for a decrease in variance across all countries.

4.3 INDEPENDENT VARIABLES: OPERATIONALISATION AND DATA COLLECTION

4.3.1 Institutional interlinkage

In chapter 3, a central role for the explanation of convergence is assigned to the influence of integration into international institutions. The operationalisation of institutional influence is thus of great importance for the analysis of convergence. There is no standard tool for the operationalisation. The effects of international institutions on domestic policy change are only sporadically included in quantitative empirical studies, mainly through the inclusion of membership in certain international organisations like the EU or the OECD.

Two different mechanisms are supposed to effect policy convergence through international institutions: international harmonisation and transnational communication. Therefore, two variables will be developed and later tested separately: the obligatory potential and the communicative potential of institutional interlinkage.

Although differentiated according to the respective mechanisms, both variables are based on national membership data. This is necessary, as the data on international institutions has to be linked to the national level at a certain point: policy convergence is measured at the level of countries or country pairs. As a first step of operationalisation of institutional interlinkage, a 'membership' variable is calculated based on the membership of countries in thirty-five selected international institutions. Second, the membership data are weighted according to the institutions' 'encompassingness', as international institutions differ in size and range of activities. Third, two indicators of the obligatory and communicative potential of an international institution are introduced, by which the 'membership and encompassingness' variable is weighted. This provides us with the two indicators for the mechanisms of international harmonisation and transnational communication. Altogether, we thus develop four different variables of institutional interlinkage that will be used for different purposes in the quantitative models.

Membership in international institutions As outlined above, this project attempts to deliver a comprehensive view of the interactions in the field of European environmental policy. This is not just a matter of a wide-ranging selection of policies for the dependent variable; it should also represent the various influences at the level of international cooperation and coordination in the field of environmental policy. Therefore, all relevant institutions are included in an aggregate variable of institutional interlinkage in the environmental field (see annex table A4.3).

Altogether thirty-five international institutions were selected. The selection of institutions is based on the *Yearbook of International Cooperation on Environment and Development* (2002), complemented by some other institutions. Only those institutions which have at least three contracting parties are included, and at least two countries from our sample should be members of these institutions. This excludes the vast amount of bilateral agreements – including them would have been very time consuming without adding much variance.

The institutions listed in table A4.4 in the annex can be classified into five different categories. The first category involves political institutions with a very broad field of activity (general multi-issue organisations). They are of major importance for international relations in general, and, among others, possess a department for environmental policy. Examples are the EU and the OECD. A second group consists of institutions that are predominantly occupied with environmental policy, for example the UN Environmental Programme (UNEP) or the International Union on the Conservation of Nature (IUCN) (environmental multi-issue organisations). Thirdly, there are international institutions that have their main focus on a different field but include environmental aspects as policy tasks, such as the WTO or the Organisation for Security and Cooperation in Europe (OSCE) (non-environmental single-issue organisations). Global or European environmental regimes are a fourth category of institutions (environmental single-issue organisations). An example is the Vienna Convention for the Protection of the Ozone Layer of 1985. Finally, regional regimes like the Conventions on river protection or the Alpine Convention were included.

Encompassingness The aggregation of institutional scores necessitates some sort of weighting. Differences in size and relative importance in international relations are considerable, for example, between the EU and single-issue regimes like the Espoo Convention. To differentiate for size effects, we develop an index for the encompassingness of international institution that is used as a weighting factor.

The weighting factor for encompassingness includes three indicators that are supposed to represent various dimensions of size effects. First and foremost, the importance of an international institution is measured by the breadth of its fields of activity. On the one hand, this represents the relative size of an organisation in general, not only for environmental policy; on the other hand, it is important to note that environmental protection is a cross-sectional policy, hence other policy fields are of importance, as well. We count the number of policy areas, assuming that the level of encompassingness increases with the number of policy areas an institution includes. An almost nation state-like jurisdiction, such as the EU, constitutes the top of the scale. The scheme for the classification of fourteen policy areas is borrowed from the structure of the General Directorates of the European Commission. The original scale from one to fourteen is transformed into a simpler one with three categories only: more than ten areas, five to ten areas, and fewer than five areas (see table A4.3 in the annex).

This first indicator represents the influence of an international organisation or regime only in very general terms, and it is obviously not sufficient. Therefore, a second indicator is included that reflects the scope of environmental problems that are regulated by this institution. They are categorised into three different classes: the institution deals either with all aspects of environmental policies, with various issues, or with one environmental issue only, such as the Convention on Biological Diversity. This indicator increases the difference between encompassing international organisations and single-issue regimes.

The final indicator of encompassingness refers to differences in the relative importance of environmental aspects for an institution. Although, for example, the scope of environmental issues addressed by the WTO is broader than for environmental regimes, it is obvious that environmental protection is not the main subject in this organisation. Here, we distinguish between three different degrees of priority of environmental problems: in an international institution, they can play a dominant role, be an issue amongst others, or be of no special importance at all. This indicator leads to a downgrading of institutions like the WTO that are large and influential in general, but not in the field of environmental protection.

For the index of institutional encompassingness, these three indicators are summed up and comprised into a weighting factor with a scale from 0–9 that is normalised to 0–1 (see table A4.3 in the annex).[6] The value for each institution is given in the ENC column of table A4.4 in the annex.

Date of 'signature' v. 'entry into force' Across all institutions, we collected two different types of membership data, according to differences in the indices for obligatory and communicative potential that will be introduced below as further weighting factors for the data on national membership. The date of accession is operationalised differently for the two factors. For obligatory potential, we apply the date of 'entry into force' because a treaty is not binding for a country before the national ratification process has been finished. For communicative potential, the date of 'signature' is used, since we assume that transnational communication starts even before an international agreement is ratified. For some institutions, the difference between 'signature' and 'entry into force' is up to five years. All institutions are captured according to that scheme except for one: for the EU only one date is collected, that is the beginning of accession talks. We assume that the process of taking over the *acquis communautaire* starts already with the beginning of accession talks.

Obligatory potential International harmonisation will be tested by adding an index of obligatory potential (OP in table A4.4 in the annex)

---

[6] The reliability for the scale of the index is confirmed by a test of Cronbachs α.

to the data on institutional membership and encompassingness. The obligatory potential of an institution strongly depends on the legal status of its regulatory output. In a first step, this output can be categorised by its degree of bindingness for domestic policy-makers. Categories for bindingness can be deduced from common categories of international law (Abbott *et al.* 2000), leading to a scale with three different types of regulatory output results.

The highest degree of obligation in the sphere of international legislation emanates from supranational law. Even though in international law studies its distinction from other types of law is not unchallenged (cf. Bogdandy 1999; Neyer 1999; Zürn 2000), this category finds wide support. Regulations of this type are implemented prior to national law and can also be enforced by national courts or specific international courts; regulatory output is directly binding without a process of ratification through national parliaments. In supranational law, one finds three different types of output. Determinate and interpretable regulations, represented in EU legislation by regulations and directives, are complemented by the category 'decision', which is also known from EU regulations and comprises regulations with a limited or individual scope of application, such that the binding effect on policy-making in general will be lower. Decisions of the WTO dispute resolution panel also belong to this category.

International hard law is the second most binding category. This is the traditional category of international law on the basis of multilateral contract law. It is also binding, but not as directly as in the case of supranational law. In international hard law, we mainly find international treaties or protocols that have to be ratified by the national parliaments. With respect to their legal bindingness the latter are not equal to treaties. However, protocols like the Kyoto protocol to the International Framework Convention on Climate Change are instruments for interpretation of treaties. Thus, they rank lower in their obligatory potential, but are definitely more obligatory than international soft law.[7] Examples for international hard law are found in international conventions, such as the 1979 Convention on Long-Range Transboundary Air Pollution.

The third category comprises international soft law; any regulatory output of an international institution that does not explicitly fall under the first two categories is subsumed under this category. Thus, a wide range of different regulatory output belongs to international soft law.

First, we find resolutions that are decisions of the institution or of one of its organisational bodies with the intention to bind, but not in the form of international contract law. Second, and less binding, there are coordinating measures and third, there are recommendations. Finally, there are measures like benchmarking or opinion statements.[8] The scale for 'type of law' is an additive one, as different types of regulatory outputs exist in parallel and complement each other. It is calculated as a weighted sum, resulting in a scale from 0 to 6 (1+2+3; see table A4.3 in the annex).

Whereas type of law is an obvious indicator for an institution's obligatory potential, it is not the only one. A second indicator is used to differentiate between institutional capacities to monitor the compliance of its members. Four categories are distinguished, defined by different types of monitoring found in international institutions. Monitoring by courts is the strictest category (e.g., the European Court of Justice). Specialised monitoring bodies, which fall into the second category, are found in many international institutions (e.g., the Implementation Committee for the Vienna Convention). Such a monitoring body is not equivalent to a court; however, it

---

[7] According to the Vienna Convention on the Law of Treaties from 1969, the disregard of international hard law has severe consequences. Also, by definition of the UN Charter, hard law gains its obligatory potential from the possibility of settling disputes before international courts; in addition, reprisals are legitimate for other members, if a 'black sheep' fails to comply with the rules.

[8] The bindingness of international soft law is defined by the fact that against a non-complying member, the instrument of retortion as an unfriendly measure of self-help as a response to mis-conduct is allowed according to the UN Charter.

also controls the efforts to implement international law. The third category comprises reporting duties found in many international regimes. An example is the UN Framework Convention on Climatic Change, where national reports are obligatory for national governments. The weakest monitoring instrument is found in the classical institution of diplomacy that can also exert pressure on domestic policy-makers where no other means are available at the international level.

Both indicators are combined into an index of obligatory potential with a scale from 0 to 10, where the type of law has a slightly higher weight (see table A4.3 in the annex).[9] To build a variable representing the effects of legal obligation through institutional interlinkage, this index for all thirty-five institutions is used as a second weighting factor (after encompassingness) for the institutional membership data on country level.

Communicative potential To measure effects of transnational communication, we develop an index of communicative potential (CP in table A4.4 in the annex). It measures the influence of international institutions that goes beyond effects of international law and supranational legislation. Four indicators are selected to cover the relevant dimensions of communication in international institutions.

The first indicator is frequency of interaction. It captures how often members of national governments or ministerial bureaucracies meet in international institutions. The communicative link between the international and the national level is very direct in this case, as the actors themselves are involved in national policy-making. The data on the frequency of meetings have been gathered for all organisational bodies that are concerned with environmental issues, such as committees and working groups on environmental policy, as well as for all organisational bodies that are higher in the hierarchy than these former ones, such as a conference of parties or a general council;

---

[9] The reliability for the scale of the index is confirmed by a test of Cronbachs α.

there, environmental aspects may also be discussed among other issues. Unit of measurement is the number of meetings per year. Of all organisational bodies, the one with the maximum frequency of interaction is chosen, as it best represents the potential of informational exchange. The original scale for the number of meetings (0.33–150) is transformed to a scale from 0–10 (see table A4.3 in the annex).

The information on frequency of meetings is complemented by the number of organisational bodies where members of national governments or ministerial bureaucracies meet on environmental issues or on general issues. There may be cases where the maximum frequency of interaction is low, whereas the actual communicative potential is higher due to the presence of many organisational bodies. As for frequency of interaction, only those organisational bodies are included where representatives of national governments meet. The original scale already reaches from 0 to 10; thus, it does not have to be transformed.

The third indicator captures the extent to which national governments are represented permanently in international institutions or not. The communicative potential of an institution is supposed to be higher if there is a permanent delegate coordinating the informational exchange between international institutions and national governments. Presence of delegates is simply measured 'yes/no' and finally transformed to the same normalised scale as the other indicators for communicative potential.

The fourth indicator, size of staff, includes information on the professional staff permanently working for international institutions. The more employees working for an international organisation, the larger the amount of informational output this institution is able to spread, even without the initiative of national governments. The number of permanent employees in environmental departments reaches from 0 to 574, which is again transformed to a scale from 1–10.

These four indicators are aggregated to an index of communicative potential, with a scale from 0–40 (see table A4.3 in the annex).[10] As for obligatory potential, the institutional scores for communicative potential are used as weighting factors for membership data, in addition to information on encompassingness of institutions. As mentioned above, membership data for the communicative potential variable differ from obligatory potential, as the relevant point of reference for a country's accession is 'signature', not 'entry into force'. Furthermore, information on the length of membership is included in the membership data, as we assume that communication through international institutions works more efficiently in long-established networks than for newcomers.

Data collection The basic data needed with regard to membership of individual countries in individual institutions over time were taken from the *Yearbook of International Cooperation on Environment and Development*, published annually by the Fridtjof Nansen Institute (FNI) in Oslo, which provides a comprehensive collection of international environmental organisations. In addition, websites of institutions and national governments were used.

Further data were needed for weighing institutions according to their encompassingness, their obligatory and their communicative potential. This information was gathered mainly by consulting and comparing websites of the respective institutions, as well as by studying the wording of the relevant treaties. In cases where the information provided by the websites was incomplete or unclear, people directly involved in those institutions were asked.

The institutional data, with the exception of membership over time and type of law, were collected only for 2000, because data for earlier years were not available for all indicators. For some of the indicators, it may be safely argued that substantive change over time is not very likely, for example monitoring capacity. For other indicators, for example the number of contacts with national

---

[10] The reliability for the scale of the index is confirmed by a test of Cronbachs α.

representatives, development over time is more likely to occur. However, the overriding trend is one of increasing international institutional involvement around environmental issues between 1970 and 2000. Therefore, even if individual institutions have followed this trend somewhat more rapidly than others, it may be assumed that the overall *relative* picture among our thirty-five institutions has remained more or less stable.

4.3.2 Economic interlinkage

The classical approach to operationalising economic interlinkage is trade dependence. The intensity of an economy's integration with the rest of the world can be measured by trade flows. The variable conventionally used is trade openness, i.e., trade volume weighted by the size of a country's GDP (e.g., Li and Reuveny 2003). With regard to trade, we use figures on exports and imports of goods only, as imports and exports of services are not related to competitive pressure on products or production as a result of environmental regulation. For each country and each point in time, we use the rather common formula of trade figures as a percentage of total GDP (see table A4.3 in the annex).[11]

While the index of trade openness will be used for the analysis of delta-convergence in chapter 7, for the analysis of sigma-convergence by the pair approach (chapter 6), a different version of trade openness is applied. The pair approach is based on the comparison of each country pair in the sample. Thus, the data used have to be based on bilateral trade figures. These allow the competitive situation between two national economies to be captured in a more

---

[11] See, for example, Alesina and Waczirg 1998; Garrett and Mitchell 2001; Hallerberg and Basinger 1998: 334; Korpi and Palme 2003; Li and Reuveny 2003; Rudra 2004; for a concise discussion see Dowrick and Golley 2004. We rely on this approach, although some authors work with trade/PPP GDP (GDP expressed in purchasing power parities). This measure of 'real openness' (Alcalá and Ciccone 2004), however, is criticised with convincing arguments by Rodrik, Subramanian and Trebbi (2002: 18) for being strongly correlated with income levels.

direct way. The trade volume is weighted by the size of the smaller national market of a country pair in order to represent the degree of dependence in bilateral trade relations. To operationalise further conditions that can be derived from theories of regulatory competition (chapter 3), bilateral trade openness is corrected by the existence of integrated market economies: if one of the countries is not a member of GATT/WTO and does not have a market economy, there is no competition between a country pair (for the formula see table A4.3 in the annex). Both types of data could be easily obtained from OECD and World Bank sources.

4.3.3 Other variables

Cultural similarity is operationalised as the sum of three different indicators: (1) the existence of a common border between a country pair,[12] (2) the sharing of a common language and (3) the existence of common historical and religious tradition, expressed by the similarity of religion between two countries.[13] Hence, this indicator can vary between 0 and 3 for each country pair (see table A4.3 in the annex). We conceive this variable as static, which means that cultural ties and geographic proximity are assumed to be highly stable factors that are not subject to far-reaching changes over time.

Economic development is based on the income figures measured as GDP per capita (see table A4.3 in the annex). In the pair approach the income figure is multiplied by the difference in income between the two countries.

Domestic political demand for a comprehensive and stringent environmental policy could possibly be expressed in several ways, such as the number of environmental organisations or the public

---

[12] Sea borders count, if located within a 200-mile zone. This results, for example, in a common border between the Netherlands and the UK or Denmark and Sweden.

[13] All languages and all dominant religions count. Because of the pairwise-comparison, countries with more than one language or dominant religion cause no problems. Whenever two countries have a language or dominant religion in common they are rated similar.

opinion data on environmental awareness. In view of their important role in bringing about political changes in domestic environmental policy, we concentrate on the political influence of national green parties. Green parties' political influence can also be seen as a very general proxy for environmental problem pressure that is otherwise difficult to grasp for environmental policy in general. The influence of green parties is measured with three indicators: electoral success, membership in parliament and participation in government. The scores are calculated as follows: a score of 1 (instead of 0) is assigned if the national vote share of green parties is above 1 per cent, considering the closest national election for the lower chamber to the four points in time. An additional score of 1 is assigned if green parties are represented in parliaments. Finally, a country receives a third score of 1 if green parties govern at the time of measurement or if the government representation has not ended more than one year before. Thus, the overall score of the variable for political demand similarity varies between 0 and 3 (see table A4.3 in the annex).

Two further variables express environmental problem pressure: population density per capita/km^2 and the level of environmental pollution as measured by CO_2 emissions per capita (see table A4.3 in the annex). Finally, the effects of pre-existing similarity of policies on convergence in later periods will be investigated in the pair approach. An overview over all variables and indicators is given in figure 4.2.

For most of the above variables, well-known and widely used data sources exist. Other variable data are simple proxies for the concepts, e.g., common border or common language, expressing geographical proximity and cultural similarity, respectively. For prevalent religion, we consulted and compared three different data sources. Only the data on green party strength, expressing political pressure, were collected from a wider range of published and often used sources as well as from existing data sets. Table A4.5 summarises the other variables and the data sources that were consulted.

Dependent variable	Main independent variables	Other variables	Indicators
	Economic interlinkage		Trade openness Bilateral trade openness
	Institutional interlinkage		
	Obligatory potential		Institutional membership, weighed by – Encompassingness – Type of law – Monitoring capacity
	Communicative potential		Institutional membership, weighed by – Encompassingness – Length of membership – Frequency of interaction – Permanence of delegation – Number of organisational bodies – Size of staff
		Cultural similarity	Language, religion Geographical proximity
		Environmental problem pressure	CO_2 emissions Population density
Policy convergence Policy similarity		Level of income	GDP per capita
		Political demand	Green parties
		Pre-existing similarity	Policy similarity in $t-1$

Figure 4.2 Variables and indicators

4.4 CONCLUSION

This chapter provides an overview of the research design of this study and of the operationalisation of the variables. As to the dependent variable, environmental policy convergence, there are two important innovations. First, environmental policy convergence is based on a very broad selection of individual measures, namely forty policies representing several policy types and covering the full range of environmental media, including metrical data on limit values. Second, as the study strives to test theories that have a micro foundation and focus on governmental decisions, we use policy output data rather than outcome data. These data had to be collected for twenty-four countries and a period of thirty years. The process of data collection, in particular for the environmental policies but also for the institutional data, was very demanding and almost a 'project in its own right'. As to the main independent variables, the construction of the institutional indicators deserves attention. This project constitutes the first attempt to measure the integration of countries in international institutions in order to estimate their potential to harmonise policies and their potential to enhance policy learning among the member states.

5 Degree and direction of environmental policy convergence: analysis of aggregate data

CHRISTOPH KNILL, THOMAS SOMMERER AND
KATHARINA HOLZINGER

5.1 INTRODUCTION

This chapter provides an overview of the empirically found patterns of cross-national policy convergence. The central questions addressed are the following. First, are the environmental policies of the countries under study actually converging and, if so, to what extent? Second, what is the direction of policy convergence; i.e., does convergence coincide with an upward or downward shift of regulatory levels? Third, to what extent do our empirical findings vary across different policy dimensions (presence-of-policies, policy instruments and policy settings) and policy types (trade-related versus non-trade-related policies, obligatory versus non-obligatory policies)?

To answer these questions, we rely on aggregate data analysis to measure the degree and direction of convergence. This way, it is possible to highlight general convergence patterns for the countries and policies under study. In addition to the presentation of aggregate data, we illustrate different convergence patterns for individual policy items. The items reflect the different dimensions (policy presence, instruments and settings) and policy types under study.

For measuring the degree of convergence (i.e., the extent of changes in policy similarity over time), we use several concepts that are commonly applied in the literature (cf. Heichel, Pape and Sommerer 2005 and chapter 3 above). First, to analyse convergence with regard to the presence of policies and policy instruments, we rely on the concept of adoption rates. This approach, which is typically used in research on policy diffusion, gives us information on the spread of policies and instruments across countries. The more countries adopt a certain policy or instrument, the more the variation of their policy and instrument repertoires will decrease. Hence, from this perspective, an increase in adoption rates implies growing policy similarity across countries.

This approach is closely related to the second concept of sigma-convergence which we apply to analyse cross-national convergence with regard to the dimension of policy settings. According to this approach, convergence reflects the result of a decrease in the variation coefficient. By calculating changes in the regulatory mean, this way of measurement at the same time allows us to answer the second question raised above, namely, the extent to which we can observe a change in regulatory levels over time.

In addition and complementarily to sigma-convergence, two further convergence concepts have been applied in the literature. The concept of beta-convergence complements the assessments of changes in variation coefficients by analysing the extent to which laggard countries over time have caught up with the leader countries. While beta-convergence only allows for the identification of processes of catching up or further drifting apart between countries, the concept of gamma-convergence, which is based on the analysis of changes in country rankings with respect to the regulatory strictness of their policies, provides an instrument for measuring the extent to which catching up actually was accompanied by processes of overtaking. Gamma-convergence is measured by the degree of rank correlation; convergence presumes that the ranking in t_0 does not correlate to the ranking in t_1.

The remainder of this chapter is structured as follows. In section 5.2, we analyse convergence patterns regarding the presence of policies, taking adoption rates as analytical starting point. In section 5.3, the focus is on convergence of policy instruments, while section 5.4 is dedicated to the investigation of mean changes and convergence of policy settings. The concluding section (5.5) summarises the results and discusses the limits of aggregate approaches to analyse policy convergence.

5.2 CONVERGENCE IN TERMS OF POLICY PRESENCE: ADOPTION RATES

The least demanding indicator for policy convergence is to focus on the extent to which countries have developed a policy at all in response to a certain environmental problem. According to this criterion, policy convergence increases with the extent to which countries have a certain policy in place, regardless of the instrument types and setting levels that are applied to achieve the policy objectives.

In the literature on policy diffusion, adoption rates are the most common approach to investigating convergence with regard to the presence of policies. Adoption rates not only include information on the number of countries that have introduced a certain policy, but also on the extent to which the number of adopters changes over time. In the following, we first give a comprehensive overview over adoption rates for the whole policy sample under investigation. In a second step, we illustrate typical adoption patterns that can be observed empirically.

5.2.1 General patterns

Starting with the development for the whole sample of the forty policies under investigation, we find a continuous spread of environmental policies across countries (see table 5.1). So, the average adoption rate continuously grew over time, with almost a doubling of the rate during each decade under investigation. From a modest average adoption rate of 11 per cent in 1970, all of the forty environmental policies under study had already been adopted in 46 per cent of all countries in the sample by 1990. By 2000, the average adoption rate had further increased to 78 per cent, including several policies with an adoption rate of 100 per cent. By contrast, there are only few policies in our sample that were spreading comparatively slowly so far, implying rather low adoption rates.

Table 5.1 *Environmental policies: average adoption rates*

	1970	1980	1990	2000	No. of policies[1]
All policies	11.23%	25.97%	45.98%	77.70%	40
Product-related policies	11.00%	41.31%	55.32%	79.95%	11
Production-process-related policies	13.00%	23.88%	50.10%	83.69%	15
Non product-/process-related policies	9.50%	16.14%	34.23%	69.50%	14
Obligatory policies	20.83%	55.73%	73.72%	86.18%	3/8/13/19
Non-obligatory policies	10.59%	18.48%	32.56%	70.04%	37/32/27/21

Note:
[1] The respective numbers for obligatory and non-obligatory policy items vary over the investigation period, as over time more and more policies became subject to international or supranational regulation. The respective numbers given in the outer right column refer in their order to the four decades distinguished in the table.

A closer look at the different policy sub-groups reveals, however, that average adoption rates vary across policy types. First, until 1990 adoption rates for obligatory policies (which are subject to international harmonisation) are more than two times higher than for non-obligatory policies. However, convergence degrees for non-obligatory policies were considerably catching up during the 1990s: whereas obligatory policies are on average adopted by 86 per cent of the twenty-four countries under study, the respective rate for non-obligatory policies is already around 70 per cent. Second, with the exception of the values for 1980, the spreading patterns for trade-related policies are rather similar, regardless whether product or process-related measures are concerned. Third, and similar to the difference between obligatory and non-obligatory policies, we can observe a considerable, albeit less pronounced, gap in adoption rates between trade-related and non-trade-related policies, including a similar process of catching-up of the latter from the 1990s onwards.

Table 5.2 presents a more detailed overview, covering adoption rates for all forty policies under investigation. According to their adoption rate level in the year 2000, the policies are divided into four sub-groups, including policies which have been adopted in 25, 50, 75 and 90 per cent of all countries under study by the year 2000. Moreover, the table gives information on the policy type. While the extent to which policies are trade-related or not does not change, the nature of the policies as non-obligatory or obligatory might vary over time, as a result of growing harmonisation activities at the supranational or international level. This development is indicated by bold type in the table.

The table indicates several patterns with regard to the cross-national spread of environmental policies. First, the data show that the extent to which policies are trade-related and obligatory has a positive influence on the level of the adoption rates. For the two groups with relatively high adoption rates in the year 2000 (over 75 per cent and over 90 per cent), the numbers of policies that are

Table 5.2 *Environmental policies: adoption rates over time*

	Trade-related	1970	1980	1990	2000
Forest protection	NPP	79.0%	95.8%	100.0%	100.0%
Lead in petrol	P	29.2%	**70.8%**	**91.7%**	**100.0%**
Passenger cars CO emissions	P	**16.7%**	**66.7%**	83.3%	**100.0%**
Passenger cars HC emissions	P	**8.3%**	**62.5%**	79.2%	95.8%
Industrial discharges in surface water copper	PP	25.0%	41.7%	70.8%	95.8%
Industrial discharges in surface water lead	PP	25.0%	41.7%	70.8%	95.8%
Industrial discharges in surface water chromium	PP	25.0%	41.7%	70.8%	95.8%
Industrial discharges in surface water zinc	PP	25.0%	41.7%	70.8%	95.8%
Large combustion plants SO_2 emissions	PP	16.7%	29.2%	**66.7%**	**95.8%**
Large combustion plants dust emissions	PP	8.3%	29.2%	**62.5%**	**95.8%**
Environmental impact assessment	NPP	4.2%	8.3%	**62.5%**	**95.8%**
Large combustion plants NOx emissions	PP	8.3%	16.7%	**58.3%**	**95.8%**
Coliforms in bathing water	NPP	20.8%	**45.8%**	83.3%	**91.7%**
Passenger cars NOx emissions	P	–	**54.2%**	**75.0%**	**91.7%**
Electricity from renewable sources	PP	4.2%	8.3%	41.7%	91.7%

Table 5.2 (*cont.*)

	Trade-related	1970	1980	1990	2000
Hazardous substances in detergents	P	8.3%	**54.2%**	**75.0%**	**87.5%**
Noise level working environment	PP	8.3%	**25.0%**	**70.8%**	**87.5%**
Industrial discharges in surface water BOD	PP	25.0%	37.5%	58.3%	87.5%
Sustainability: reference in legislation	NPP	–	–	25.0%	87.5%
Energy efficiency of refrigerators	P	–	4.2%	–	**87.5%**
Noise emissions standard from lorries	P	**37.5%**	**66.7%**	**79.2%**	**83.3%**
Sulphur content in gas oil	P	12.5%	**54.2%**	**70.8%**	**83.3%**
Contaminated sites policy	NPP	12.5%	29.2%	50.0%	83.3%
Precautionary principle: reference in legislation	NPP	–	8.3%	25.0%	79.2%
Eco-labelling	P	–	4.2%	20.8%	**79.2%**
Eco-audit	PP	–	–	8.3%	**75.0%**
Heavy fuel oil levy for industry	PP	20.8%	25.0%	45.8%	**70.8%**
Motorway noise emissions	NPP	8.3%	12.5%	41.7%	70.8%
Environmental/ sustainable development plan	NPP	–	–	25.0%	70.8%
CO_2 emissions from heavy industry	PP	–	–	12.5%	70.8%
Waste landfill target	NPP	–	–	4.2%	**66.7%**
Soil protection	NPP	8.3%	12.5%	41.7%	62.5%

Table 5.2 (cont.)

	Trade-related	1970	1980	1990	2000
Recycling construction waste	PP	–	4.2%	12.5%	58.3%
Waste recovery target	NPP	–	–	4.2%	**54.2%**
Promotion of refillable beverage containers	P	12.5%	20.8%	29.2%	50.0%
Efficient use of water in industry	PP	4.2%	16.7%	29.2%	41.7%
Electricity tax for households	NPP	–	8.3%	8.3%	37.5%
Glass reuse/recycling target	NPP	–	–	4.2%	37.5%
Paper reuse/recycling target	NPP	–	–	–	37.5%
Voluntary deposit system beverage containers	P	–	–	8.3%	20.8%

P: Product Standard; PP: Process Standard; NPP: Non-trade-related
Policy; obligatory items in bold.

trade-related and are or have become obligatory are considerably
higher than for the groups characterised by lower adoption rates.
Notwithstanding this general pattern, there are notable exceptions
to this trend. Forest protection policies, for instance, had been adopted
by all countries under investigation already by the year 1990,
although they are not directly related to trade and had never been
subject to international harmonisation.[1] By contrast, despite their
trade-related and obligatory nature, the policies on noise emissions

---

[1] This can be attributed to the fact that forest protection is a very old policy field already originating in earlier centuries.

from lorries and the sulphur content of gas oil rank comparatively low in terms of adoption rates by the year 2000.

Second, those policies characterised by an early introduction generally reveal higher adoption rates than those measures only introduced for the first time during the 1980s or 1990s. However, also for this pattern, exceptional cases can be observed. For instance, policies on the efficient use of water in industry, the promotion of refillable beverage containers or soil protection display rather low adoption rates by the year 2000, notwithstanding the fact that they had already been introduced by 1970. On the other hand, there are also several 'late-comers' in our sample which nevertheless had been adopted rather quickly across the countries under study. The most outstanding case refers to policies regarding the energy efficiency of refrigerators, for which the adoption rate increased from 0 per cent to 87.5 per cent between 1990 and 2000.[2]

Table 5.3 offers an overview over the extent to which the twenty-four countries in our sample have adopted the forty policies over time (ranking the countries according to the number of policies adopted by the year 2000). While the table confirms the general findings of a rather broad policy spread, we find differences across the countries under study. First, the data reveal a difference in adoption rates between countries typically known as environmental leaders (Denmark, the Netherlands, the Scandinavian countries and Germany) and environmental laggards (led by the US, Bulgaria, Romania and Ireland).

Second, the data show that EU membership need not automatically imply that the respective countries adopt a high number of environmental policies. While a lot of the 'top adopters' are members of the EU, there are also several countries that – in spite of EU membership – rank rather low (including the 'old members' Spain

---

[2] Japan had introduced such a policy already by 1980, which was, however, terminated during the subsequent decade. Hence, by 1990 no country in our sample pursued a policy promoting the energy efficiency of refrigerators.

Table 5.3 *Policy adoptions over time by country (number of countries)*

	1970	1980	1990	2000
Denmark	1	13	23	39
Netherlands	8	14	24	39
Finland	9	16	23	37
Sweden	14	20	25	37
Germany	5	12	24	36
Norway	2	9	24	35
Austria	3	9	23	34
France	6	11	22	33
Italy	4	18	21	33
Switzerland	5	13	25	33
UK	6	11	19	32
Greece	0	2	16	31
Hungary	9	18	22	31
Japan	13	20	20	31
Portugal	1	3	21	31
Spain	1	7	20	31
Mexico	1	1	11	28
Belgium	8	14	17	27
Poland	1	4	12	27
Slovakia	3	7	9	27
Ireland	1	8	13	26
Romania	0	1	4	26
Bulgaria	4	6	11	25
USA	4	13	13	17

and Ireland).[3] This development can be traced to the fact that a considerable part of the policies under investigation is not subject to European harmonisation.

---

[3] A similar statement applies to Belgium. In this case, however, the strong decentralisation of environmental policy competencies to the regional level has to be taken into account, implying that the number of policy adoptions at the federal level remain at a lower level. This argument might also account for the rather weak performance of the US.

Third, we observe different dynamics regarding the change of adoption rates over time. Hardly surprising in this context are the strong increases in policy adoptions during the 1990s in the CEE countries and Mexico, which reflect the overall processes of economic catching-up and political transformation taking place in these states. An exception to this pattern is Hungary, which belonged to the group of 'top adopters' already during the first two decades of the observation period. In contrast to the pattern of strongly increasing adoption rates over time, we also find countries where policy adoption is characterised by rather low growth rates and even stagnation (examples are the US and Japan for the periods of the 1980s and 1990s) or a rather linear increase in policy adoptions over time (Denmark, the Netherlands, Finland, Sweden, Germany).

5.2.2 Illustration of different spreading patterns: adoption curves

In addition to these general aspects regarding the adoption rate levels of the policies under study, there are distinctive patterns characterising the spreading of policies and countries over time. To illustrate the latter, we will have a closer look at adoption curves of selected policy items. More specifically, we differentiate between three general empirically observable adoption patterns, namely, policies characterised by widespread adoption in the beginning of the observation period, policies characterised by a rather linear spreading process over the whole observation period, and policies where adoption took off towards the end of the observation period. We chose six examples for each pattern, thus analysing the respective developments for eighteen out of the forty environmental policies under study.

Figure 5.1 shows the adoption curves for six policies which were spreading broadly across the countries under study already during the 1970s, including the regulation of passenger car emissions, forest protection, noise emission from lorries, hazardous substances in detergents, lead in petrol and sulphur content in gas oil. All of

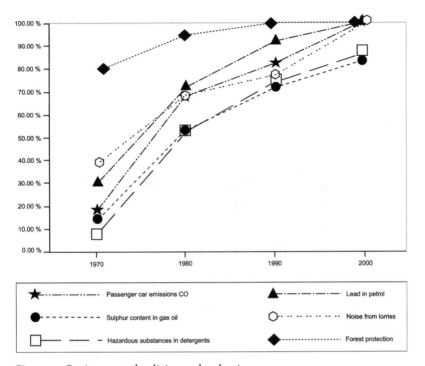

Figure 5.1 Environmental policies: early adoptions, 1970–2000

these policies have in common that, while their adoption curves rise permanently over time, the numbers of adoptions were particularly high in the beginning of the observation period and, due to saturation effects, gradually decreased over time. Three policies (passenger car emissions, lead in petrol, forest protection) reach a spread of 100 per cent by the year 2000, implying full convergence in terms of policy presence. For the three remaining policies (hazardous substances in detergents, lorry noise emissions and sulphur content in gas oil), the respective adoption rate is around 85 per cent.

In contrast to the above-mentioned development of early diffusion, figure 5.2 shows adoption curves for six policies which are characterised by a relatively linear spreading pattern. A similar development can be observed for the policies on airborne emissions from large combustion plants and on the quality of bathing water.

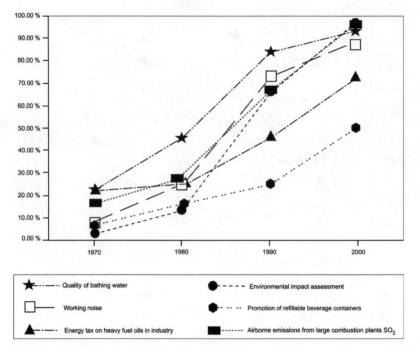

Figure 5.2 Environmental policies: linear adoptions, 1970–2000

While only few countries had adopted such policies by 1970, almost all of the countries under investigation followed the early adopters over the observation period. The number of new adoptions is distributed rather equally over time, implying a linear shape of the adoption curve. Also the policies on noise emissions at workplaces and environmental impact assessment share a rather similar adoption path. In these cases, however, it becomes apparent that a rather linear spreading process took off only from 1980 onwards, nevertheless leading to a high adoption rate and hence degree of convergence by the year 2000. Steadily increasing numbers of adoptions are also observed for policies on the promotion of refillable beverage containers and on the introduction of levies on the industrial use of heavy fuel oil, although in these cases, adoption rates and convergence remain at a lower level when compared to the other cases.

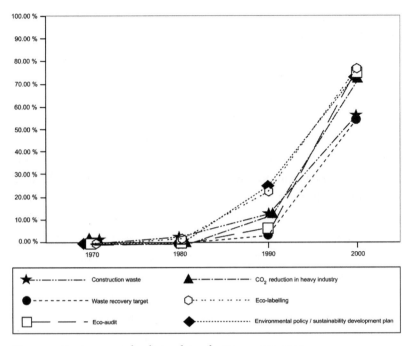

Figure 5.3 Environmental policies: late adoptions, 1970–2000

Finally, six environmental policies that are characterised by a late rather than early or linear process of diffusion are presented in figure 5.3. Notwithstanding their only recent emergence, they have been adopted by a large number of countries within a comparatively short period of time. For example, eco-labels, eco-audits and national environmental plans were reported for less than a quarter of the twenty-four countries by 1990. In 2000, they had spread to over 70 per cent. The same applies to policies on the reduction of CO_2 emission in heavy industries that are found in seventeen countries by 2000. In the latter case, only Austria, Finland and Sweden had adopted such measures in 1990. Similar figures are found for policies on construction waste and on waste recovery targets.

One could certainly argue that the impressive spread of these measures can be traced to respective harmonisation activities at the EU level. This scenario, however, only applies to three out of the six policies listed, namely the eco-label (EU directive in 1992), the eco-audit (EU regulation in 1993) and waste targets (EU directive in 1994). European harmonisation thus cannot fully account for the sharp increase in adoption rates during the 1990s.

The aggregate analysis of policy convergence with regard to policy presence indicates several general developments. First, changes in rates of policy adoption reveal a picture of strongly growing policy similarity over time. Second, while this statement holds for the whole policy sample, convergence is particularly pronounced for policies that share one or more of the following characteristics: trade-relatedness, obligatory nature and early introduction. Third, three different patterns of adoption can be identified, including processes of early, linear and late cross-national spreading of policies. Fourth, differences exist with regard to country-specific adoption patterns. In this context, our empirical findings confirm generally made distinctions between environmental leader and laggard countries.

5.3 CONVERGENCE OF POLICY INSTRUMENTS

Depending on the underlying indicators, judgements on the occurrence or non-occurrence of policy convergence can be based on different policy dimensions. One option is to investigate the convergence on the basis of the mere presence of certain policies (as done in the previous section). This implies the application of a very broad conception of policy convergence, because convergence on that dimension need not imply that countries also converge with regard to the use of respective instruments. In this section, we focus on this latter policy dimension, hence applying a more demanding indicator for assessing cross-national convergence. While convergence of instruments coincides with convergence of policies (to converge on instruments, countries must have a relevant policy in place), countries using similar instruments might still reveal considerable differences with regard to the settings of each instrument.

When analysing the convergence of policy instruments, the focus is on the question whether different countries apply the same means to reach their policy goals. Convergence of instruments occurs if one instrument type (e.g., obligatory standard, tax or levy, information-based instruments or planning instruments) is preferred to others across countries.

5.3.1 General patterns

To provide an overview of the relative importance of policy instruments for the different policy items under study, table 5.4 contains the distribution of frequencies for each of the eleven instrument types that have been distinguished in the context of the underlying project. In this regard, the data presented below refer to information on what has been identified as the dominant instrument by national environmental policy experts. Thus, the data do not refer to the entire repertoire of instruments that could be found in a country, but only to a pre-structured distinction of instrument types that can be considered as the most important in the environmental field and that have also been identified in other analyses (cf. Holzinger, Knill and Schäfer 2003).

When analysing the distribution of dominant instruments in closer detail, several general developments can be identified. First, the data reveal that the overall repertoire of the adopted instruments is rather broad, including all of the eleven instrument types under study. Second, there is strong variation with regard to the relative importance of different instrument types over time.

In this context, obligatory standards constitute the instrument type most frequently reported as the dominant one. The number of obligatory standards as dominant instrument type with respect to a certain policy steadily increased over time, from 45 observations in 1970 up to 128 for the year 2000. This general judgement on the dominance of obligatory standards is somewhat modified, however, if we look at the share of this instrument type relative to other types. Taking into account the general cross-national spread of environmental policies during the investigation period, we find a decreasing share of obligatory standards relative to other policy

Table 5.4 Overview of dominant policy instruments, 1970–2000

	1970		1980		1990		2000	
	N	%	N	%	N	%	N	%
Obligatory standard, prohibition or ban	45	65.2%	87	65.9%	109	61.9%	128	51.8%
Technological prescription	3	4.3%	5	3.8%	3	1.7%	3	1.2%
Tax or levy	0	0%	3	2.3%	3	1.7%	3	1.2%
Subsidy or tax reduction	1	1.5%	4	3.0%	9	5.1%	20	8.1%
Liability scheme(s)	2	2.9%	3	2.3%	7	4.0%	10	4.0%
Planning instrument	9	13.0%	10	7.6%	11	6.3%	13	5.3%
Public investment	1	1.5%	2	1.5%	4	2.3%	5	2.0%
Data collection/monitoring programme(s)	3	4.3%	11	8.3%	17	9.6%	19	7.7%
Information based instrument	1	1.5%	6	4.5%	8	4.6%	28	11.3%
Voluntary instrument	4	5.8%	1	0.8%	1	0.5%	9	3.7%
Legal obligation to purchase energy from renewable sources	0	0%	0	0%	4	2.3%	9	3.7%
N	69	100.0%	132	100.0%	176	100.0%	247	100.0%

instruments that had already started during the 1980s. Whereas in 1980, 66 per cent of all dominant instruments were obligatory standards, this share decreases to 52 per cent in 2000. A similar decrease in importance can be observed for planning instruments, the second most popular dominant instrument type at the beginning of the observation period in 1970.

By contrast, the relative importance of so-called NEPIs, such as information-based or monitoring instruments, slightly increases during the 1990s. The same holds true for economic instruments like subsidies and taxes. However, the only slight increase in importance is in strong contrast to political statements which emphasise the increasing relevance of new instruments (for similar findings see, for instance, Holzinger, Knill and Schäfer 2003; Jordan, Wurzel and Zito 2003). Moreover, the relatively low importance of other instruments that are also subsumed under the heading of new instruments might be traced to the fact that some of them are only relevant for certain policy items, for example liability schemes (contaminated sites), voluntary agreements (CO_2 emissions from heavy industry) or legal obligation to purchase energy from renewable sources. Finally, public investment plans or technological prescriptions are not commonly used as dominant instruments in our sample, which does not mean that they could not be used in addition to other policy instruments.

5.3.2 Illustration of different adoption patterns

To illustrate different patterns of convergence in the use of policy instruments, we have selected three examples. In the first case, the regulation of industrial discharges into the surface water, we observe one instrument type developing into the single dominant approach over time. The second example refers to instruments that are applied to promote the use of energy from renewable sources. Instead of a development towards one dominant instrument, this case is characterised by the emergence of two dominant approaches over time. Finally, in the third example, the reduction of CO_2 emissions from heavy industry, a diversification rather than concentration in the adoption of dominant policy instruments takes place, hence indicating patterns of divergence rather than convergence in instrument repertoires.

Figure 5.4 shows the repertoire of dominant policy instruments reported for each country for the regulation of industrial emissions of zinc into the surface water. Apparently, from 1970 to 2000, obligatory standards developed into the most commonly used policy instrument for the regulation of industrial discharges. Out of five different instrument types (including technological prescriptions, planning instruments, information-based instruments and taxes or levies), obligatory standards are the only remaining dominant

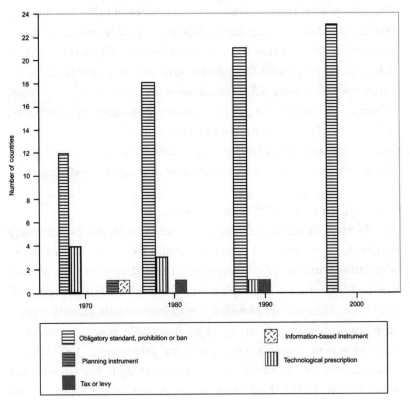

Figure 5.4 Policy instruments: industrial discharges of zinc into the surface water

instrument reported in 2000. The variation of the instrument repertoire across countries is thus clearly reduced.

A different pattern can be observed for dominant instrument types that are applied to promote the use of energy from renewable sources (figure 5.5). This example refers to a rather recent policy innovation in the environmental field. It is only from the mid-1980s onwards that policies to promote the production and use of energy from renewable sources have started to spread across countries. Since that time, however, instruments to promote renewable energy have been widely adopted. In 2000, twenty-two out of the twenty-four countries under study had introduced such measures.

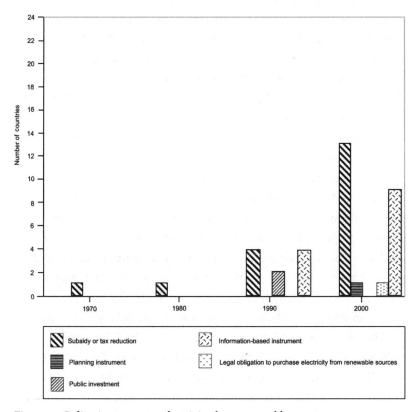

Figure 5.5 Policy instruments: electricity from renewable sources

In 2000, two approaches have emerged as most commonly applied instruments. The first approach refers to subsidies or tax reductions for producers of renewable energy. While Finland relied on this approach already in 1970, the number of countries applying this instrument as the dominant national approach to promote renewable energy rose to eleven in 2000. The second approach is the reliance on legal obligations for energy users to purchase a certain amount of renewable energy. This instrument has been applied in four countries by the year 1990 (Germany, Greece, the Netherlands and the UK), with the number of countries following this approach rising to nine in 2000. Apart from these two dominant approaches, other instruments are of minor importance. In 1990, two countries (Austria and Poland) predominantly relied on public investment for the promotion of renewable energy. Both countries switched to legal purchasing obligations by 2000. In addition, two other instruments have been reported as dominant approaches in 2000, namely information-based and planning instruments. Both are of very limited relevance, as they are applied as dominant instruments only in Switzerland and in France. In view of this constellation, we thus find convergence towards two different instrument types.

In contrast to the above-mentioned examples, patterns of adoption indicate a less clear picture of convergence with regard to dominant instruments applied to reduce CO_2 emissions from heavy industry (figure 5.6). Prior to 1990, only three countries had adopted a relevant policy, relying on different instruments to achieve their policy objectives. The adoption of data collection and monitoring programmes in Austria was paralleled by the use of planning instruments in Sweden and the introduction of tax schemes in Finland. By the year 2000, seven further countries had introduced such policies. While France, Germany, Ireland, Norway, Switzerland and the UK primarily rely upon the use of voluntary instruments, the Netherlands applies tax reduction schemes, hence following the approach of Finland.

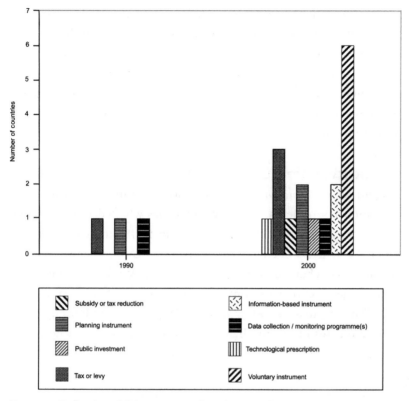

Figure 5.6 Reduction of CO_2 emissions from heavy industry

Although it is obvious that one instrument type is dominantly applied across countries, statements about convergence are difficult to make on the basis of the underlying frequency analysis. This can be traced to the fact that the emergence of voluntary instruments as a dominant instrument coincides with an expansion of the repertoire of dominant instruments applied across countries. While for 1990, only three instrument types were reported, their number rose to seven by the year 2000.

In sum, our analysis of cross-national convergence on the dimension of environmental policy instruments indicates a less clear trend towards similarity increases over time than is the case when the focus is solely on the presence of policies. While absolute figures point to the increasing dominance of obligatory standards, the growing use of other instruments over time modifies this picture. This ambivalent statement is underlined by the illustration of different convergence patterns, including cases in which we observe the emergence of one or two dominant instruments over time, but also constellations characterised by a growing diversification of instruments.

5.4 CONVERGENCE OF POLICY SETTINGS

In contrast to the analysis of convergence in terms of policy presence and policy instruments, it is only for policies which define a concrete setting, i.e., an environmental standard or tax, that we can complement the analysis of changes in variation (sigma-convergence) with an analysis of changes in the regulatory mean. While the study of the degree and direction of convergence constitutes the first step of the following analysis, we will complement these findings by interpreting our results in the light of alternative concepts of beta- and gamma-convergence.

5.4.1 Sigma-convergence and mean changes

In a first step, we look at the changes of the variation coefficient for the whole group and different sub-groups of the twenty-one setting items analysed in our research project. The coefficient of variation (CV) is defined as

$$CV = \frac{\frac{1}{N}\sqrt{\sum_{i=1}^{N}(X_i - \overline{X})^2}}{\overline{X}},$$

with N referring to the number of countries, X_i constituting the relevant policy setting of country i and $\overline{X}$ being the arithmetic mean across the country sample. The results of this analysis are summarised in table 5.5.

To assess the convergence of setting items along these lines, two perspectives are distinguished. According to the first perspective,

Table 5.5 *Variation coefficients for setting items*

	1970	1980	1990	2000	No. of policies[a]
All settings	0.58	0.73	0.72	0.68	21
Countries with policy from 1980		0.73	0.85	0.67	21
Countries with policy from 1990			0.70	0.62	21
Product-related settings	0.20	0.38	0.69	0.72	6
Countries with policy from 1980		0.38	0.69	0.53	6
Countries with policy from 1990			0.69	0.64	6
Production-process-related settings	0.96	1.00	0.79	0.79	9
Countries with policy from 1980		0.84	0.88	0.68	9
Countries with policy from 1990			0.80	0.64	9
Non-product-/process-related settings	0.38	0.72	0.63	0.48	6
Countries with policy from 1980		0.76	0.87	0.71	6
Countries with policy from 1990			0.65	0.63	6
Obligatory settings	0.10	0.43	0.64	0.66	3/8/11/12
Countries with policy from 1980		0.43	0.72	0.51	3/8/11/12
Countries with policy from 1990			0.67	0.52	3/8/11/12
Non-obligatory settings	0.72	0.97	0.84	0.71	18/13/10/9
Countries with policy from 1980		0.86	0.93	0.83	18/13/10/9
Countries with policy from 1990			0.82	0.85	18/13/10/9

Note:

[a] The respective numbers for obligatory and non-obligatory policy items vary over the investigation period, as over time more and more policies became subject to international or supranational regulation. The respective numbers given in the outer right column refer in their order to the four decades distinguished in the table.

for each point in time, all available values are included (implying that the number of countries might change over time): regarding x countries in t_i and y countries in t_j, is there a decrease in variation over time? This way, it is possible to show how countries that introduced a policy in a certain period contributed to convergence or divergence (perspective 1). In the second perspective, by contrast, only those countries are included in the analysis for which a value existed in t_i, that is, the number of countries is held constant throughout the observation period (perspective 2).

First, when looking at the average variation coefficient for all twenty-one setting items from perspective 1, the figures show that convergence only occurred during the period from 1990 to 2000. Moreover, the similarity increase remains rather low, with the variation coefficient shifting from 0.72 to 0.68. Perspective 2 reveals that those countries having introduced a policy by 1980 further diverged during the following decade. Moreover, from perspective 2, the convergence development during the 1990s is more pronounced, indicating that countries which introduced a policy after 1990 converged to a lesser degree towards all others than those countries which had already adopted a relevant regulation before that time. In combination with stable coefficients in perspective 1, this means that those countries adopting new policies during the 1980s oriented themselves more strongly towards the policy in specific countries (i.e., the frontrunner states).

Second, we can compare the development of the variation coefficient for setting items that refer to trade-related policies (i.e., product or production standards) and policies that are not subject to competitive pressures emerging from economic integration. Our findings reveal patterns that are striking from the perspective of theories of regulatory competition. So, the variation coefficients indicate divergence rather than convergence for product standards. For production standards, weak convergence trends can only be observed during the 1980s. By contrast, increases of similarity are reported for policies that are not related to trade; the difference between perspective 1 and perspective 2 shows that this is mainly caused by countries that adopted a limit value after 1990. This finding is in contradiction with expectations derived from theories of regulatory competition, stating that convergence tendencies through mutual adjustment of national policies should be more pronounced in policies subject to competitive pressures through economic integration.

Third, variation coefficients for the sub-groups of setting items can be compared for obligatory and non-obligatory policies. Also in this case, empirical findings seem to be contradictory with the expectation that convergence for obligatory items should be more pronounced than for non-obligatory items. While there is convergence for non-obligatory items since 1980, the picture looks quite different for obligatory items. While perspective 1 even suggests divergence, perspective 2 reveals convergence only for the period between 1990 and 2000 for those countries that had established a relevant policy either in 1980 or 1990. This general statement holds regardless of the fact that absolute coefficient values for obligatory items are generally lower than those for non-obligatory items.

Table 5.6 provides an overview of the development of variation coefficients (on the basis of perspective 1) and changes of the regulatory mean for all twenty-one setting items under investigation. On the basis of these data, several general developments become apparent. First, the changes in the variation coefficients underline the above finding of rather limited sigma-convergence. While for the 1970s and the 1980s there is an overall, generally rather slight, increase of variation, the period of the 1990s is characterised by a highly mixed pattern including cases of strong convergence as well as strong divergence. Moreover, the partially surprising differences in similarity changes for the varying policy types again become apparent. In this context, we also observe that the similarity changes for non-trade-related policies in general are characterised by less volatile patterns than is the case for product or process regulation.

Second, we find partially strong differences in convergence patterns within the different policy sub-groups. With respect to product standards, cases of strong convergence during the 1990s for passenger car emission standards coincide with constellations of strong divergence during the same period (lead in petrol, sulphur content of gas oil). Similarly opposite trends can also be found for process standards. These differences seem to be largely unaffected

Table 5.6 Changes in variation coefficients and regulatory mean (21 settings)

	Trade-related	VC Changes			Mean Changes		
		1970s	1980s	1990s	1970s	1980s	1990s
Passenger cars CO emissions	P	0.13	0.73	-0.76	+	+	+
Passenger cars NOx emissions	P	0.00	0.61	-0.36	0	+	+
Passenger cars HC emissions	P	0.33	0.23	-0.06	+	+	+
Noise emissions standard from lorries	P	0.02	0.00	0.04	+	+	+
Sulphur content in gas oil	P	0.24	-0.02	0.55	+	+	0
Lead in petrol	P	0.24	0.32	1.09	+	+	+
Large combustion plants SO_2 emissions	PP	0.00	0.08	-0.75	-	+	+
Heavy fuel oil levy for industry	PP	-0.21	0.99	-0.30	+	+	-
Large combustion plants NOx emissions	PP	0.00	0.00	-0.29	0	0	+
Industrial discharges in surface water BOD	PP	-0.17	0.24	-0.10	0	+	+
Noise level working environment	PP	0.00	0.03	-0.01	-	-	+

Industrial discharges in surface water lead	PP	0.41	−0.96	0.03	+	+	+
Industrial discharges in surface water copper	PP	0.42	−0.84	0.27	+	+	+
Large combustion plants dust emissions	PP	−0.30	**−0.16**	**0.27**	+	+	−
Industrial discharges in surface water chromium	PP	0.42	−1.31	0.32	+	+	+
Industrial discharges in surface water zinc	PP	0.54	0.10	0.54	+	+	+
Coliforms in bathing water	NPP	**1.16**	**−0.25**	**−0.21**	−	−	−
Motorway noise emissions	NPP	0.00	−0.09	−0.02	−	−	+
Glass reuse/recycling target	NPP	0.00	0.00	0.00	0	0	0
Paper reuse/recycling target	NPP	0.00	0.00	0.00	0	0	0
Electricity tax for households	NPP	0.00	0.14	0.00	0	+	−

P: Product Standard; PP: Process Standard; NPP: Non-trade-related Policy; obligatory items in bold.
+: upward shift of the mean; 0: no mean change; −: downward shift of the mean.

by the extent to which the policies are obligatory or non-obligatory in nature.[4]

Third, with regard to the direction of convergence, our empirical findings indicate a general trend towards increasing regulatory strictness over time. This pattern is most pronounced for product standards, for which an average strengthening of standards can be observed throughout the whole observation period. This development, with minor and periodical exceptions, also holds for production standards. Hence, our findings provide no support for the race-to-the-bottom scenarios developed in theories of regulatory competition. While the picture is rather unclear for most of the non-trade-related policies, the regulation of coliforms in bathing water seems to reflect a case of a race-to-the-bottom, with a weakening of the regulatory mean throughout the whole observation period.[5]

5.4.2 Beta-convergence

The concept of beta-convergence is applied in particular in studies on economic convergence. Beta-convergence occurs when poor economies grow faster than rich ones. It often goes along with sigma-convergence, as 'growing together' presupposes a process of catching-up. However, we can also conceive of constellations in which catching-up may entail overtaking and thus a greater dissimilarity than before, hence implying sigma-divergence (Heichel,

---

[4] As already mentioned in chapter 4 above, we have no product standards in our sample that are not subject to international or supranational harmonisation, implying that all product items are marked as obligatory. This does not mean, however, that they are obligatory for all countries under study, given their variance in membership in international and supranational institutions.

[5] The major reason for this development is that the rather strict standards of the early adopters Sweden and Finland were followed by a much weaker standard defined at the level of the EU that had subsequently to be implemented by the member states. As the countries with stricter limit values did not depart from their regulatory levels, the decreases in the regulatory mean reflect no race-to-the-top, but result from the fact that new adopters introduced less demanding standards as the early innovators. This development is due to high scientific uncertainty in this matter.

Pape and Sommerer 2005; Sala-i-Martin 1996: 1022f.). The concept of beta-convergence can also be applied to the study of policy convergence (see chapter 4). In this context, the growth rate of an economy is substituted by the change rate of a policy setting.

Beta-convergence offers a complementary view to the study of convergence in general, as it includes the dynamics of policy changes across countries. However, the concept as such provides no sufficient basis to make an overall judgement on policy convergence. Beta-convergence does not directly refer to the absolute level of the respective policy, nor does it include a measurement of the relative position of a country's policy towards the rest.[6]

To provide an overview of the extent to which we can observe beta-convergence for the twenty-one policy settings under study (see table 5.7), we estimate beta-convergence on the basis of the following bivariate regression:

$$\Delta s_{i,t_0-t_1} = c + \beta(s_{i,t_0}) + e_{i,t_0}$$

where Δs_i refers to the change rate of a policy setting between t_0 and t_1, c is the constant, s_{i,t_0} is the initial level of regulation of the respective setting and e_{i,t_0} the error term. The standardised coefficients (scale from -1.00 to 1.00) are given in table 5.7. A positive coefficient is equivalent to a process of catching up where countries with formerly lax regulations have higher change rates for their policies than their counterparts with stricter regulations.

The findings reveal an overall pattern of beta-convergence. For most of the policy settings, a process of catching up can be observed. In these cases, countries with less stringent environmental regulations strengthened their policies to a higher degree than former frontrunner countries. It is only for six items that we find beta-divergence, albeit not for the whole observation period. The latter process is indicated by a negative coefficient in table 5.7. For CO

---

[6] Further criticisms on the concept of beta-convergence referring to the insufficient inclusion of cross-country dynamics are developed by Boyle and McCarthy (1999).

Table 5.7 *Beta-convergence (21 settings)*

	Trade-related	1970s	1980s	1990s
Passenger cars HC emissions	P	**1.00**	**0.87**	**1.00**
Passenger cars CO emissions	P	−1.00	0.69	1.00
Passenger cars NOx emissions	P	–	0.47	1.00
Lead in petrol	P	−0.23	0.57	0.60
Sulphur content in gas oil	P	**1.00**	**0.98**	**0.35**
Noise emissions standard from lorries	P	**0.66**	**0.44**	−0.08
Heavy fuel oil levy for industry	PP	0.60	0.13	**1.00**
Large combustion plants SO$_2$ emissions	PP	–	−1.00	0.99
Large combustion plants dust emissions	PP	1.00	**0.98**	**0.88**
Large combustion plants NOx emissions	PP	–	–	**0.83**
Industrial discharges in surface water lead	PP	–	1.00	0.53
Industrial discharges in surface water chromium	PP	1.00	1.00	0.48
Noise level working environment	PP	–	–	**0.39**
Industrial discharges in surface water zinc	PP	–	0.32	0.38
Industrial discharges in surface water copper	PP	–	0.99	0.33
Industrial discharges in surface water BOD	PP	–	−0.03	−0.10
Coliforms in bathing water	NPP	–	**0.61**	**0.27**
Motorway noise emissions	NPP	–	–	0.04
Electricity tax for households	NPP	–	−1.00	−1.00
Glass reuse/recycling target	NPP	–	–	–
Paper reuse/recycling target	NPP	–	–	–

P: Product Standard; PP: Process Standard; NPP: Non-trade-related Policy; obligatory items in bold.

emissions from passenger cars, for instance, a negative sign is given for 1970s only. During this decade, two pioneer countries, the US and France, diverged. Compared to its initial level, the American standard was strengthened in a much stronger way than was the case for the respective French limit value.

5.4.3 Gamma-convergence

While the concept of beta-convergence allows us to identify processes of catching up between leaders and laggards, we still have no information on the extent to which the countries actually changed their ranks in terms of regulatory strictness over time. This can be traced to the fact that catching up need not necessarily mean overtaking. To grasp the latter aspect, the concept of gamma-convergence has been developed. This way, gamma-convergence offers complementary information about the overall trend of observed sigma-convergence. For instance, we might interpret a process of growing together that coincides with a complete overthrow of country rankings differently than a situation in which national limit values become similar over time, but with pioneer and laggard countries holding their rank positions. Moreover, in addition to the identification of changes in country rankings (that are not covered by beta-convergence), gamma-convergence also allows us to detect policy changes which are not perceived when relying on sigma-convergence, as country rankings may change, for example, without a significant decrease in cross-country variation.

For the analysis of gamma-convergence, country rankings based on the strictness of domestic policies are compared over time. For instance, if countries with strict environmental regulations in the first ranks fall behind over time, gamma-convergence occurs. Policy change is assessed with the gamma coefficient, a simple measure of correlation for ordinal scales based on the calculation of rank concordance for two points in time. Thus, we speak of gamma-convergence if the ranking in t_0 is not associated with the ranking in t_1. The gamma coefficient is based on differences between concordant pairs (p) and discordant pairs (q) and computed as

$$\gamma = \frac{(p-q)}{(p+q)},$$

with a scale from -1.00 to 1.00. The more values we find below 1.00, the higher the mobility of countries over time and hence gamma-convergence.

Table 5.8 shows the correlation of country rankings for all twenty-one setting items. First, it becomes apparent that there are only two policy items (the recycling targets for glass and paper reuse) for which no changes in country rankings occurred throughout the whole observation period. This can mainly be traced to the fact that in these cases no policy adoptions occurred during the first half of the observation period. For all other items, we observe in part far-reaching changes, including two policies with relatively high mobility for all decades, namely, limit values for lead in petrol (gamma between .36 and .69) and noise emission from lorries (gamma between .45 and .77).

Second, the table reveals that mobility changes are considerably higher for trade-related policies, while gamma-convergence for policies that are not related to trade is rather low. This statement holds for the whole observation period.

Third, we find different convergence movements across the policies under investigation. For some policies, gamma-convergence occurred primarily at the beginning of the observation period (e.g., limit values for the sulphur content in gas oil). Other cases, by contrast, reveal an opposite pattern, with gamma-convergence being most pronounced throughout the 1980s and 1990s (e.g., the regulation of industrial discharges into surface water).

5.4.4 Comparative assessment for different convergence concepts

The concepts of sigma-, beta- and gamma-convergence analyse and evaluate cross-national policy change on the basis of different

Table 5.8 *Gamma-convergence (21 settings)*

	Trade-related	1970s	1980s	1990s
Passenger cars CO emissions	P	**0.95**	**0.76**	**0.33**
Lead in petrol	P	**0.56**	**0.69**	**0.36**
Passenger cars NOx emissions	P	**1.00**	**0.70**	**0.45**
Noise emissions standard from lorries	P	**0.52**	**0.77**	**0.45**
Passenger cars HC emissions	P	**0.85**	**0.78**	**0.48**
Sulphur content in gas oil	P	**0.02**	**0.52**	**0.93**
Industrial discharges in surface water chromium	PP	0.87	0.83	0.22
Industrial discharges in surface water BOD	PP	0.96	0.64	0.37
Large combustion plants SO$_2$ emissions	PP	1.00	**0.47**	**0.43**
Industrial discharges in surface water zinc	PP	0.81	0.81	0.45
Industrial discharges in surface water lead	PP	0.87	0.82	0.52
Heavy fuel oil levy for industry	PP	0.79	0.59	**0.56**
Large combustion plants NOx emissions	PP	1.00	**1.00**	**0.56**
Industrial discharges in surface water copper	PP	0.87	0.78	0.63
Noise level working environment	PP	**1.00**	**1.00**	**0.72**
Large combustion plants dust emissions	PP	0.96	**0.22**	**1.00**
Motorway noise emissions	NPP	1.00	0.77	0.72
Coliforms in bathing water	NPP	**0.60**	**0.96**	**0.73**
Electricity tax for households	NPP	1.00	1.00	0.78
Glass reuse/recycling target	NPP	1.00	1.00	1.00
Paper reuse/recycling target	NPP	1.00	1.00	1.00

P: Product Standard; PP: Process Standard; NPP: Non-trade-related Policy; obligatory items in bold.

but complementary perspectives and indicators. While with sigma-convergence, the focus is on changes in the variation of policies, the concept of beta-convergence is applied to investigate whether changes in variation actually coincide with processes of catching-up between leader and laggard countries. The concept of gamma-convergence further complements our understanding of processes of policy convergence, as it sheds light on the different ways countries become similar, from a complete change of role from former frontrunners and latecomers on the one hand to sigma-convergence without major turbulences in terms of country rankings on the other hand.

Table 5.9 provides a synthesis of the convergence results for the twenty-one policy setting items under investigation, listing the convergence record for each item in light of the three different approaches mentioned above. In this context, we can identify several patterns with regard to the results obtained by different convergence concepts.

First, there are cases in which we find concurrent evaluations for all convergence concepts. For instance, for NOx emissions from large combustion plants, we find high levels of sigma-, beta- and gamma-convergence for the period of the 1990s, while no convergence (regardless of the concept applied) is found for the previous decades. This suggests that during the 1990s, the setting values for this item were not only characterised by a strong decrease in variation, but also that laggard countries were catching up with the leaders. Moreover, catching-up coincided with considerable changes in country rankings (i.e., processes of overtaking).

Second, there are constellations which are characterised by rather similar assessments for two convergence approaches. This applies, for instance, to the regulation of SO_2 emissions from large combustion plants with respect to sigma- and beta-convergence. Similar evaluations in terms of beta- and gamma-convergence, by contrast, can be found for NOx emissions from passenger cars and the regulation of noise levels for the working environment. In these

Table 5.9 *Synthesis of convergence results*

	Sigma-convergence (VC)			Beta-convergence			Gamma-convergence		
	1970s	1980s	1990s	1970s	1980s	1990s	1970s	1980s	1990s
Large combustion plants SO_2 emissions	0	–	+++	0	– – –	+++	0	+++	+++
Coliforms in bathing water	– – –	++	++	0	+++	++	++	+	++
Industrial discharges in surface water lead	– –	+++	–	0	+++	+++	+	+	++
Passenger cars CO emissions	–	– – –	+++	– – –	+++	+++	+	++	+++
Industrial discharges in surface water chromium	– –	+++	– –	+++	+++	++	+	+	+++
Industrial discharges in surface water copper	– –	+++	– –	0	+++	++	+	++	++
Heavy fuel oil levy for industry	++	– – –	++	+++	+	+++	++	++	++
Large combustion plants dust emissions	++	+	– –	+++	+++	+++	+	+++	0
Large combustion plants NOx emissions	0	0	++	0	0	+++	0	0	++
Passenger cars NOx emissions	0	– – –	++	0	++	+++	0	++	+++
Motorway noise emissions	0	+	+	0	0	+	0	++	++
Industrial discharges in surface water BOD	+	– –	+	0	–	–	+	++	+++
Noise level working environment4	0	–	+	0	0	++	0	0	++
Passenger cars HC emissions	– –	– –	+	+++	+++	+++	+	++	+++

Table 5.9 (cont.)

	Sigma-convergence (VC)			Beta-convergence			Gamma-convergence		
	1970s	1980s	1990s	1970s	1980s	1990s	1970s	1980s	1990s
Sulphur content in gas oil	--	+	---	+++	+++	++	+++	++	+
Glass reuse/recycling target	0	0	0	0	0	0	0	0	0
Paper reuse/recycling target	0	0	0	0	0	0	0	0	0
Electricity tax for households	0	-	0	0	---	---	0	0	++
Noise emissions standard from lorries	-	0	-	+++	++	+++	++	++	+++
Lead in petrol	--	--	---	--	+++	+++	++	+	+++
Industrial discharges in surface water zinc	---	-	---	0	++	++	+	+	+++

	Sigma-convergence	Beta-convergence	Gamma-convergence
+++	very strong convergence	$\Delta vc > -0.5$	$\beta > 0.5$	$\gamma < 0.2$
++	strong convergence	$-0.2 < \Delta vc < -0.5$	$0.2 < \beta < 0.5$	$0.2 < \gamma < 0.5$
+	weak convergence	$0 < \Delta vc < -0.2$	$0 < \beta < 0.2$	$0.5 < \gamma < 1.0$
0	no convergence	$\Delta vc = 0$	$\beta = 0$	$\gamma = 1$
-	weak divergence	$0 < \Delta vc < 0.2$	$0 < \beta < -0.2$	not included in the concept
--	strong divergence	$0.2 < \Delta vc < 0.5$	$-0.2 < \beta < -0.5$	not included in the concept
---	very strong divergence	$\Delta vc > 0.5$	$\beta < -0.5$	not included in the concept

cases, processes of catching-up were accompanied by respective changes in country rankings.

Third, there are several constellations in which the different approaches arrive at rather different assessments of convergence. We find cases in which mobility changes took place without parallel processes of catching-up (e.g., dust emissions from large combustion plants, industrial discharges of BOD into the surface water). We also observe the occurrence of mobility changes that are accompanied by neither sigma- nor beta-convergence (e.g., electricity tax levels for households). Moreover, there are cases of beta- and gamma-convergence which did not result in corresponding reductions in the variation coefficient. Examples for this scenario refer to the regulation of sulphur content of gas oil, noise emissions standard from lorries, lead in petrol and industrial discharges of zinc into the surface water.

In order to illustrate the varying assessments of convergence based on these different approaches, we have selected two policy items for a more detailed analysis, namely CO emissions from passenger cars and industrial discharges of zinc into the surface water. In the first case, we find a rather mixed pattern of concurrent and contradictory assessments of sigma-, beta- and gamma-convergence over time, while for the latter example, as mentioned above, assessments differ for sigma-convergence on the one hand and beta- and gamma-convergence on the other hand.

Figure 5.7 shows the development of CO emission standards for passenger cars, an environmental product standard for which international harmonisation at the level of the EU existed since 1970 (the beginning of our observation period). The development for the 1970s can hardly be interpreted in view of the low number of cases (only the standards for France and the US can be displayed).[7] The development is similar for other car emissions.

---

[7] From the selected ten countries, Germany had also adopted a limit value by 1970. However, for lack of comparability with the standards of the other countries, the German value is not displayed in the table.

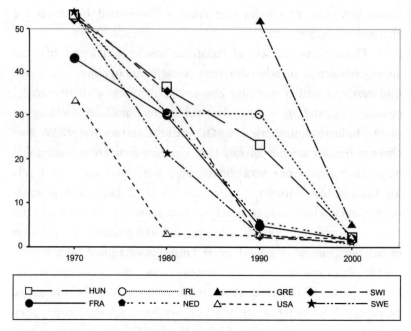

Figure 5.7 CO emissions from passenger cars (g/km)

The increase of the variation coefficient indicates sigma-divergence between 1980 and 1990 but convergence between 1990 and 2000 (compare table 5.6 above). This is caused by the fact that during this period, Scandinavian countries as well as Austria and Switzerland introduced the US standards that were stricter than EU standards at that time. As a result, we find considerable changes in country rankings and strong beta-convergence for this period. Interestingly, however, the evidence of sigma-divergence (measured by an increase in the variation coefficient) seems to be in contradiction with the optical impression of convergence – a problem we will take up again below.

By contrast, for the 1990s, strong sigma-convergence can be observed which coincides with parallel developments of catching-up and ranking changes. The latter can be illustrated by the US which turned from a leader country and early adopter into a laggard country during the 1990, being overtaken by the stricter EU standard. An inverse pattern can be observed for Hungary which introduced a rather weak standard in 1980 and adopted the strict EU standard during the 1990s.

As already mentioned above, the observation of increasing variance during the 1980s is somewhat contradictory with the optical impression – a phenomenon that can be traced to the fact that sigma-divergence is basically triggered by outlier countries. In order to take these effects into consideration, figure 5.8 analyses the variation of settings on the basis of box plots. Box plots display the distribution of values for each point in time. Each box includes 50 per cent of all values: the upper and the lower quartiles delimit the box on both sides. In contrast with convergence analysis based on the variation coefficient, outliers and extreme values are displayed separately. This way, they do not influence the length of the box. The line in the middle of each box represents the median: 50 per cent of all values are below, 50 per cent above this value.[8] The length of the box represents the degree of variation: the longer the boxes, the less similar are values on this variable. Decrease in the length of a box can be interpreted as the occurrence of sigma-convergence.

Figure 5.9 displays changes in variation on the basis of both perspectives distinguished in section 5.4.1 above. The figure on the left includes the data for all countries, implying that the number of countries might vary over time. On the right side, by contrast, only those countries are taken into account that had introduced a policy by the year 1980. For both perspectives, the box plots indicate strong decreases in variation throughout the whole observation period, including the period of the 1980s. This finding points to certain shortcomings of convergence analysis solely based on changes in the variation coefficient, which does not take into account potential effects emerging from outlier values.

---

[8] In some cases, the median is at the level of the upper or lower end of the box and hence not displayed separately. The additional line below or above the box describes the range for 90 per cent of all values. This line is not always displayed, as in some cases all values are within the 50 per cent range displayed by the box.

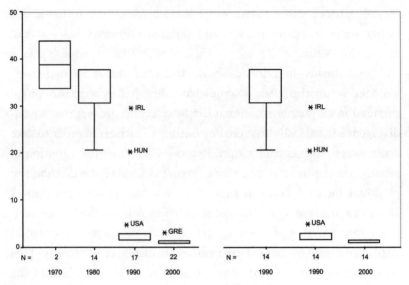

Figure 5.8 CO emissions from passenger cars (g/km) – box plots

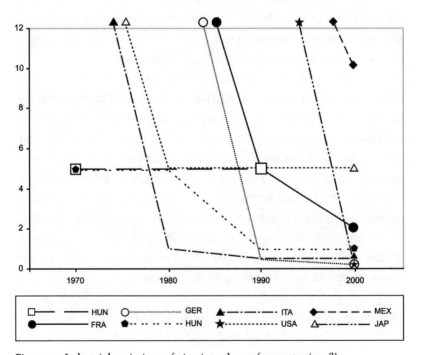

Figure 5.9 Industrial emissions of zinc into the surface water (mg/l)

Similar patterns emerge when looking at our second example, the regulation of industrial discharges of zinc into the surface water. The zinc standards share with the regulation of car emissions that they are trade-related (although constituting process rather than product standards). In contrast to car emissions, however, zinc standards constitute a non-obligatory item; i.e., for this policy, no obligatory policy at the international level has been adopted during the observation period. Figure 5.9 shows the development of setting values for this item. The development is similar for the other heavy metal emissions in our sample.

The coefficient of variation throughout the whole period under study reveals a clear pattern of divergence (see table 5.6 above). Again, this result is strikingly different from the optical impression. An important reason accounting for divergence has to be seen in the number of new policy adoptions during the 1980s and 1990s. As a result, the range of values and their variance significantly changed over time. But even if only those countries are taken into account for which a value was existing already in the previous time period, no clear tendency of convergence can be observed.

During the 1980s and the 1990s, we find increasing variance, notwithstanding the fact that in both decades processes of catching-up and changes in country rankings have taken place. Looking at individual countries, the shift of Japan from an early leader to a laggard country is striking. This is in strong contrast with the German development. Germany introduced a limit value only in 1990, but quickly emerged as the strictest regulator in the following years. Contrary to the Germans, Hungary was one of the first countries to introduce limit values. Moreover, the Hungarian standards have been significantly strengthened during the 1980s and the 1990s – again illustrating the rather progressive environmental policy in this country (at least with respect to legally defined level of regulation, leaving questions of practical enforcement aside).

However, as with passenger car emissions, the finding of sigma-divergence is modified when relying on box plot analysis. Figure 5.10

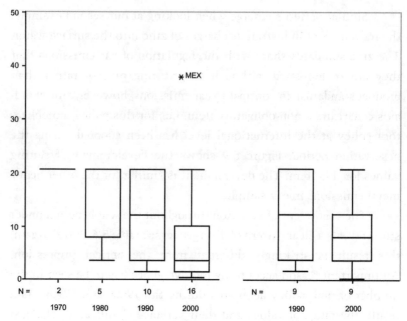

Figure 5.10 Industrial discharges of zinc into the surface water (mg/l) – box plots

indicates policy convergence during the 1990s for a core group of countries, whereas the outlying countries keep their position. While for the earlier periods under investigation, both box plot analysis and the variation coefficient indicate divergence, the interpretation offered by both instruments points to different directions for the period between 1990 and 2000.[9] This picture of different interpretations is confirmed, regardless of the selected convergence perspective (perspective 1 on the left, perspective 2 on the right side of the figure).

In summarising our analysis of convergence on policy settings, the following aspects are of particular importance. First, when looking at the coefficient of variation, we find only modest increases in the similarity of policy settings (sigma-convergence) for the period

[9] One of the ten countries in 1990, Belgium, has a missing value in 2000.

of the 1990s. With regard to different policy types, we find convergence for non-trade-related settings, while the variation coefficient indicates even diverging tendencies for trade-related settings – a finding that seems to be in contradiction with the expectations derived from theories of regulatory competition. Similarly striking is the fact that convergence on non-obligatory setting items is slightly stronger than is the case for obligatory settings.

Second, in contrast with the assessment for sigma-convergence, there is a general picture of catching-up (beta-convergence), with laggard countries displaying higher change rates in terms of policy strengthening than the leader countries. This development coincides with considerable changes in country rankings (gamma-convergence). Both patterns are more pronounced for trade-related policies than for non-trade-related items.

Third, as regards the direction of convergence, empirical results show that there is a general tendency of a continuous strengthening of environmental standards, which is most pronounced for trade-related policies. These findings therefore provide no support for any races-to-the-bottom, as predicted by theories of regulatory competition.

Fourth, the partially different assessments of variance changes, as obtained by variation coefficients and box plot analysis, indicate potential limits of an aggregate analysis based on the former instrument, given the possibly 'disturbing' influence of outlier countries on the assessment.

5.5 CONCLUSION

In this chapter, we have relied on common approaches to analyse cross-national policy convergence on the basis of aggregate data. In particular, we analysed if and to what extent (1) the variance in environmental policies in the twenty-four countries under study decreased or increased over time, (2) changes in average levels of regulation took place and (3) there are developments of catching-up and ranking changes between leader and laggard countries. On the basis of our analysis, several general empirical patterns can be identified.

First, there is a differentiated picture with regard to the occurrence of cross-national policy convergence (in terms of variance decreases over time). While for the policy settings and policy instruments, we can identify both decreases and increases in variation over time, there is strong convergence when it comes to the dimension of policy presence. Moreover, convergence patterns vary across different item sub-groups. Second, when analysing convergence for the different decades under investigation, the 1990s emerge as the period during which the strongest developments of sigma-convergence took place, regardless of the policy dimension and sub-group under investigation. Third, our empirical results indicate a very clear trend with regard to the direction of convergence. There is no evidence for races-to-the-bottom. On the opposite side, the development of policy settings is generally characterised by an upwards shift of regulatory requirements. Finally, there is evidence of considerable processes of catching-up and ranking changes between leader and laggard countries throughout the whole observation period, notwithstanding the fact that these developments need not necessarily coincide with sigma-convergence.

While the application of complementary concepts of and perspectives on convergence offers a highly differentiated assessment of complex empirical developments, the analysis of aggregate data, on which these concepts are based, is nevertheless characterised by several shortcomings.

On the one hand, the analysis of aggregate data might imply misleading or incomplete interpretations of our empirical data. These deficits are closely related to the concept used to determine sigma-convergence and are not fully compensated for by alternative concepts of beta- or gamma-convergence. As the variation coefficient is calculated on the basis of the whole sample of countries, similarity increases among country sub-groups might be overlooked. It is even conceivable that one or two outliers may lead to an increase in the variation coefficient, although the other countries are converging. This point is driven home by the fact that, in many instances, our finding of increasing variation coefficients coincided with the contradictory graphical impression of convergence. What is more, on the basis of the variation coefficient, convergence can only be assessed for metrical, but not for nominal, data. From this it follows that sigma-convergence on policy instruments or the presence of policies cannot be analysed on the basis of this approach. To provide evidence on convergence with respect to the latter policy dimensions, we therefore had to rely on alternative forms of illustration.

On the other hand, in relying on aggregate data, we are not able to account for the performance of individual countries or groups of countries in comparison to the whole sample. The variation coefficient constitutes no reference point against which developments in one or more countries can be assessed. As a consequence, it is impossible to test theoretical explanations for country-specific patterns. In view of these deficits associated with aggregate data analysis of convergence, the following chapters offer two innovative tools for the assessment of cross-national policy convergence, which take account of these limitations.

6 The pair approach: what causes convergence of environmental policies?

THOMAS SOMMERER, KATHARINA HOLZINGER
AND CHRISTOPH KNILL

6.1 INTRODUCTION

The central objective of this chapter is to assess the influence of three international mechanisms on the convergence of environmental policies in Europe, namely international harmonisation, transnational communication and regulatory competition. In so doing, we apply a novel concept – the pair approach – for measuring and explaining convergence.

In this chapter, three central research questions underlying this study are addressed. First, on the basis of the pair approach, we provide further insights into the extent of cross-national policy convergence, which complement the aggregate analysis in chapter 5. Second, and this is the primary concern of this chapter, we investigate the specific impact of economic and institutional interlinkages between nation states on policy convergence. Third, and related to this point, we are interested in the explanatory relevance of possible alternative explanations (in particular domestic factors) that were introduced in the theoretical part of this book (chapter 3). In answering these questions, we merely concentrate on potential changes in the similarity of individual environmental policies and of policy repertoires of countries over time. The direction of convergence, i.e., movements to the top or to the bottom of regulation, is not the subject of the analysis in this chapter, but will be analysed in chapter 7.

Our analysis is based on the following steps. We first introduce the concept of the pair approach (section 6.2). The reasons for using this approach are given first, followed by a description of the calculation of pair similarity and convergence under this conception, and of the selection of policy items used for the dependent variable in the pair approach. Section 6.3 gives the descriptive results on policy convergence according to the measurement concept used for the pair approach. Section 6.4 specifies the independent variables used in the quantitative model, as well as the hypotheses to be tested in the pair approach. These hypotheses are precise formulations of the general expectations on causal relationships between the independent variables and the degree of policy convergence expressed in chapter 3. Section 6.5 outlines the characteristics of the quantitative model. Finally, section 6.6 provides the findings of the regression analysis for the whole sample of environmental policies, as well as for some policy sub-groups that are of theoretical interest.

6.2 THE PAIR APPROACH

6.2.1 Characteristics of the pair approach

Some forms of sigma-convergence were already presented in chapter 5, for example the coefficient of variation, adoption rates and box plot distributions. None of them, however, allows the testing of hypotheses on causal mechanisms at the country level, as they are aggregate descriptive measures of convergence. Therefore, it proved necessary to develop a more sophisticated measurement concept of sigma-convergence that can overcome the limitations of the measures used in chapter 5.

The concept of policy convergence is based on the comparison of policy changes across a number of countries. Thus, the assessment of convergence requires a point of reference. An aggregate measure, such as the sample mean, can serve as the point of reference. However, if the analytical focus is on the degree rather than the direction of convergence the most direct approach is to compare each country to all other countries by way of a dyadic approach. This represents the lowest possible level of aggregation for any assessment of similarity. This way, no divergence or convergence shifts will be filtered out by reference to an aggregate figure. A pairwise comparison is the basic starting point for the study of sigma-convergence. It is possible to extend the concept from dyads to triads and tetrads and so on, up to the level of the whole country sample in subsequent steps.

In the pair approach the units of analysis are country pairs and not single countries. Consequently, the concept of convergence implies an increase of policy similarity between a certain pair of countries over time. The use of country pairs or dyads is new to the study of policy convergence, whereas it is common in other research areas, e.g., in the study of international conflict (Bremer 1992; Hewitt 2003; Kinsella and Russett 2002). Barrios, Görg and Strobl (2003) is an example from the economic literature applying a similar approach to the study of convergence of firm types.

The pair approach is not only the most direct way to compare policy changes with respect to their divergence or convergence; it involves several additional advantages for the study of convergence. First, any movement of convergence or divergence between countries is taken into consideration. Second, it can be used for both categorical and metrical data, whereas the coefficient of variation can only be applied to metrical data. Thus, using the pair approach, the various dimensions of policies in our sample (presence-of-policy, instrument and setting) can be integrated into one measure. Third, as it is not based on aggregate figures like the coefficient of variation, it allows for using a convergence variable instead of a similarity variable as the explanandum in a quantitative model. The variation coefficient is a measure of similarity at a given point in time, and not an appropriate measure of the development over time. Fourth, the hypotheses can be tested more directly with country pairs than at the level of individual countries: it is the *common* membership of a pair of countries in an international institution which is assumed to increase policy convergence among these countries via international harmonisation or via transnational communication. Likewise, it is the *bilateral* trade exchange that gives reason to assume that a pair of countries is exposed to regulatory competition. The whole quantitative model, that is, not only the dependent variable but also the independents, is based on country pairs. All variables are transformed to the pair level: the data set includes the *common* institutional membership of a certain pair, the *bilateral* trade exchange, a *common* border, a *common* language, and so on. The hypotheses specified in section 6.4 hence refer to country pairs; i.e., the more two countries are interlinked institutionally and economically, the more their policies will converge.

To be sure, there are also certain weaknesses inherent to the pair approach. At first glance, the logic of country pairs may not be intuitive to the reader. Methodologically, the pair approach may not be entirely independent from the composition of the sample: the score of a certain country pair can be determined by the score of other country pairs. However, this disadvantage also holds for other approaches, such as convergence towards the mean, because the comparison to a point of reference that is defined by the composition of the sample is immanent to the concept of convergence. Finally, the pair approach raises the number of cases from 24 countries to 276 country pairs. As the number of original subjects does not change, this increase may lead to overconfidence in the quantitative models. Therefore the significance of these models has to be interpreted carefully. Weighing up strengths and weaknesses, the pair approach offers the opportunity of an innovative and direct access to the study of sigma-convergence, measuring the increase or decrease of policy similarity between countries on the bilateral level.

6.2.2 Selection of policy items for the dependent variable

The dependent variable of the pair approach includes the whole policy repertoire of countries in our sample, i.e., all policy items introduced in chapter 4. However, as the theoretical expectations outlined in chapter 3 vary for different policy sub-groups (e.g., trade-related versus non-trade-related policies) we complement the general dependent variable with a number of sub-group variables (see table A6.1 for a list of all policies and variables). This way we answer different research questions and obtain more robust estimations.

In the most encompassing variable all forty policies of the data set are included. The general variable aggregates presence-of-policy, policy instruments and policy settings. It comprises twenty-one setting items, twenty-eight policy instrument items as well as forty presence-of-policy items, which add up to eighty-nine items altogether. The difference in numbers has substantive reasons: while presence-of-policy applies can be assessed for all forty policies under investigation, this does not hold in a similar way for the instruments and settings. For example, for car emissions policy, it can be asked whether there is a policy present, which instrument is used (e.g., limit value), and finally, at which level the limit value is set. However, when the question is about the sustainability principle one cannot ask for the instrument or actual settings of limit values used, but only for its presence in laws. As a consequence, for each of the forty policies there is information in the data set on the presence of this policy in a certain country (yes-no), for twenty-eight policies there is information on the instrument used,[1] and for twenty-one policies there is information on the precise setting of a value (limit value, tax rate).

We use the following sub-group variables. First, for each dimension of policy, there is a variable for presence-of-policy items, policy instrument items and policy setting items. This allows us to assess whether convergence effects are stronger with respect to the simple adoption of a policy and an instrument or with respect to a precise setting of the level of protection (see hypothesis 1 in chapter 3). Second, there is a variable for trade-related and non-trade-related

---

[1] The questionnaire included twelve explicit questions for instruments; in five cases the question was followed by a settings question, in seven cases there was no settings question possible. However, we have additional implicit information on instruments, as for all settings policies we know automatically the instrument used. Thus, this adds up to twenty-eight policy instrument items (twenty-one settings plus seven pure instruments).

policies within each sub-group. According to the theory of regulatory competition, convergence effects should be stronger for trade-related policies (see chapter 3). Third, we include in a similar way variables for obligatory and non-obligatory policies. The reason for this distinction is our theoretical expectation that the effects of international harmonisation on cross-national convergence should be more pronounced for obligatory measures, whereas for non-obligatory policies convergence effects should primarily be the result of transnational communication. Over time, the type of policy may shift from non-obligatory to obligatory, given respective harmonisation activities at the international level. Table A6.1 indicates at which point in time policies became obligatory.

6.2.3 Calculation of pair similarity

In order to measure policy convergence, in a first step the data set is transformed from the country level to dyads for each pair of countries. This way the number of cases extends from 24 countries to 276 country pairs. The number of combinations is calculated by the binomial coefficient, with double pairs (countries A and B, countries B and A) being eliminated, such that each pair is unique:

$$\binom{24}{2} = \frac{24!}{2!(24-2)!}$$

In the raw data set, for the pair $\underline{AB}$ information on policy x is included for both countries separately. These two values are compared in order to calculate similarity scores. In table 6.1 the values for two policy items are given as examples: sulphur content in gas oil and the presence of bathing water policy for two points in time, 1990 and 2000. For instance, for Austria and Belgium, the respective values for the sulphur content in gas oil policies in the year 2000 are as follows: Austria: 0.10 limit value, 1: policy present and Belgium: 0.20 limit value, 1: policy present.

The similarity scores are calculated as follows: the assessment of similarity is trivial for presence-of-policy items and for policy

Table 6.1 *Structure of the pair dataset*

Case	Country	ID	Sulp 1990	Bath 1990	Sulp 2000	Bath 2000	Country	ID	Sulp 1990	Bath 1990	Sulp 2000	Bath 2000	Sim Sulp 1990	Sim Bath 1990	Sim Sulp 2000	Sim Bath 2000	Conv Sulp 1990s	Conv Bath 1990s
1	AUT	1	0.2	1	0.1	1	BEL	2	0.2	1	0.2	1	1.00	1	0.90	1	−0.10	0
2	AUT	1	0.2	1	0.1	1	BUL	3	1.25	1	1.25	1	0.00	1	0.00	1	0.00	0
3	AUT	1	0.2	1	0.1	1	DEN	4	0.3	1	0.3	1	0.86	1	0.80	1	−0.06	0
...	...	...	...	...	...	...	...	...	...	...	...	...	...	...	...	...	...	...
110	FRA	6	0.3	1	0.2	1	ITA	11	0.3	1	0.2	1	1.00	0	1.00	0	0	0
111	FRA	6	0.3	1	0.2	1	JAP	12	–	1	–	1	0.00	0	0.00	0	0	0
112	FRA	6	0.3	1	0.2	1	MEX	13	–	0	2.00	1	0.00	0	0.00	0	0	1
...	...	...	...	...	...	...	...	...	...	...	...	...	...	...	...	...	...	...
226	NED	14	0.2	1	0.2	1	SLO	19	0.3	1	0.2	1	0.86	1	1.00	1	0.14	0
227	NED	14	0.2	1	0.2	1	SPA	20	0.3	1	0.2	1	0.86	1	1.00	1	0.14	0
228	NED	14	0.2	1	0.2	1	SWE	21	0.8	1	0.2	1	0.13	1	1.00	1	0.87	0
...	...	...	...	...	...	...	...	...	...	...	...	...	...	...	...	...	...	...
274	SWI	22	0.2	0	0.2	0	UKD	23	0.3	1	0.2	1	0.86	0	1.00	0	0.14	0
275	SWI	22	0.2	0	0.2	0	USA	24	–	0	–	1	0.00	0	0.00	0	0	0
276	UKD	23	0.3	1	0.2	1	USA	24	–	0	–	1	0.00	0	0.00	0	0	1

instrument items. When comparing the presence-of-policies and similarity of instruments, score '1' means that the countries A and B have the same policy or the same instrument, whereas '0' means that they are dissimilar. Equations (1) and (2) give this simple intuition formally:

$$SP_{x,\underline{AB}} = 1 \Leftrightarrow P_{x,A} = P_{x,B} > 0$$
$$SP_{x,\underline{AB}} = 0 \Leftrightarrow P_{x,A} \neq P_{x,B} > 0 \tag{1}$$

$$SI_{y,\underline{AB}} = 1 \Leftrightarrow I_{y,A} = I_{y,B} > 0$$
$$SI_{y,\underline{AB}} = 0 \Leftrightarrow I_{y,A} \neq I_{y,B} > 0, \tag{2}$$

where SP_x is the similarity of policy x, SI_y the similarity of instrument y, P_x is the presence-of-policy x and I_y the instrument y, and $\underline{AB}$ the dyad of countries A and B.

For setting items, by contrast, we apply a normalised metrical score from 0 to 1 based on differences between limit values of country A and B, leading to a similarity scale between 1 (limit values are identical) and 0 (country pair with the most dissimilar setting values). For all other values gradual similarity is assessed by weighting the distance between two settings with the maximum distance for each item and for each point in time. The maximum distance is controlled for outliers by calculating the range between the 90 per cent and the 10 per cent quantile of the empirical distribution. Again, this is formalised in equation (3):

$$SS_{z,\underline{AB}} = 1 - \frac{|S_{z,A} - S_{z,B}|}{S_{z,90} - S_{z,10}}, \tag{3}$$

where SS_z is the similarity of setting z, $S_{z,A}$ and $S_{z,B}$ the level of policy setting z for countries A and B and $S_{z,90}$ and $S_{z,10}$ the 90 per cent and the 10 per cent quantile of the empirical distribution of setting z in the sample.

As already mentioned, we analyse not only the whole sample of forty policies, but also different sub-groups. For the presence-of-policy, the instrument and the setting items, as well as for all sub-groups of them (see table A6.1) the scores are simply summed up for the respective policy items included. For example, if the dependent variable consists of all twenty-one setting items a maximum score of 21 can be reached by a country pair; in case of all presence-of-policy items the maximum score is 40, in case of trade-related settings the maximum score is 16, etc.

For the encompassing general dependent variable that includes all policies and all dimensions of policies (presence, instrument and setting), the similarity scores across all forty presence-of-policy, twenty-eight instruments and twenty-one settings are summed up. We thus arrive at a similarity scale from 0 to 89 points. For better interpretation and for reasons of comparability with other scales, all scores are transformed to percentage scales, with the maximum of 89 (40, 28, 21) points corresponding to 100 per cent similarity of environmental policies. An important aspect of the procedure of summing up over the policy items is that it introduces a second dimension to policy similarity: we learn not only about the similarity of single policies across countries but also about the similarity of the whole environmental policy repertoire across countries.

One important methodological point related to the rating of country pairs needs to be mentioned here: in constellations in which neither of the two countries of a pair had adopted a policy, instrument or setting, the countries are – by definition – treated as dissimilar, as we do not observe '0' on both sides, but an 'empty set' that cannot be compared.[2] In the case of settings, it does not seem logical to assign the same maximum score (full similarity = 1) to a pair of countries that both have no limit value and to a pair of countries that have adopted exactly the same limit value. In table 6.1, for instance, neither Switzerland nor the US had adopted a policy

---

[2] If a policy were abolished in both countries, then non-existence of policy would be interpreted as similarity. Empirically, however, such a case does not appear in our data set.

on bathing water in 1990. They are hence given a similarity score of 0 on that policy. A consequence of this decision is that we might overestimate convergence effects for the early periods under investigation, as there are a number of countries that had not adopted many environmental policies in 1970.

Notwithstanding this problem, however, the analysis of our data strongly supports our methodological decision. Table 6.2 shows that defining non-existent policies in a country pair as similarity leads to similarity scores that do not allow for a meaningful interpretation of the data. The table gives the results of the pair approach for policy similarity and policy convergence for presence-of-policy items. Two versions are compared: in version 1 country pairs which do not yet have a policy are rated as dissimilar, while in version 2 they are rated as similar. Whereas there is a clear increase in similarity over time and thus convergence in version 1, similarity in version 2 stays roughly the same over the three decades or even decreases. Thus, version 2 implies a strong overestimation of similarity in the early periods, which is a consequence of the fact that in 1970 most countries had not yet adopted many environmental policies. Rating them as similar in this respect clearly disturbs the estimation of the convergence movements: converging or diverging moves disappear in the aggregate perspective although they are present at the micro level.

Table 6.2 *Policy similarity and policy convergence: mean values in % from different analytical perspectives*

	Policy similarity				Policy convergence		
	1970	1980	1990	2000	1970s	1980s	1990s
Presence-of-policy – Version 1	0.03	0.12	0.30	0.65	0.09	0.20	0.51
Presence-of-policy – Version 2	0.82	0.73	0.67	0.74	−0.09	−0.06	0.07

6.2.4 Calculation of policy convergence

The similarity scores are of particular interest for the descriptive analysis of environmental policies at one point in time. The main research questions of the project, however, deal with convergence, i.e., increasing similarity over time. Therefore, for the regression analysis of the effects of causal factors on convergence, the dependent variable should include information on convergence over a given period, not on similarity at a given point in time.

The similarity scores developed in the last section can easily be transformed to convergence scores. Convergence is measured by changes in percentage points of absolute similarity between t_0 and t_1, as expressed in the following equation:

$$
\begin{aligned}
CP_{x\Delta t_1;\underline{AB}} &= SP_{x,t_1;\underline{AB}} - SP_{x,t_0;\underline{AB}} \\
CI_{y\Delta t_1;\underline{AB}} &= SI_{y,t_1;\underline{AB}} - SI_{y,t_0;\underline{AB}} \\
CS_{z\Delta t_1;\underline{AB}} &= SS_{z,t_1;\underline{AB}} - SS_{z,t_0;\underline{AB}}
\end{aligned}
\tag{4}
$$

where CP_x is the convergence of policy x, CI_y the convergence of instrument y and CS_z the changes in similarity scores of setting z; $SP_{x,t_1(t_0)}$, $SI_{y,t_1(t_0)}$, $SS_{z,t_1(t_0)}$ are similarity scores at $t_1(t_0)$ and Δt_1 is the period between t_0 and t_1. To give an example, table 6.1 shows a strong increase in similarity between the Netherlands and Sweden during the 1990s (0.87) for sulphur content in gas oil.

For the aggregated convergence variables comprising groups of policy items, changes in similarity scores are summed up such that

$$
\begin{aligned}
\sum_{x_1}^{x_n} CP_{x_i,\Delta t_1;\underline{AB}} &= \frac{\sum_{x_1}^{x_n} SP_{x_i,t_1;\underline{AB}} - SP_{x_i,t_0,\underline{AB}}}{n-k} \\[2ex]
\sum_{y_1}^{y_n} CI_{y_i,\Delta t_1;\underline{AB}} &= \frac{\sum_{x_1}^{y_n} SI_{y_i,t_1;\underline{AB}} - SI_{y_i,t_0,\underline{AB}}}{n-k} \\[2ex]
\sum_{z_1}^{z_n} CS_{z_i,\Delta t_1;\underline{AB}} &= \frac{\sum_{z_1}^{z_n} SS_{z_i,t_1;\underline{AB}} - SS_{z_i,t_0,\underline{AB}}}{n-k}
\end{aligned}
\tag{5}
$$

where n is the size of the sub-group of policies x_i, instruments y_i and settings z_i, and $k \in \{1, 2, \ldots i, \ldots n\}$ is the number of policies, instruments, or settings with $SP_{x_i, t_0; \underline{AB}} = SP_{x_i, t_1; \underline{AB}} = 1$ ($SI_{y_i, t_0; \underline{AB}} = SI_{y_i, t_1; \underline{AB}} = 1$ or $SS_{z_i, t_0; \underline{AB}} = SS_{z_i, t_1; \underline{AB}} = 1$). The difference is weighted not by the number of policy items but with the factor $1/(n - k)$. Those policy items that have shown complete similarity between t_0 and t_1 for country pair $\underline{AB}$ are excluded from a policy sub-group. This operation avoids the inclusion of saturation effects, which would imply an underestimation of convergence. For example, imagine a country pair that has a high degree of totally similar policies in t_0 that stay stable until t_1: there is no possibility for convergence on these items any more. If the number of policies n were not corrected by k, a larger denominator in equation (5) would decrease convergence rates for the respective period.

6.3 DESCRIPTIVE ANALYSIS OF THE DEPENDENT VARIABLE

The pair approach produces measures of policy similarity and policy convergence which are introduced into the explanatory model later on. However, the first result of the application of the pair approach is an aggregated version of the dependent variable. Thus, the pair approach provides also answers to the first research question of the project: To what extent can we observe convergence of environmental policies in Europe? In this section some important descriptive results are presented which complement the analysis given in chapter 5. The following figures and tables show patterns of convergence at various levels of aggregation. Since for the basic levels of analysis it is impossible to present the complete results, section 6.3.1 starts with the selective presentation of several policy setting examples and aggregate variables. Section 6.3.2 gives an overview on similarity and convergence of all policy groups.

6.3.1 Graphical display of pair similarity

The most basic level of analysis is the similarity of country pairs with respect to single policies. Figure 6.1 uses 'limit values for lead in petrol' as an example of a policy. The graph displays the development of similarity between country pairs from 1970 to 2000. The percentage scale relates to the maximum similarity score as outlined in the previous section. The graph shows five selected country pairs representing different developments: three pairs that converge, one pair that converges with divergence in between and one pair without significant convergence.

The country pair Switzerland and UK starts in 1970 already with some similarity (20 per cent), then shows a strong increase in similarity during the 1970s and a slight increase during the 1980s,

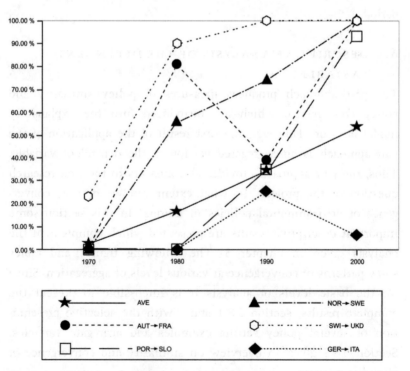

Figure 6.1 Similarity of selected country pairs, 1970–2000, limit values for lead in petrol

reaching perfect similarity already in 1990. Norway and Sweden, both having no policy in 1970, converge strongly during the 1970s. This approximation continues over time until they reach total similarity of their limit values in 2000. Portugal and Slovakia had dissimilar policies during the 1970s, converged slightly during the 1980s, and have almost the same policy in 2000. Austria and France reach already high similarity during the 1970s, but they diverge significantly during the 1980s. A closer look at the data reveals that this divergence occurred although both countries strengthened their policies during that period; however, Austria did so to a much higher degree. In 2000, this pair ends up with identical limit values (100 per cent similarity). Finally, Germany and Italy do not show a significant pattern of convergence. Whereas in 1990 their limit values are modestly similar (27 per cent), they become almost totally dissimilar again during the 1990s, due to a unilateral strengthening of the German limit value.

Additionally, figure 6.1 gives the development of the 'average country pair' (the solid line). The average country pair is a first way of aggregation, as it represents the similarity of *all* 276 country pairs with respect to a certain policy. The average country pair shows a strong increase in similarity, starting with 2 per cent similarity in 1970 and ending up with 55 per cent in 2000. 'Lead in petrol' is a policy with very clear convergence over the observation period.

There are other setting items that show a similar trend. Figure 6.2 shows convergence trends for lead in petrol, CO emissions from passenger cars and industrial discharges of zinc into surface water. While we can observe similarity increases for all of these items during the observation period, both similarity levels and similarity changes differ across policies and over time. Whereas in the case of CO emissions, the average pair reaches a similarity degree of 42 per cent in 2000, respective figures for zinc discharges in surface water only reach a level of 28 per cent. The preliminary explanation for this difference is the existence of harmonised EU standards for lead in petrol (Directive 78/611) and CO emissions (Directive 70/220).

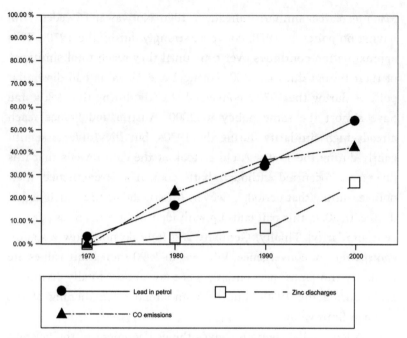

Figure 6.2 Similarity of average country pairs for selected policies, 1970–2000

For zinc discharges, international harmonisation is completely lacking. Nevertheless, this item reveals at least some convergence.

The second form of aggregation is the summation of similarity scores of country pairs over all policies. Figure 6.3 illustrates convergence trends of five selected country pairs as well as the development of the average pair. The graph shows a permanent increase of average similarity of all country pairs over time, with slight convergence during the 1970s and stronger convergence during the last decade, implying that in 2000, the average country pair reaches the level of 56 per cent similarity. Having a reputation for early and strict environmental regulation, the pair Japan/Sweden has been the most similar pair in 1970 as well as in 1980. In 1990 and 2000, by contrast, the pairs with the highest similarity are Germany/Switzerland and Denmark/Netherlands. Moving from single policies to the aggregate

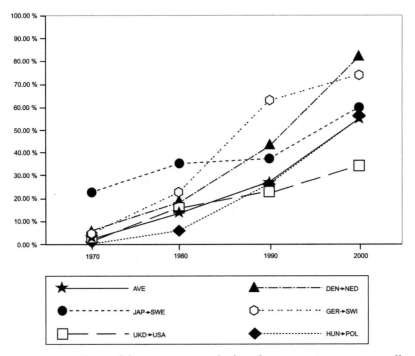

Figure 6.3 Similarity of the average pair and selected country pairs, 1970–2000, all policy items

level of all policies under investigation, the overall impression of a manifest convergence trend is quite obvious.

As not all country pairs can be displayed in one diagram, figure 6.4 summarises policy similarity of all policies and all country pairs for each point in time from 1970 to 2000. It illustrates the distribution of all country pairs around the average pair. While the average pair reaches a similarity degree of 56 per cent, the pair with maximum similarity in 2000 reaches 82 per cent, and the minimum pair a value only slightly above 20 per cent. What can be observed is that the dispersion of values around the average (in particular, for the 25 per cent and 75 per cent quantiles) increased until 1990 and decreased during the last ten years. Thus, we observe a clear general convergence trend over the whole policy sample and the whole period.

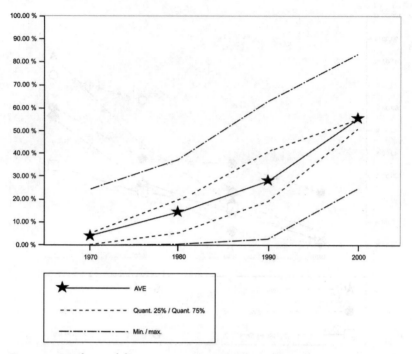

Figure 6.4 Similarity of the average, minimum and maximum pairs, 1970–2000, all policy items

6.3.2 Mean values for policy similarity and policy convergence

An overall summary of the descriptive findings for all dependent variables that will be used in the regression analysis is presented in table 6.3. The table provides results for the whole sample used in the pair approach and for all policy sub-groups. It gives information about mean values of policy similarity for 276 country pairs (in per cent) with respect to four points of time (1970, 1980, 1990 and 2000). Additionally, the results for similarity increases, i.e., policy convergence, between these points are provided. The last column gives the convergence results for the average of all three decades.

Several findings seem of particular interest. First, in general, similarity grows considerably from 1970 to 2000 (from 0.04 to 0.56). Moreover, we observe an increase of similarity from 1970 to 2000 not only for all items but also for all sub-groups of items. Second,

Table 6.3 *Policy similarity and policy convergence: mean values in % for 276 country pairs*

	Policy similarity				Policy convergence			
	1970	1980	1990	2000	1970s	1980s	1990s	Average
Pair approach, all policies (89 items)	0.04	0.14	0.29	0.56	0.10	0.18	0.37	**0.22**
Presence-of-policy (40)	0.03	0.12	0.30	0.65	0.09	0.20	0.51	**0.27**
Policy instruments (28)	0.06	0.21	0.38	0.61	0.16	0.21	0.36	**0.24**
Settings (21)	0.00	0.07	0.17	0.33	0.06	0.10	0.18	**0.12**
Presence-of-policy trade-related (26)	0.02	0.14	0.34	0.72	0.13	0.24	0.59	**0.32**
Presence-of-policy non-trade-related (14)	0.05	0.09	0.22	0.52	0.04	0.14	0.39	**0.19**
Presence-of-policy obligatory (3/8/13/19)	0.05	0.32	0.55	0.75	0.27	0.44	0.62	**0.44**
Presence-of-policy non-obligatory (37/32/27/21)	0.06	0.07	0.18	0.56	0.05	0.11	0.44	**0.20**
Instrument trade-related (21)	0.07	0.25	0.46	0.73	0.20	0.27	0.46	**0.31**
Instrument non-trade-related (7)	0.04	0.07	0.14	0.26	0.04	0.07	0.14	**0.08**
Instrument obligatory (3/8/12/14)	0.06	0.28	0.50	0.76	0.27	0.38	0.55	**0.40**
Instrument non-obligatory (25/20/16/14)	0.06	0.18	0.28	0.46	0.10	0.09	0.19	**0.13**
Setting trade-related (16)	0.01	0.09	0.20	0.39	0.08	0.12	0.21	**0.14**
Setting non-trade-related (5)	0.00	0.00	0.05	0.14	0.00	0.05	0.10	**0.05**
Setting obligatory (3/8/11/12)	0.02	0.16	0.27	0.44	0.15	0.16	0.22	**0.18**
Setting non-obligatory (18/13/10/9)	0.00	0.01	0.06	0.19	0.01	0.05	0.14	**0.07**

convergence effects are highest during the 1990s (0.37). Third, in 2000 similarity effects are most pronounced with regard to presence-of-policy items (0.65) followed by instruments (0.61), with settings being least developed (0.33). The picture is similar for policy convergence (average: 0.27; 0.24; 0.12). Fourth, when looking at policy types, it becomes apparent that similarity increases for trade-related policies are more pronounced than for policies not related to trade. A similar statement applies to the distinction between obligatory and non-obligatory items, with similarity effects being generally stronger in the former case. The highest rate of convergence across all policy groups is found for obligatory presence-of-policy items (average: 0.44), while the respective figures are lowest for non-obligatory settings (average: 0.07).

All of these results are in line with our theoretical expectations formulated in chapter 3. We expected lower similarity increases, the more specific the policy dimension under investigation. Expected convergence is most pronounced for presence-of-policy and least for settings, with instruments lying somewhere in between. We also hypothesised that as a result of regulatory competition, convergence on trade-related policies should be higher than for policies not related to trade. Moreover, effects of international harmonisation should lead to higher convergence for obligatory items than for non-obligatory policies.

The overall picture of convergence is the result of aggregation: table 6.3 presents the mean values for 276 country pairs aggregated over a group of policies. Among them, of course, are also pairs that diverge for a certain policy in a given decade. However, there are not so many of such instances of divergence. Table 6.4 shows the number of items for which divergence occurred, distinguishing between different policy dimensions and observation periods. Divergence happens more often with setting and instrument items than with presence-of-policy items. This is not surprising as the setting items are much more specific than the presence-of-policy items which are based on a yes/no scale. Furthermore, in table 6.4 the diverging pairs are compared to the converging pairs. The share of converging pairs clearly

Table 6.4 *Instances of divergence*

		Number of items without diverging pairs	Number of diverging pairs in %[a]	Number of converging pairs in %[a]	Number of persisting pairs in %[a]
40 Presence-of-policy	1970s	40/40	0.0	7.9	92.1
	1980s	39/40	0.1	17.4	82.5
	1990s	36/40	0.3	35.7	64.0
28 Instruments	1970s	26/28	0.1	14.5	85.4
	1980s	19/28	0.5	17.4	82.1
	1990s	18/28	1.8	25.1	73.1
21 Settings	1970s	17/21	0.5	8.6	90.9
	1980s	8/21	4.0	18.2	77.8
	1990s	3/21	8.1	33.4	58.5

Note:
[a] Relative to 276 country pairs for each item, i.e., 11,040 for presence-of-policy, 7,728 for instruments and 5,796 for settings.

outnumbers the share of diverging pairs for all decades. Most pairs, however, do not move at all. The share of persisting pairs decreases significantly over time. The table shows that this is predominantly a result of increasing convergence, not of increasing divergence.

6.4 INDEPENDENT VARIABLES AND HYPOTHESES

After having elaborated on the measurements of convergence and the descriptive findings of the pair approach, we now turn to the question of theoretical explanation. For this purpose, we first have to specify the operationalisation of the independent variables under study in a way that makes them suitable for the pair approach. On this basis, we are also able to specify the general hypotheses formulated in chapter 3 for the analysis of country pairs. These adjustments are necessary since for the pair approach all variables are based on dyadic data, e.g., the *common* membership in institutions. Similarly, the hypotheses relate to country pairs and will thus be reformulated in order to fit the pair approach. The same numbering system will be used in order to allow identification easily.

The dependent variable used in the explanatory models is the convergence of policies, not their similarity at one point in time; i.e., we use the 'change rate' figures given in the right half of table 6.3. Policy convergence in each period of observation will be explained by independent variables that refer not to change rates but to absolute figures at the beginning of the decade. These are conceived as 'potentials' that are supposed to cause convergence in the following years, such as communicative potential through membership in international institutions or cultural similarity.

6.4.1 International harmonisation

The effects of international harmonisation (and also transnational communication) as a causal mechanism of cross-national policy convergence are based on the impact of international institutions. To grasp these effects, we rely on an indicator of institutional interlinkage that is built on a sample of thirty-five institutions (see table A4.4 in the annex). We distinguish two types of international institutions relevant in the field of environmental policy: international environmental organisations, treaties, protocols or regimes (hereafter 'international institutions') and the EU.

The harmonisation effects of international institutions arise from accession: members ratify the treaty and have to comply immediately. This implies that convergence effects from accession occur only once. While such 'harmonisation effects through accession' are also given for the EU it also has 'harmonisation effects through membership': the institution continuously produces regulatory output that is directly legally binding on its member states. This leads to enduring and steadily renewed harmonisation effects. Hence, in contrast with accession effects EU membership in t_0 will imply convergence in subsequent periods.

To measure the effect of institutional harmonisation, we distinguish between three variables to cover both 'membership effects' and 'accession effects'. The first variable refers to convergence effects of membership in international institutions with obligatory potential. From the international institutions relevant in the environmental field, only the EU has this opportunity of internal harmonisation by adopting rules that are obligatory for its members.[3] Hence, we use a dummy variable of common EU membership of a country pair to test the following hypothesis (this and the next two hypotheses are specifications of hypothesis H 2.1 developed in chapter 3):

(H 2.1.1): *If two countries are members of the EU in t_0, the environmental policies of both countries will converge in the following periods.*

As already mentioned, the EU may also cause harmonisation through accession. To distinguish these effects from accession effects of other international organisations and regimes, we include a second dummy

---

[3] Internal decisions of other international institutions, e.g., conference or party decisions, do not have an equivalent status in terms of international law.

for the common accession to the EU of a country pair. As date of accession we use the beginning of the accession talks, as usually the candidate country already begins with the adoption of the *acquis communautaire* at that point in time.

>(H 2.1.2): *If one or both countries of a pair accede to the EU from t_0 to t_1, such that both are EU members afterwards, the environmental policies of both countries will converge during the same period.*

The treatment of EU membership and accession to the EU as separate variables can also be justified on the grounds that the EU could be expected to play a dominant role in the convergence of environmental policies in Europe. It is thus useful to be able to single out EU effects from the effects of other international institutions.

The third variable takes account of the effects of accession to other international institutions. To measure these effects, we collected data on the membership of countries in the above-mentioned thirty-four international organisations and regimes (thirty-five minus EU). The common membership score is weighted by the institutions' encompassingness and obligatory potential. Changes of the score between t_0 and t_1 are taken as a proxy for convergence effects through accession to international institutions. The exact calculation of the indices can be found in table A4.3 in the annex.

>(H 2.1.3): *The higher the score of common institutional accession (weighed by obligatory potential) of a country pair from t_0 to t_1, the more the environmental policies of both countries will converge during the same period.*

6.4.2 Transnational communication

Potential effects of international institutions on the convergence of national policies are not restricted to the adoption of legally binding rules. Rather these institutions represent an arena for communication and information exchange among their members – an aspect that can trigger cross-national convergence by itself and independent of an institution's regulatory output (see chapter 3). The institutional influence that exceeds effects of harmonisation is included in the variable 'institutional membership'. With this variable, we grasp effects of membership in international institutions in t_0 on policy convergence between t_0 and t_1. This is based on the assumption that convergence effects emerging from transnational communication will not unfold immediately with accession, but become relevant only after a certain period of membership. The variable consists of common membership data for all (including EU) international institutions, weighted by encompassingness, the length of membership and the institutions' communicative potential (see table A4.3 for details).

(**H 3.1**): *The higher the score of common institutional membership (weighed by communicative potential) of a country pair in t_0, the more the environmental policies of both countries will converge in the following periods.*

6.4.3 Regulatory competition

Theories of regulatory competition commonly refer to trade figures as a proxy for the economic interlinkage between countries. Trade flows are usually captured by an index of trade openness. For the pair approach, a different type of trade data is used, namely bilateral trade flows (see chapter 4 for details). As for other indices of openness, the trade volume is weighted by the size of the national economy. We apply the GDP of the smaller market in order to operationalise more precisely the dependence on international trade. Using bilateral data, the competitive situation between two national economies can be better captured. We include only trade flows between market economies, as trade between non-market economies (e.g., CEE countries before 1989) is not expected to unfold the effects focused upon by theories of regulatory competition.

(**H 4.1**): *The higher the trade flows between a country pair in t_0, the more the environmental policies of both countries will converge in the period between t_0 and t_1.*

6.4.4 Other factors

It is the central objective of this project to analyse the extent to which international economic and institutional interlinkages among countries lead to similarity increases in their environmental policies. In focusing on these factors, however, we do not imply that other convergence causes might not be relevant. In the following, we therefore specify the other explanatory factors of convergence mentioned in chapter 3. This way, we are able to make a more comprehensive judgement about the relative explanatory power of the convergence causes in which we are primarily interested.

A first variable can be derived from the theoretical literature on policy diffusion, policy transfer and policy learning (cf. Holzinger and Knill 2005b; Simmons and Elkins 2004). Among others, emphasis is placed in these theories on two factors that facilitate the transfer and emulation of policies, hence leading to increases in cross-national policy similarity over time, namely cultural ties between countries (e.g., in terms of language or religion) and geographical proximity. These factors are expected to work even in the absence of strong international institutional interlinkages between countries. One important advantage of the pair approach is the possibility to directly include an index of cultural similarity in the quantitative analysis (see table A4.3 in the annex).

A second control variable refers to the well-documented relationship between the level of economic development of a country and the comprehensiveness and strictness of its environmental policy as expressed by the Environmental Kuznets Curve (see chapter 3). For the pair approach, we use an interaction variable of per capita income difference between two countries and absolute income figures. We use the GDP per capita of the poorer country in order to measure the economic development of a country pair.[4]

---

[4] Taking the average income rate of both countries would lead to an inaccurate estimation for country pairs with a high difference in income levels.

A third variable refers to the existence of domestic political demand for a comprehensive and stringent environmental policy. For the pair approach, the influence of green parties is measured by commonalities of a country pair regarding electoral success, membership in parliament, and participation in government of green parties (see table A4.3). A high score is attributed to a country pair if green parties are equally highly influential in both countries. As with income, we use an interaction variable that also includes the difference between the two countries.

A fourth control factor to be considered is environmental problem pressure. The effect of this factor is tested with two variables, the level of CO_2 emissions per capita and population density. Although both are rather rough indicators, they should serve as general proxies for problem pressure through environmental pollution. To represent the common pressure in a county pair, the lower level of emissions and the lower figures for population density are included. Again, the difference between the two countries is accounted for by using an interaction term.

Fifth, we control for effects of pre-existing similarity of policies on convergence in later periods. Theories of policy convergence through transnational communication and learning emphasise that the degree of existing similarity (or the number of earlier adopters of a policy) may influence the degree of convergence in the future (social emulation and herding effects; see chapter 3). Moreover, the presence of a 'saturation effect' can be assumed: if a group of countries has already very similar environmental policies, convergence towards each other will necessarily decrease over time.

These specifications of hypothesis H 5.1 on the other variables developed in chapter 3 are summarised in the following. A list of all independent variables and their descriptive statistics is given in table A6.2.

(H 5.1.1): *The higher the cultural similarity between a country pair, the more the environmental policies of both countries will converge.*

(**H 5.1.2**): *The higher the common income level of a country pair and the more similar it is in t_0, the more the environmental policies of both countries will converge in the following periods.*

(**H 5.1.3**): *The higher the influence of green parties in a country pair and the more similar it is in t_0, the more the environmental policies of both countries will converge in the following periods.*

(**H 5.1.4**): *The higher the level of CO_2 emissions per capita of a country pair and the more similar it is in t_0, the more the environmental policies of both countries will converge in the following periods.*

The higher the level of population density of a country pair and the more similar it is in t_0, the more the environmental policies of both countries will converge in the following periods.

(**H 5.1.5**): *The more similar policies of a country pair in t_0, the more the environmental policies of both countries will converge during the following periods, as long as the degree of similarity already reached is not yet very high.*

6.5 METHOD OF ANALYSIS

In the following analysis of the empirical data we assess the influence of the explanatory factors on the changes in policy similarity between pairs of countries. The models basically refer to a pooled data set of three cross-sectional assessments of convergence for the 1970s, the 1980s and the 1990s. Each of the three cross-sectional models includes observations on 276 country pairs. As noted above, the dependent variable for all models refers to the change rate of policy similarity from the beginning of a decade to its end, indicated in percentage points (see table 6.3). We begin with the most encompassing dependent variable: the complete sample of forty environmental policies, including all eighty-nine items on the presence of a policy, on instruments and settings. The regression results for the pooled data and the encompassing dependent variable are presented in tables 6.5 and 6.6.

Table 6.5 Regression results: policy convergence of 89 items, pooled data

	1	2	3	4	5	6	7	8	9
Constant	—**	—**	—**	—**	—**	—**	—**	—	—**
EU membership	.182**	-.029		.130**	-.020			-.029	.052**
EU accession	.110**	.058**		.108**	.057**			.060**	.044**
Accession to institutions		.479**			.474**			.476**	.400**
Institutional membership		.489**			.505**			.518**	.161**
Bilateral trade			.204**	.146**	-.038			-.067**	-.070**
Cultural similarity						.022	.016	.061**	.084**
GDP per capita						.207**	-.045	.022	.151**
Existence of green parties						.274**	.159**	-.008	-.016
CO$_2$						-.074**	-.042	-.054**	-.053**
Population density						.128**	.044	.030	.024
Policy similarity in t–1							.514**	-.019	-.104**
Time									.442**
R^2	0.05	0.63	0.04	0.07	0.63	0.15	0.32	0.63	0.67
N	828	828	828	828	828	828	828	828	828

Table 6.6 Regression results: policy convergence of 89 items, partialised models, pooled data

	9	10	11	12	13	14	15
Constant	–**	–**	–**	–**	–**	–**	–**
EU membership	.052**	.132**	−.027	.075**	.077**	.077**	.112**
EU accession	.044**	.104**	.057**	.102**	.093**	.061**	.041**
Accession to institutions	.400**	.629**	.451**	.628**	.648**	.501**	.317**
Institutional membership	.161**	.426**	.650**	.405**	.357**	.260**	.120**
Bilateral trade	−.070**	−.033	−.033	.204**	−.033*	−.032	−.013
Cultural similarity	.084**	.054**	.054**	.054**	.053**	.056**	.073**
GDP per capita	.151**	.017	.017	.017	.224**	−.013	.104**
Existence of green parties	−.016	−.007	−.007	−.007	−.007	−.056**	−.014
CO_2	−.053**	−.053**	−.053**	−.053**	−.052**	−.061	−.051**
Population density	.024	.029	.029	.029	.029	.097**	.023
Policy similarity in t–1	−.104**	−.011	−.011	−.011	−.010	.546**	−.056**
Time	.442**	.185**	.185**	.185**	.185**	.160**	.721**
R^2	0.67	0.67	0.67	0.67	0.67	0.67	0.67
N	828	828	828	828	828	828	828

We apply simple regression models with standard OLS estimations. In order to answer the main research question on the influence of international driving forces behind growing similarity of domestic environmental policies, we use a stepwise approach. We start with regression models that show the explanatory potential of variables for institutional interlinkage (models 1 and 2, table 6.5) and for economic interlinkage (model 3) separately. Next, we provide two common models of these main variables, one including EU and trade effects, the other including all institutions and trade effects (models 4 and 5). In a further step, the common explanatory power of all control variables is assessed in two models, the second one additionally including the pre-existing similarity of policies as an explanatory factor (models 6 and 7). Finally, all variables are taken together in one common model (8). The last model (9) adds a time variable. This procedure not only enables us to interpret the direction of the effects of the main independent variables, but also allows for assessing the importance of these explanatory factors relative to the set of control variables.

Through the inclusion of eleven independent variables and one time variable, we hope to get a model that is sufficiently specified, covering all major explanatory mechanisms. This set of variables, however, introduces statistical complications. We are confronted with the multicollinearity of independent variables, a problem that often emerges with this type of analysis. Trade figures, for example, correlate with EU membership, and wealthier countries can be assumed to be institutionally interlinked to a higher degree. In particular, some variables, such as the rise of green parties and the increase of institutional interlinkage, are highly correlated with time. This correlation of independent variables is hardly astonishing, as it is obvious that all institutional variables are endogenous factors; that is, they are themselves influenced by other factors, such as the level of economic development. Thus, some independent variables in the data set are correlated. Moreover, the variance in inflation statistics indicates problems for a robust estimation of coefficients.

The methodological literature is divided over how to deal with multicollinearity. Whereas some propose to ignore it as long as results are significant, others propose various methods to control for it, and in particular, to search for ways of specifying the relationship among the variables (for an overview see chapter 13 in Kennedy 2003). We pursue an approach along the second road, trying to make multicollinearity among our independent variables visible and at least to give an impression of its extent and direction. Although the stepwise approach outlined above may already uncover changes in coefficients, and hence give information on multicollinearity, two further steps are undertaken in order to cope with this problem.

First, table A6.3 gives the bivariate regression coefficients of all independent variables with policy convergence. These figures can be interpreted as showing the maximum potential of each variable to explain the variance of the dependent variable, serving as a point of reference for the multivariate models.

The second step is displayed in table 6.6. For the models 10 to 15, the common influence of covariates is systematically (i.e., sequentially) partialised out of the regression coefficients. That is, after bringing all variables into a hierarchical order, the common explanatory potential of two independent variables regarding the variance of policy convergence is attributed to the higher-ranking variable. Thus, all independent variables are orthogonalised: through bivariate regression and subsequent residualisation, they are made stochastically independent from each other. For subordinate variables in the order, only the unstandardised residual from the bivariate regression with their respective higher-ranking variables is included in the equation. This way we can speak of partialised or residualised models. The coefficient of a subordinated independent variable only includes information on effects *which go beyond* the (common) effect of higher-ranking covariates. This procedure allows for an assessment of the relative importance of the main variables compared to the other independent variables. This way, we capture the effects that go beyond the influence of international factors. The goodness of fit of the multivariate model is not affected by this orthogonalisation of independent variables.

The partialising out of effects of lower-ranking variables takes place stepwise. Variables are brought into an order and categorised into different groups. Each single variable is orthogonalised by all variables of higher-ranking groups. The procedure will be explained using the example of model 10 (table 6.6). The regression equation is given below:

$$y = c + \beta_{1y}x_1 + \beta_{2y}x_2 + \beta_{3y}x_3 + \beta_{(4-123)y}x_{4-123}$$
$$+ \beta_{(5-1234)y}x_{5-1234} + \beta_{(ci-12345)y}x_{ci-12345}$$
$$+ \beta_{(t-12345ci)y}x_{t-12345ci} + e$$

In this basic version of the partialised regression, five different groups for orthogonalisation are composed by the following twelve variables: variables x_1 to x_3 are harmonisation variables (group one), x_4 is communicative potential (group two), x_5 is trade (group three), x_{ci} represents the control variables c_i (group four) and x_t the time variable (group five).

The hierarchical order chosen in model 10 implies the following theoretical expectations (that is, variables are ordered *as if* we expected . . .). First, the expectation is that the strongest effects on environmental policy convergence arise from international harmonisation. Second, it is assumed that convergence effects of communication will be somewhat weaker than harmonisation effects, thus 'institutional membership' follows after the harmonisation variables. Third, the trade variable is expected to have even weaker effects. For the other variables (cultural similarity, income, political demand, problem pressure and pre-existing similarity of policies) we are not primarily interested in their contribution to the explanation of convergence, but in a potential effect that might go beyond the main variables. Thus, they are ranked lower in order. Except for the time variable, we do not differentiate between the control variables; all of them are residualised on the five variables referring to the three main driving forces of convergence. The time variable is the last one, as it is correlated with many covariates and no explicit theoretical expectation can be formulated. This way only the time effect that goes beyond the influence of all other variables enters the regression. Its coefficient is thus expected to be much lower than in the non-partialised model.

In addition to model 10 with the harmonisation variables at the top of the ranking, five other partialised regression models are run with different hierarchical orderings, implying different theoretical expectations. This way we avoid arbitrariness in choosing the hierarchy of variables, as we do not possess a confirmed theory telling us which factor is the most relevant. At the top of the rankings in models 11 to 15 are the communicative potential variable, the trade variable, and those control variables that are most important according to bivariate regression (table A6.3), i.e., the level of economic development, pre-existing similarity, as well as the time variable. The equation is similar to the one for model 10. In table 6.6, the variable in the highest rank is marked in bold for each model.

So far, all models are based on the most encompassing dependent variable including all forty policies. These models are complemented by others with different dependent variables for the various sub-groups of policies of theoretical interest (as developed in chapter 3 and section 6.3). They also serve as a further test of robustness for the estimated effects of the explanatory variables (see table 6.7).

Moreover, the pooled model will then be compared to the cross-sectional ones (table 6.8). This way we can compare causal effects in the decade models with effects over the whole period and draw conclusions on the changing importance of causal mechanisms over time. The analyses thus provide more differentiated and more reliable results. For the models in tables 6.7 and 6.8, we use the partialised model 10 as a basis. The reason for this choice is that the harmonisation variables in group one show not only the largest effect in model 10, where they are ranked highest, but also turn out to be very important in all other partialised models.

Table 6.7 *Regression results: policy convergence of different policy sub-groups, pooled data, partialised, based on model 10*

		Policies					Instruments	Settings				
	All	All	OB	NO	TR	NT	All	All	OB	NO	TR	NT
Constant	–**	–**	–**	–	–**	–**	–**	–**	–**	–**	–	–**
EU membership	.132**	.123**	.318**	.006	.136**	.084**	.052*	.185**	.267**	-.037	.185**	.061**
EU accession	.104**	.118**	.058**	.118**	.123**	.104**	.093**	.054*	.017	.089**	-.005	.232**
Accession to institutions	.629**	.581**	.457**	.545**	.589**	.405**	.511**	.505**	.299**	.463**	.508**	.060**
Institutional membership	.426**	.588**	.416**	.547**	.554**	.578**	.251**	.123**	-.017	.157**	.028	.410**
Bilateral trade	-.033	-.037**	-.039	.015	-.020	-.038*	-.028	.016	.000	.042	.004	.035
Cultural similarity	.054**	.007	.096**	-.027	.044**	-.045**	.078*	.122**	.184**	.109**	.189**	-.027
GDP per capita	.017	-.018	.062**	.005	.055**	-.059**	.023	.065**	.149**	-.005	.066**	.046
Existence of green parties	-.007	.052**	-.050*	.101**	.034*	.096**	-.070**	-.043	-.057	.076**	-.029	.099**
CO_2	-.053**	-.046**	.074**	-.091**	-.049**	-.022	-.038	-.050*	.039	-.162**	-.075**	.001
Population density	.029	-.001	-.025	.037*	.018	.018	.003	.094**	.010	.221**	.144**	.019
PSim	-.011	.112**	.126**	.099**	.002	.140*	-.156**	.032	-.247**	-.230**	-.248**	-.227**
	.185**	.157**	-.026	.229**	.098**	.234**	.154**	.131**	-.005	.167**	.118**	.027
R^2	0.67	0.77	0.57	0.69	0.73	0.62	0.40	0.37	0.30	0.37	0.41	0.30
N	828	828	828	828	828	828	828	828	828	828	828	828

Table 6.8 *Regression results: policy convergence of 89 items, pooled data and decades, based on model 10*

	All	1970s	1980s	1990s
Constant	$-$**	$-$**	$-$**	$-$**
EU membership	.132**	.326**	.063	.165**
EU accession	.104**	−.093	$-$[a]	.062
Accession to institutions	.629**	.383**	.564**	.435**
Institutional membership	.426**	.103**	.197**	.003
Bilateral trade	−.033	.125**	−.009	−.055
Cultural similarity	.054**	.083*	.192**	.021
GDP per capita	.017	.228**	.179**	.092*
Existence of green parties	−.007	$-$[b]	−.004	−.039
CO_2	−.053**	.049	−.112**	.099*
Population density	.029	.019	.224**	−.151**
PSim	−.011	.105*	−.318**	.024
R^2	0.67	0.34	0.51	0.20
N	828	276	276	276

Note:
[a] No accession during the 1980s, as accession negotiations with Spain, Portugal and Greece started before 1980 (see chapter 4).
[b] No green parties before 1980.

6.6 FINDINGS

6.6.1 Overall model fit

Tables 6.5 to 6.8 present the results of the regression analysis. The models show satisfying results for the overall explanation of variance and the fit of the model. For the pooled model that includes all explanatory variables (table 6.5, *model 9*), referring to the whole eighty-nine policy-item sample, the degree of explained variance is very high, with corrected r^2 of .67. The explanatory potential of *model 5* that includes only the main project variables shows a high fit as well (r^2 .63), confirming their high relevance for the process of sigma-convergence. On the other hand, the stepwise approach demonstrates that the contribution of the control variables is rather limited. *Model 6* (r^2 .15) and *model 7* (r^2 .32) including solely the control variables present a less efficient estimation of policy convergence. The latter includes the level of pre-existing similarity of policies between countries.

Differences regarding the goodness of fit occur when we look at sub-groups of environmental policy. The degree of explained variance is on average slightly higher than for the overall sample of policies if only the convergence of the presence-of-policy items is regarded (r^2 .57 to .77 in table 6.7). R^2 is significantly lower for the convergence of policy instruments (r^2 .40) and for policy settings (r^2 .30 to .41).

The fit of the model also varies strongly if the three decades are analysed separately. Table 6.8 shows that the explanatory potential of the model for convergence between 1980 and 1990 is rather high (r^2 .51). It is less for the 1970s (r^2 .34) and even lower for the 1990s (r^2 .20). This variation can be related to changes in the effectiveness of some causal mechanisms. The difference from the pooled model is caused by a parallel development over time of the dependent variable and some crucial independent variables that leads to a much higher correlation than for the cross-sectional approach.

In the following sections the results of the regression analysis are presented separately for each of the explanatory factors. For the main independent variables we proceed in the following way. First, we analyse the effects for the whole policy sample for each variable. Second, we differentiate between policy sub-groups. Third, we compare the effects for the different decades under study. For the control variables we are less systematic and present only the most interesting results. Sometimes reference is made to bivariate correlations (cf. table A6.3 in the annex).

6.6.2 International harmonisation
We start with the variables relating to international harmonisation. While international harmonisation is generally of great importance across all explanatory models, differences exist with respect to the three variables which are supposed to represent this mechanism: common EU membership, EU accession and the accession to other international institutions.

EU membership   *Model 1* in table 6.5 illustrates the results for the impact of EU membership on convergence of environmental policies. The effect of harmonisation among member states confirms the expectation from hypothesis H 2.1.1: EU membership is positively correlated with changes in policy similarity (.182). The EU effect, however, is not as dominant as one would expect. The models including all variables show that, although significant, EU membership is not the strongest predictor of convergence, not even for obligatory policy items. In *model 9*, the standardised coefficient declines to .052, whereas the coefficient is .132 in the partialised *model 10*, where the common explanatory potential of EU and other covariates is totally assigned to EU membership.

Table 6.7 validates the expectations with regard to varying EU effects for different policy types. EU membership has a strong positive effect on the convergence of obligatory presence-of-policy (.318) and obligatory setting items (.267), i.e., on convergence of policies where binding regulations exist at the international level. On the other hand, there is no significant effect for convergence of non-obligatory policies and settings, a cross-check which confirms the validity of this indicator. The difference in the EU effect for changes in similarity of trade-related policy items points in the same direction. They are higher for trade-related presence-of-policy items (.136) and setting items (.185) than for the group of non-trade-related policies (.084) and settings (.061). This result is consistent with the fact that environmental policy at the European level has been strongly influenced by the concern for the creation of a common market (Holzinger 1994; Knill 2003). Finally, while the effect is similar for settings and for policies, it is much weaker when it comes to policy instruments (.052, table 6.7).

The correlation between EU membership and convergence also varies over time (table 6.8). The general impact of EU membership is strongly positive for the 1970s (.326) and, to a lower degree, for the 1990s (.165), but very weak for the 1980s (.062). This observation is in line with what is known about the development of EU environmental policy. For the 1970s, the increasing environmental activities of the EU caused strong convergence effects for its members.[5] During that time, the EU introduced binding regulation on nine out of nineteen obligatory policies in our data set (see table 4.1 in chapter 4), whereas only two additional directives that refer to four items of our selection of policies were introduced between 1978 and 1990. Thus, except for changes in existing legislation, almost no additional harmonisation pressure emerged at the European level. From 1990 until 2000, however, five directives and regulations relating to six items were launched by the EU, which explains the higher effect on convergence observed for the 1990s.

What are the reasons for the surprising lack of predominance of EU membership? First, until 1990 only twelve countries were members of the EU, and, for the two decades before, significantly less than half of the sample. Second, non-member countries oriented their policy towards EU legislation.[6] Third, our data show significant differences between EU member states due to discrepancies in implementation, as environmental directives usually leave considerable leeway to domestic policy-makers.[7] Finally, in the case of minimum harmonisation, one would not expect total convergence among EU member states anyway.

EU accession Also EU accession and prospective membership show effects on policy convergence (H 2.1.2). In *model 1* (table 6.5), a positive correlation can be observed that is slightly weaker (.110) than the one for EU membership. This proportion can be found almost across all models, e.g. in *model 10* in table 6.6 (.104).

---

[5] EU member states at the beginning of the 1970s: Belgium, Denmark, France, Germany, Ireland, Italy, Netherlands, UK.

[6] Austria and Switzerland, for example, applied the same limit values for sulphur content in gas oil as the EU during the 1980s.

[7] For example, Germany and the Netherlands had different car emission standards in 1980 in spite of being subject to the same EU requirement.

The clear difference between accession effects on convergence of the presence-of-policy items and convergence of setting items is striking. The latter is very low and barely significant. A plausible explanation for this difference might be that candidate states broadly implemented the environmental *acquis*, but lagged behind most other member states with respect to the level of policy settings before entering the Community. There is no such difference between the effects on convergence of obligatory policies and non-obligatory policies.

The separate analysis for each decade sheds light on the dynamics of EU accession effects. For the 1970s a negative though not significant effect has been found (−.093). Greece, Portugal and Spain are responsible for this effect. This implies that they did not implement the environmental *acquis* already from the beginning of the accession talks in 1978 but only after actual accession. The coefficient for accession during the 1990s is positive (.062), however not very accentuated. This could be the consequence of the two enlargements during the 1990s, the EFTA enlargement and the beginning Eastern European enlargement process. In this decade there are two groups of accession candidates: the Scandinavian states and Austria for the early 1990s, and the CEE states Poland, Hungary, Slovakia, Bulgaria and Romania. A differentiation between the two groups showed that for the first group, there is even a negative effect, while for the second, a more pronounced positive effect can be found. The EFTA countries already had environmental policies similar to the EU members; thus, there was almost no potential to converge any further for this group, whereas for the CEE countries the accession process produced significant convergence.

Accession to institutions In hypothesis H 2.1.3, we expect that international harmonisation can also be effective through the accession to international institutions other than the EU. Our results show that this variable does a very good job at explaining convergence. The variable's influence is clearly stronger than the influence of EU variables. In *model 2* (table 6.5) the coefficient shows the expected positive sign (.479). The size and direction of the effect are quite robust. This can be seen in *model 9* (.400) that includes the whole set of variables. This indicator of the degree to which national governments are subjected to international hard law seems to be a very precise predictor of policy convergence. This is not surprising, as the variable is a fine-tuned indicator of institutional interlinkage. In spite of its explanatory power, this variable should not be seen as too close to the dependent variable in causal terms: there are many steps from the adoption of international agreements to the domestic implementation of these agreements and therefore many obstacles to overcome. The two variables are not interchangeable and their relation is thus not tautological.

A very pronounced positive effect does not only exist for convergence of all policy items, but also for the majority of policy subgroups. We find only minor differences regarding the effects on the convergence of settings, instruments and presence of policies, with a somewhat higher coefficient for the latter. The influence of accession to international institutions is insignificantly low only for non-trade-related settings, where the regression model in general shows a lower fit. Finally, the explanatory potential of this variable seems to be lower for obligatory policies and settings, whereas it turns out to be a powerful predictor for non-obligatory settings and policies.

More variation exists regarding the accession effects over time (table 6.8). For the convergence of all items in our data set, coefficients are lowest for the 1970s (.383), and higher for the 1980s (.575) than for the 1990s (.435). The weaker effect during the 1970s, as well as the peak in the second decade, can be traced back to the fact that many international environmental regimes like the Convention on Long-Range Transboundary Air Pollution or the Vienna Convention for the Protection of the Ozone Layer entered into force after 1980. The slight decrease of the positive effect for the 1990s may be a result of the high level that institutional integration had already reached in our country sample.

In general, international harmonisation turns out to be an influential mechanism for the occurrence of policy convergence from 1970 to 2000. This effect is the dominant one for the regression *model 9* in table 6.5 that includes all independent variables. Therefore, the partialised version with all other variables orthogonalised according to harmonisation variables, i.e., *model 10* in table 6.6, was chosen for the presentation of further regression models for single decades and for policy sub-groups in tables 6.7 and 6.8. Harmonisation effects may be overestimated with respect to their absolute size in these models; however, not with respect to their relative size.

6.6.3 Transnational communication

Our regression results not only indicate strong convergence effects resulting from international harmonisation, but also provide support for the expected impact of communication and information exchange in transnational networks (H 3.1). The effect of common membership in international institutions on cross-national policy convergence as an effect of international interlinkage that cannot be linked to the outcome of international law is – with a standardised coefficient of .489 (*model 2* in table 6.5) – comparable in size to the influence of international harmonisation. It only decreases in *model 9* with the inclusion of time (.161), although it keeps its positive sign and is still significant. Obviously, the influence of communicative networks increases over time. *Model 11* in table 6.6 shows the variable's maximum explanatory potential in a partialised multivariate model (.650); all other coefficients can be interpreted only in terms of their effect beyond the effect of membership in international institutions. It turns out that here the harmonisation variables explain less. *Model 10* shows that the strong positive influence persists (.426), even when only the effects of common institutional membership are included that go beyond harmonisation.

Differences can be observed for the effect of common institutional membership on sub-groups of policies. In table 6.7, transnational communication effects seem to be most pronounced for the convergence of presence-of-policy items (.588). It is only half as strong for the convergence of instruments (.251) and even weaker for the convergence of setting items (.123).[8] These results are in line with our theoretical expectation for the role of transnational communication. It is not surprising that transnational communication through institutional networks exerts a higher influence on the approximation of policy repertoires and on the diffusion of broader ideas of policies than on the exact similarity of a policy setting.

Moreover, coefficients are higher for non-obligatory and non-trade-related policy items. On the other hand, for the convergence of obligatory as well as for trade-related setting items, there is no significant communication effect exceeding the one of harmonisation variables. This shows that the effect of communication relates especially to 'voluntary' convergence not caused by international interdependencies and international harmonisation. It need not constitute a contradictory finding that transnational communication plays an important role for the convergence of obligatory presence-of-policy items. For instance, it is rather plausible that policies adopted at the level of the EU might receive broader international attention, hence fostering the spread of these policies also between those countries that are not (yet) EU member states. It should be noted that until 1990, only 30 per cent of all country pairs shared EU membership. Moreover, countries that are interlinked for a longer time might introduce obligatory policies more quickly.

The influence of common membership also varies across decades. For the 1970s (.103) and 1980s (.197), this variable makes a positive contribution to the explanation of convergence of all policy items (table 6.8 and table A6.3). For the 1990s, however, this effect disappears completely. This striking change in the effects of transnational communication can be explained by the interaction of two developments. On the one hand, it is conceivable that country

---

[8] This difference holds for the bivariate relation as well and is not caused by the multivariate orthogonalised version (see table A6.2).

pairs with strong communicative interlinkage, due to saturation effects, converged to a lesser extent during the 1990s than in earlier periods. If one looks at the degree of similarity of the policy repertoires already reached before the 1990s (see the effect on presence-of-policy above), it becomes clear that communication did not affect the growing together of those countries in the 1990s. On the other hand, our data showed that country pairs characterised by weak communicative interlinkage strongly converged during the 1990s. It should be remembered that this variable includes information on the length of membership – countries that only recently acceded to international institutions weigh less. This holds true in particular for the CEE countries where convergence was driven by harmonisation effects emerging from the accession to international institutions.

What can be said of the explanatory potential of this variable in general? Obviously, it confirms that there are institutional effects beyond harmonisation. Common membership in institutions with high communicative potential is one of the most influential factors in order to account for similarity increases. However, a direct attribution of these effects to voluntary processes of learning, policy transfer or diffusion is not easy, as we do not trace single processes. Nonetheless we found that communication effects have been particularly pronounced for items that are either non-obligatory or not related to trade, as well as higher coefficients for the presence of policies than for instruments and precise settings.

6.6.4 Regulatory competition

Just like the other main explanatory variables analysed so far, convergence effects through regulatory competition confirmed theoretical expectations from hypothesis H 4.1 in general. It can be stated that for a pair of countries, a high degree of economic interlinkage leads to increasing similarity of domestic policies. In *model 3* in table 6.5 the correlation between bilateral trade openness and convergence is significant and clearly positive (.204).

As many empirical studies did not find support for such a trade effect on convergence or diffusion (cf. Drezner 2001; Potoski 2001; Simmons and Elkins 2004), this result should be interpreted carefully for two reasons. First, it should be noted that the trade effect disappears in more comprehensive models; the coefficient is even slightly negative in *model 8* (−.070). A second caveat comes from the comparison of partialised *models 10* and *12* in table 6.6, where the former are orthogonalised with harmonisation variables in first order, the latter with bilateral trade. It is obvious from theoretical considerations that there will be some endogenity between economic interlinkage and institutional integration, in particular in the EU: institutional integration leads to increased trade flows, and the existence of economic interlinkage is a strong incentive to cooperate in political institutions at the international level. Our results suggest that the latter factor is more important than the first. While there is no trade effect beyond harmonisation and communication in *model 10* (−.033), the coefficients for institutional variables are relatively stable regarding their subordination to trade openness in *model 12*. This supports the conjecture that the influence of competition is less important and overridden by institutional integration. It seems plausible that potential competition effects were anticipated by the involved countries and subsequently reduced by international harmonisation. EU environmental policy was to a large extent based on market integration: member states aimed at the creation of the internal market; however, they were interested in the correction of market results by environmental regulation as well. This paved the way for harmonisation of trade-related environmental problems. This interpretation is supported by our descriptive results, showing that convergence was much stronger for trade-related rather than non-trade-related items (see section 6.4).

Regardless of the absolute influence of bilateral trade openness, differences in its relative influence in sub-group models are of interest. It is striking that for no group of policy items do we find a significant influence of bilateral trade openness on increasing similarity (table 6.8). In particular, trade effects found for the convergence of trade-related policies and settings are not more pronounced than for their non-trade-related counterparts, neither for the partialised models in table 6.6, nor for bivariate regression (table A6.3).

However, differences exist with regard to trade effects over time, confirming the interpretation that competition seems to be substituted by regulatory cooperation and transnational communication. Trade effects that go beyond harmonisation and cooperation are pronounced and significantly positive for the 1970s (.125; see table 6.8), when international cooperation in environmental policy has just started. This effect completely disappears over time, and for the 1990s, the model shows a negative relation between economic interlinkage and convergence (−.055), which is confirmed at the bivariate level as well (−.097, table A6.3). Thus, for convergence in recent years, trade dependence seems to play a minor role.

6.6.5 Other variables

Our findings in *model 6* (table 6.5) show that other variables than the ones discussed above contribute to the explanation of policy convergence in the environmental field. Most of them have significant effects, if the main variables are left out.

Cultural similarity We hypothesised that cultural similarity constitutes an influential factor for the occurrence of policy convergence (H 5.1.1). As shown in the bivariate regression in table A6.3, this expectation is confirmed. There is a positive influence on convergence of environmental policies except for the 1990s, where increasing policy similarity is less linked to culturally similar and neighbouring countries. The partialised models in tables 6.6, 6.7 and 6.8 show that the influence of cultural similarity beyond the main variables under investigation is rather limited.

We find significant positive effects for the convergence of setting items (.122), for convergence in the 1970s (.082) and, most pronounced, in the 1980s (.192). The strong effects of cultural similarity during the 1980s are observed in a period that is characterised by a strong expansion of environmental policies, both at the European and the national level. It is well conceivable that this dynamic development particularly inspired countries to transfer and copy innovative policies from other countries. This interpretation is supported by the fact that for the 1990s (which is generally seen as an era of environmental policy stagnation) cultural similarity is not a relevant causal factor behind convergence. This development goes along with the increasing importance of international institutions and seems to become substituted by harmonisation. The increasing similarity of domestic environmental policies is not limited to neighbourhood effects any more. Astonishingly, cultural similarity effects are also strong for obligatory policies. As this cannot be attributed to EU effects (this is excluded because of the partialisation), the explanation might again be found in the emulation of EU policies by culturally similar countries that were not yet EU member states.

Income In the literature, environmental policy is often related to the wealth of a country. With regard to the impact of economic development, we find support for our hypothesis H 5.1.2 that a high and similar level of income of a country pair leads to convergence. We observe positive income effects on convergence in the bivariate analysis (.225, table A6.3) and a positive effect in *model 9* that includes all variables (.151, table 6.5). However, the coefficients decrease strongly when it comes to effects beyond institutional interlinkage. Comparing partialised *models 10, 11* and *13* in table 6.6, the same can be said as for regulatory competition above. Whereas institutional effects are robust in *model 13* that is orthogonalised by the income level, income effects disappear in *models 10* and *11*. Again this can be interpreted as the non-existence of an independent effect of economic development on convergence.

A second parallelism to trade effects is the fact that we find positive influence on convergence independent from institutional effects only for the first and second decade, but not for the 1990s.

Here bivariate regression even reports a strong negative correlation (−.160). The negative correlation is a consequence of two developments: rich countries were already very similar and did not converge any further, whereas poor countries converged during the 1990s (see the descriptive results in chapter 5).

Green parties The expectations on the influence of political demand on cross-national policy convergence (hypothesis H 5.1.3) are partially confirmed. The rise and success of green parties had a significant positive effect at the bivariate level for the 1980s (.182) and 1990s (.074, table A6.3), but not for the 1970s because green parties did not exist in that period. This influence is, however, not visible when all other variables are included (*model 9* in table 6.5).

The only policy sub-group models where the effect goes beyond the influence of the main variables under study are those for convergence on non-obligatory and non-trade-related items (tables 6.7 and A6.3). Thus we find effects on convergence of policy items that are less linked to international interdependence and harmonisation – which is in line with the expectation that political demand affects domestic policy choice. In general, however, political pressure from environmentalism does not seem to be an independent complementary mechanism that has influenced cross-national policy convergence in recent years.

Environmental problem pressure A similar conclusion can be drawn for the two variables measuring environmental problem pressure (H 5.1.4). Over time, both add little to the explanation. Almost all multivariate and pooled models show only minor or no explanatory power. A closer look, however, gives a more differentiated pattern. As can be seen from tables 6.7 and A6.3, the expected positive effect of high and similar CO_2 emissions appears in two models: for obligatory presence-of-policy items (.074) and for setting items (.039). Together with the fact that CO_2 emissions have been influential especially in the first decade (tables 6.7 and A6.3), this result points at a pattern of substitution between the mechanism of domestic problem pressure and international harmonisation: high problem pressure mainly in the field of air pollution led to the introduction of environmental policies, and subsequently international regulation followed at the end of the 1970s and during the 1980s, leading to a decrease in coefficients. A positive CO_2 effect reappears during the 1990s. This can be causally linked to the catching-up of CEE countries where environmental problem pressure was high before, although without consequences on policy-making.

The influence found for population density is slightly higher, though not as strong as expected. A very strong positive effect beyond international factors is only present for the convergence of non-obligatory (.221) and trade-related (.144) setting items. In both groups we find a large share of policies directed towards water pollution, which commonly appears more often in densely populated areas.

It should be recalled that the pair approach aims at explaining sigma-convergence and not at explaining the direction of environmental policy. Given this, it is no surprise that the effects of a common level of income or commonly experienced problem pressure diminish over time. First, these factors are gradually substituted by international harmonisation. Second, the main aspect we measure with the pair approach is the introduction of policies. As for presence-of-policy and instruments, we usually observe not many changes over time; further changes of policies are only captured by the setting dimension. The big effects, however, are caused by the introduction of policies. Therefore, convergence effects shrink over time, as they are less pronounced in the database in later periods.

Pre-existing similarity of policies   For some variables discussed so far, we observed that their influence seems to change in the 1990s. This interpretation can be advanced in interpreting the change in the pattern of convergence as a consequence of saturation effects: convergence between some countries already reached a high level in the 1980s (e.g., for Germany and Switzerland, as shown in figure 6.3).

Those country dyads did not have much potential to converge any further in the following period.

In order to test the saturation effect (H 5.1.5), we use a variable that consists of the level of similarity between country pairs in the previous period. In the bivariate analysis we find a very high positive correlation of this variable with convergence (.546; see also *model 7* in table 6.5). This suggests that those country pairs that already have a high degree of similarity of their environmental policies subsequently converge more strongly than country pairs that are more dissimilar. In the general multivariate model, however, this effect disappears or even turns negative (*models 9–10*), and no independent effect is found that goes beyond the influence of international driving forces of convergence (*models 10–12* in table 6.6).

The analysis by decades confirms the expectation of a saturation effect. In the bivariate analysis for all items, a strong positive correlation is found for the 1970s, followed by a weak positive effect in the 1980s and a significantly negative one for the 1990s (table A6.3). This decreasing effect is roughly confirmed in the multivariate partialised model (table 6.8). This effect can be explained as follows: pioneer countries, i.e., those countries which already had policies in place in 1970, became more similar during the 1970s. Consequently, in the next decades their potential to further converge shrank. At the same time, those countries which were dissimilar before show much higher convergence rates in the 1990s. That is, convergence is now better explained by previous dissimilarity. This turn can be ascribed to the fundamental changes in the environmental policies of the CEE countries and Mexico. Therefore, the negative correlation for the 1990s indicates a process of catching-up of the laggard countries.

Time As already mentioned above (section 6.6.1), time also influences convergence. We do not have explicit theoretical expectations about this variable. It represents the dynamics of this relatively new policy area and it includes various aspects that drive the development of environmental policy in general, which have not been included in this analysis, such as technological progress, diminishing costs of environmental protection, and external shock events like acid rain and 'Waldsterben', the nuclear disaster in Chernobyl, or the concerns about the greenhouse effect.

Time is highly correlated with policy convergence, even for the overall *model 9* in table 6.5 (.442). For the partialised models (table 6.6) the effect is still significantly positive (.185, *models 10–13*). *Model 15* shows the time factor has a very strong effect if all other factors are partialised out (.721) – actually, time has the strongest bivariate effect of all variables (table A6.3). Still, even in this model harmonisation, transnational communication and income have some explanatory power. The effect is largest for accession to institutions (.317), followed by institutional membership (.120) and EU membership (.112).

6.7 CONCLUSION

The statistical analysis of sigma-convergence of environmental policies on the basis of the pair approach largely confirmed the expectations and the specific hypotheses developed in section 6.4, although there are some surprises when it comes to the exact size of the effects.

First of all, at the descriptive level we saw that the similarity of environmental policies of the twenty-four countries has much increased over the observed period from 1970 to 2000. Therefore, with respect to the first main question of this research project a clear answer can be given: there is no doubt that environmental policies converged to a considerable extent. The picture of sigma-convergence resulting from the analysis of country pairs is much clearer and less ambiguous than from the country-based aggregate analysis in chapter 5.

Second, the extent of convergence varies according to the dimension of policy. Convergence is most pronounced when we look only at the presence of a certain policy. It is less strong when we look at the similarity of the instrument used, and it is even weaker when it comes to the exact setting of an instrument, such as limit values for emissions or environmental taxes. Moreover, convergence is more pronounced for obligatory and trade-related policies than for non-obligatory and non-trade-related policies.

Third, among the three main causal factors, international harmonisation contributes most to the explanation of convergence. The mechanism of international harmonisation was operationalised by three variables: EU membership, EU accession and accession to international environmental organisations other than the EU. These differentiations lead to a surprising result: accession to and membership in the EU explains clearly less than accession to other international environmental institutions. It is somewhat counter-intuitive that the effects of EU harmonisation on the environmental policies of mostly European countries are smaller than the effects of harmonisation by multilateral international treaties. This result can, however, be explained by the fact that, seen over the whole period, EU members form only a small part of the country sample.

Fourth, the effects of transnational communication on environmental policy convergence are almost in the same order of size as the effects of international harmonisation. Although we did not formulate a hypothesis on the comparative effect of these two mechanisms, it seemed more intuitive that harmonisation effects are stronger than communication effects. However, it turned out that communicative interaction has similarly strong effects on the convergence of environmental policies as harmonisation. The effect of transnational communication on convergence is particularly pronounced with respect to non-obligatory and non-trade-related policies. This is in line with expectations: when there is already a harmonised policy at the international level, there is not much room left for transnational communication to influence further convergence. The effects of transnational communication seem to vanish during the 1990s. This may be a consequence of saturation effects on the side of countries characterised by high communicative interlinkage.

Fifth, the explanatory potential of the mechanism of regulatory competition is less convincing than that of international harmonisation and transnational communication. Although there is a clear and significant trade effect in a bivariate regression model, the effect vanishes in multivariate models and in models that subordinate the trade variable to harmonisation or communication. This implies that there is no effect of regulatory competition that goes beyond the effects of harmonisation or communication. Moreover, the effects of trade are no more pronounced for trade-related policies than for those not related to trade.

Sixth, the other variables controlled for in the project to some extent contribute to the explanation of environmental policy convergence. Most pronounced are the effects of income and cultural similarity, whereas political demand and environmental problem pressure show weaker effects. The latter two do not seem to play an independent role for the explanation of convergence. The introduction of the variable 'pre-existing similarity' showed that countries with previously similar policies converged more strongly in subsequent periods. Whereas this effect is particularly strong for the 1970s, it is weaker during the 1980s and turns negative during the 1990s due to saturation.

In sum, we find that the environmental policies of the twenty-four countries in the sample converged to a great extent in the period from 1970 to 2000. Convergence is mainly caused by two mechanisms, namely international harmonisation and transnational communication. Regulatory competition and some domestic variables play a minor role in the explanation of environmental policy convergence.

7 The gap approach: what affects the direction of environmental policy convergence?

BAS ARTS, DUNCAN LIEFFERINK,
JELMER KAMSTRA AND JEROEN OOIJEVAAR

7.1 INTRODUCTION

This chapter deals with the following sub-set of questions of the research project:

(1) What is the direction of policy convergence; i.e., does convergence coincide with an upward ('race-to-the-top') or downward trend ('race-to-the-bottom')?
(2) What institutional and economic factors (as well as other potentially relevant variables) can explain upward or downward patterns of environmental policy convergence?
(3) To what extent do our empirical findings vary across different policy *dimensions* (presence-of-policies and policy settings) as well as across various policy *types* (trade-related versus non-trade-related policies and obligatory versus non-obligatory standards)?

Theoretically, this chapter builds upon delta-convergence, dealing with convergence towards an exemplary model (Heichel, Pape and Sommerer 2005). Methodologically, this chapter builds on the so-called gap approach, based on an assessment of the gaps between individual country policies on the one hand and a certain policy benchmark – for example the best practice available – on the other, over different points in time. An average policy gap change in the direction of the benchmark then points at delta-convergence as well as at a 'race-to-the-top', provided that the benchmark is the best practice.

This approach is complementary to the 'classical' ones as well as to the pair approach. On the basis of aggregate descriptive data and the concept of sigma-convergence, the 'classical' approach (chapter 5) primarily dealt with the degree of convergence. By calculating changes in the regulatory mean, furthermore, an idea of the direction of convergence could be given. In the present chapter, we further specify the direction of convergence by working with a benchmark. In addition to that, contrary to the simple calculation of the regulatory mean, the gap approach also allows for the inclusion of nominal data. The pair approach (chapter 6) then moved to the explanation of the patterns observed but only focused on the degree of convergence. The present chapter adds to the picture the explanation of the direction of convergence.

The structure of this chapter is as follows. The next section (7.2) explains in some detail how the gap approach actually works. This is followed by a descriptive analysis of the development of policy gaps in our sample of twenty-four countries in section 7.3. Thus, we obtain the necessary data for the dependent variable – policy gap change – for the subsequent explanatory analysis. Section 7.4 serves to formulate specific hypotheses for this analysis and to revisit the independent variables in the light of the gap approach. Whereas section 7.5 briefly describes the procedure followed in the explanatory analysis, section 7.6 presents the results of our regressions and discusses the findings. In section 7.7, more general conclusions are formulated and a link is established with the findings of the 'classical' analysis of chapter 5 and, particularly, the pair approach of chapter 6.

7.2 THE GAP APPROACH

7.2.1 Basic methodology

The gap approach is based on the following procedure. The level of each environmental policy item being in force in country A . . . Z – or 'policy level' (PL) – is compared to a benchmark level in order to measure the distance – or 'policy gap' (PG) – for each country to this benchmark. Since convergence is a time-related phenomenon, this is done at different points in time. As benchmark we use what we call the 'strictest available policy option' (SAPO), which is defined as the most ambitious or best practice level of the environmental policy item that is available in a country set in a certain period of time. As chapter 5 has already shown that 'races-to-the-bottom' do not occur in our data set, we have chosen the *strictest* (rather than the laxest) policy as a benchmark. This implies that sometimes the SAPO is a minimum level (e.g., limit values for polluting substances), sometimes a maximum level (e.g., eco tax). Nonetheless, in order to assess comparable policy gap changes, we opt for *positive* gap scores for both cases. In mathematical terms:

$$PG_{A...Z} = |SAPO - PL_{A...Z}|,$$
$$\text{for } T_1, T_2, T_3 \tag{1}$$

However, we are not interested in the absolute policy gaps of countries with regard to a number of policy items at different points in time, but rather in the *change* of policy gaps over time. After all, delta-convergence refers to decreasing distances of countries' policies towards an exemplary model over time. If delta-convergence occurs, in other words, policy gaps change into the direction of the exemplary model from T_1 to T_2, for example. With that, *'policy gap change'* (*PGC*) is our dependent variable.

$$PGC_{T_1-T_2} = PG_{T_1} - PG_{T_2},$$
$$\text{for country A...Z.} \tag{2}$$

If $PGC > 0$, the policy gap at T_1 is bigger than at T_2. This implies that the gap has decreased over time and that delta-convergence is present. And the higher the score, the more convergence. If $PGC < 0$, the gap has increased. If $PGC = 0$, there is obviously no change at all.

7.2.2 *Calculating policy gap change with the ENVIPOLCON data set*

As mentioned, we use as our benchmark the 'strictest available policy option' (SAPO) of each policy that is available in a country set in a certain period of time. The set of policies (N = 40), the set of countries (N = 24) and the measurement points in time (1970, 1980, 1990, 2000) are given with the ENVIPOLCON data set. Regarding the choice of the SAPO, however, two choices are still possible. On the one hand, we can take the one and only SAPO for each policy item for the *entire* period (1970–2000) or we can choose for the three SAPOs for each policy item in the respective *decades* (1970s, 1980s, 1990s). We decided to use the second option. The choice for *decade* SAPOs – instead of *overall* SAPOs – is based on substantive and methodological grounds. First of all, one can argue that it is invalid to compare, for example, a policy item of 1970 with a benchmark from the year 2000 (which is likely to be the strictest option in the ENVIPOLCON data set in most cases). Politically, socially and technically, these two policy levels are only indirectly related, or even unrelated, given the strong separation in terms of time. Therefore it is better to compare policy levels with SAPOs which are closer in time, i.e., in our case, using the decade intervals provided by our data set. Methodologically, the use of overall SAPOs would imply that many policy gaps in 1970 – and even in 1980 and 1990 – will be high, given that many policies in the year 2000 are likely to be much stricter than their predecessors. This will lead to a decreasing variance in the data set for 1970 (and, to a lesser extent, for 1980 and 1990), lowering the chance of finding significant results in the regressions.[1] These methodological effects are largely absent if we use *decade* SAPOs instead of overall SAPOs.

Using the ENVIPOLCON data set implies having both *metric* and *nominal* data. For policy settings, which are metric data, we selected the strictest values as benchmarks in each decade. The gap is then simply the (metric) difference between the decade benchmark and a country's setting. For the presence of environmental policies, which are nominal data, the benchmark is the mere existence of

---

[1] It should be noted that the effect of decreasing variance in earlier decades is further strengthened by our normalisation procedure, which has a bias towards suppressing the size of policy gaps and policy gap changes in the case of bigger absolute gaps (see below).

the policy in national environmental policy. The possible scores for those items are simply 0 (absence of policy) or 1 (presence of policy). Countries that do not have the policy at stake at a certain point in time then face a gap equal to 1 (1 minus 0). It should be noted, moreover, that the gap approach, unlike the previous chapters, does not distinguish between the categories of 'presence-of-policy' and 'policy instrument'. The reason is that instruments as such cannot possibly be ranked according to strictness.

Thus building on a mixed data set, covering both metric and nominal data, the question is how to deal with this in the gap approach. For substantive and methodological reasons, we con-structed two sub-sets of data, which can be compared in the descrip-tive and explanatory analyses below. The first sub-set consists of all forty policy items. All of those, including the settings items among them, are now dealt with as 'presence-of-policy' only, implying that the entire sub-set is *nominal* in character. The advantage is that we have all policy items included, the disadvantage that (metric) infor-mation is lost. Therefore we create a second sub-set of data, consist-ing of the twenty-one policy settings, which are now dealt with as *metric* data. In this second case, we lose information on policy items, but win information in terms of metric data. A possible third data sub-set, which combines metric and nominal data, was left out. Most notably, mixing the two types of data would lead to an overes-timation of presence-of-policy versus policy settings. This is due to the fact that in our approach the mere introduction of a policy (presence-of-policy), irrespective of its precise content, immediately brings the nominal variable from 0 to 1, whereas even a highly significant tightening of a limit value or the increase of a tax (setting) finds expression only in decimals. A similar effect occurs in the pair approach (chapter 6).

The construction of *aggregated* policy gaps (PG_{Ag}), based on all (or a sub-set) of the forty items for the twenty-four countries at the four points in time, raises another problem. To be able to aggre-gate gaps over several items – with various units of measurement, at least for the metric data (g/km, mg/l, $\mu g/m^3$, dB, etc. . . .) – we need to work with *normalised* policy levels (PL_{No}) that transform absolute gaps into comparable but relative ones (between 0 and 1). In order to standardise the settings to a value between 0 and 1, every score on an item is divided by the decade ($SAPO_{Dec}$) concerned. For example, when the decade SAPO is an environmental tax of 180 $/kJ in the 1970s[2] and when all policy levels of countries in 1970 and 1980 are *below* this figure, then this procedure will lead to the SAPO itself scoring 1 and the other values somewhere between 0 and 1. The closer the number gets to zero, the less strict the policy is:

$$PL_{No} = PL/SAPO_{Dec} \qquad (3)$$

In the case of environmental standards, however, the SAPO typically represents the lowest score, for example 0.23 mg/l with regard to a substance that pollutes water, while the other levels are *above* this figure. In this case the above procedure will lead to scores of 1 (the SAPO itself) and higher (the other levels). In order to obtain values between 0 and 1, therefore, the scores for this type of setting are once more recoded by calculating $1/x$.

$$PL_{No} = SAPO_{Dec}/PL \qquad (4)$$

In footnote 1, we have already referred to the fact that this normalisation procedure exhibits a certain bias. It tends to relatively increase the normalised policy gaps and the normalised policy gap changes in the case of lower absolute gaps. Take as a fictive example the policy levels of 2, 4, 6 and 8, with 2 being the SAPO. Normalised, these figures amount to 1.00, 0.50, 0.33 and 0.25. The absolute policy gaps then are 0, 2, 4 and 6, the normalised ones 0.00, 0.50, 0.67 and 0.75. With this example, it becomes obvious that the linear

---

[2] Remember that the *decade* SAPO has been defined as the strictest available policy option in force in the country set in the decade under consideration. In practice this means that for the 1970s, for example, the decade SAPO may in principle occur either at the measuring point at the beginning of the decade (1970) or at the end (1980) (see also below).

relationship of the absolute figures is lost in the normalised continuum. And more precisely: the lower the absolute policy gap is, the (relatively) higher the normalised one. This also implies that, over time, the normalised policy gap *change* will be relatively higher in the case of lower absolute policy gaps.[3] In an attempt to eliminate this bias, we experimented with other or corrected normalisation procedures. On the basis of fictive examples and calculations, we nonetheless decided to maintain the above normalisation procedure based on decade SAPOs, the main reason being that this procedure produced the same trends in outcomes as more complex normalisation procedures. Under these circumstances, parsimony was preferred.

Following normalisation, the *aggregated* and *mean* policy gaps for each country at each point in time can now be calculated by taking the decade SAPOs (score always 1) minus the normalised policy levels for all policy items concerned (somewhere between 0 and 1). Note that the number of policy items varies with each decade, since not all forty policy items already existed in the 1970s or 1980s ($N = 30$ for 1970s; $N = 38$ for 1980s; and $N = 40$ for 1990s). In mathematical terms, based on formula (1) in the above:

$$PG_{Ag} = \sum |1 - PL_{No}| / N \text{ policy items,}$$
for 24 countries, \hfill (5)
in 1970, 1980, 1990, 2000

When the aggregated and normalised policy gaps are known for the twenty-four countries at the four points in time, the average gap development for all countries over time can be calculated, giving an overall indication of the direction of policy convergence. Also,

[3] This bias would become particularly pressing if overall SAPOs were used (see above). In that case, the absolute gaps in the 1970s and 1980s would be typically big, but the normalised ones would be (relatively) less so. This would, in other words, suppress the policy gap change in these decades compared to the 1990s. This bias, though, is to a considerable extent overcome by using decade SAPOs instead.

the (normalised and aggregated) policy gap *changes* can be calculated, in accordance with formula (2) above. At that point we will be able to see if and to what extent our data set shows a general trend of delta-convergence and a 'race-to-the-top'.

Before turning to the findings on the basis of the ENVIPOL-CON data set, however, two other implications of the use of decade SAPOs should be addressed here. They relate to the descriptive and explanatory analyses respectively. First, by using decade SAPOs we in fact work with three distinct decades: (1) 1970–1980, the policy gaps of which are based on the SAPOs of the 1970s; (2) 1980–1990, the policy gaps of which are based on the SAPOs of the 1980s; and (3) 1990–2000, the policy gaps of which are based on the SAPOs of the 1990s. For calculating policy gap change for 1970–1980, in other words, we need values for the policy gaps in 1970 and 1980 based on the 1970s SAPO, while for calculating policy gap change for 1980–1990 we need the policy gaps in (again) 1980 as well as of course 1990, but now based on the 1980s SAPO. A similar procedure of course applies to calculating policy gap change for 1990–2000. As a result, we end up with two policy gap calculations for each item and country for 1980 and 1990, respectively, however based on different SAPOs. The second point is that for pooled regression analyses (see below) the change of N policies over time is problematic. After all, one can only pool similar variables in a regression. Two options are then possible. Either we take the thirty policy items which were already existent in the 1970s as the basis for all our calculations, but then we will miss information on ten policy items in the analyses. Or we can include all forty policy items in all decades and give those which are still non-existent in the 1970s and 1980s a zero for policy gaps and gap changes, since no policies and no SAPOs were yet available. Although the latter option is less attractive for the outcomes particularly in the 1970s, we nonetheless preferred this one in order not to lose information with regard to the ten policy items which were only introduced in the 1980s or 1990s.

7.3 DESCRIPTIVE ANALYSIS OF THE DEPENDENT VARIABLE

In this section we will present a descriptive account of our dependent variable, based on the ENVIPOLCON data set. As mentioned, the dependent variable for our analysis is policy gap *change*. However, in order to construct this dependent variable, we first have to establish (normalised) *policy gaps*. Hence, the discussion will proceed in two steps. First the normalised policy gaps resulting from our data set will be presented. After that, these gaps will be combined over time so as to map policy gap change, or delta-convergence. In both steps, we will start our discussion with two individual policy items and then move on to the aggregate level of the entire data set.

7.3.1 Two examples

In chapter 6, the example of limit values for lead in petrol was used to explain and make transparent the methodological procedures concerned. For reasons of comparability, we will do the same here. In addition, another example is added – industrial discharges of zinc to surface water – so as to show how different policies may produce different outcomes. Following the procedure set out in the previous section, the policy gaps for all twenty-four countries in the 1970s, 1980s and 1990s are calculated, normalised and averaged for both items. Tables 7.1 and 7.2 summarise the findings. Although we are not interested in the performance of individual countries, but rather in the development of the strictness of policies over time in a group of countries, we have nonetheless taken up scores of individual countries here in order to give the reader an impression of the underlying calculations. In the tables, the overall trend is clear: the policy gaps decrease in each decade. Moreover, the decade SAPOs become stricter over time in both examples.

This can be read from the tables as follows. First, the SAPOs – indicated here by a policy gap of zero (and bold type in the tables) – are consistently found at the *end* of each decade. As a consequence, secondly, the policy gaps of 1980 and 1990 increase (or remain

Table 7.1 *Policy gaps for lead content in petrol, based on decade SAPOs*

Country	1970s		1980s		1990s	
	1970	1980	1980	1990	1990	2000
Austria	1.00	0.63	0.97	0.13	0.67	**0.00**
Belgium	1.00	0.67	0.97	0.91	0.97	**0.00**
Bulgaria	1.00	1.00	1.00	1.00	1.00	0.97
Denmark	1.00	1.00	1.00	1.00	1.00	**0.00**
Finland	1.00	1.00	1.00	0.91	0.97	0.62
France	0.82	0.70	0.97	0.95	0.98	**0.00**
Germany	1.00	**0.00**	0.91	**0.00**	0.62	0.62
Greece	1.00	1.00	1.00	0.97	0.99	0.99
Hungary	0.83	0.79	0.98	0.97	0.99	0.97
Ireland	1.00	0.77	0.98	**0.00**	0.62	**0.00**
Italy	1.00	1.00	1.00	0.96	0.98	0.97
Japan	1.00	1.00	1.00	1.00	1.00	**0.00**
Mexico	1.00	1.00	1.00	1.00	1.00	**0.00**
Netherlands	1.00	0.63	0.97	0.91	0.97	**0.00**
Norway	1.00	0.61	0.97	0.91	0.97	**0.00**
Poland	1.00	1.00	1.00	0.96	0.98	0.97
Portugal	1.00	0.76	0.98	0.97	0.99	0.62
Romania	1.00	1.00	1.00	0.97	0.99	0.97
Slovakia	1.00	1.00	1.00	0.91	0.97	**0.00**
Spain	1.00	0.63	0.97	0.97	0.99	0.97
Sweden	0.79	**0.00**	0.91	0.74	0.90	**0.00**
Switzerland	0.76	0.63	0.97	0.91	0.97	**0.00**
United Kingdom	0.82	0.67	0.97	0.91	0.97	**0.00**
USA	1.00	1.00	1.00	1.00	1.00	**0.00**
Mean	*0.96*	*0.77*	*0.98*	*0.83*	*0.94*	*0.36*

constant in case there is no policy present) when they are calculated on the basis of the SAPOs of the *coming* decade, compared to the gaps based on the SAPOs of the *previous* decade. These outcomes already point at stricter decade SAPOs over time, implying delta-convergence for both cases.

On this basis, we can now calculate the development of the policy gaps over time, i.e., policy gap *change*, being the indicator of

Table 7.2 *Policy gaps for zinc in industrial discharges to surface water, based on decade SAPOs*

Country	1970s		1980s		1990s	
	1970	1980	1980	1990	1990	2000
Austria	1.00	1.00	1.00	0.83	0.93	0.80
Belgium	0.80	0.80	0.90	0.90	0.96	1.00
Bulgaria	1.00	1.00	1.00	1.00	1.00	0.80
Denmark	1.00	1.00	1.00	1.00	1.00	1.00
Finland	1.00	1.00	1.00	1.00	1.00	1.00
France	1.00	1.00	1.00	0.90	0.96	0.90
Germany	1.00	1.00	1.00	**0.00**	0.60	**0.00**
Greece	1.00	1.00	1.00	1.00	1.00	1.00
Hungary	0.80	0.80	0.90	0.50	0.80	0.80
Ireland	1.00	1.00	1.00	1.00	1.00	1.00
Italy	1.00	**0.00**	0.50	**0.00**	0.60	0.60
Japan	1.00	0.80	0.90	0.90	0.96	0.96
Mexico	1.00	1.00	1.00	1.00	1.00	0.98
Netherlands	1.00	1.00	1.00	1.00	1.00	1.00
Norway	1.00	1.00	1.00	1.00	1.00	1.00
Poland	1.00	1.00	1.00	1.00	1.00	0.90
Portugal	1.00	1.00	1.00	0.90	0.96	0.96
Romania	1.00	1.00	1.00	1.00	1.00	0.60
Slovakia	1.00	1.00	1.00	1.00	1.00	0.80
Spain	1.00	1.00	1.00	0.83	0.93	0.93
Sweden	1.00	1.00	1.00	1.00	1.00	1.00
Switzerland	1.00	0.50	0.75	0.75	0.90	0.90
United Kingdom	1.00	1.00	1.00	1.00	1.00	0.60
USA	1.00	1.00	1.00	1.00	1.00	0.32
Mean	*0.98*	*0.91*	*0.96*	*0.85*	*0.94*	*0.83*

delta-convergence. This operation leads to the results shown in table 7.3. Here only the mean policy gap changes are presented for the three decades (as we are interested in policies, not in individual countries). Obviously, delta-convergence exists for both items over the entire period, but is much higher for lead policy than for zinc policy. Also, it is shown that delta-convergence does not necessarily increase incrementally over the decades, at least not for individual

Table 7.3 *Mean policy gap changes for lead and zinc*

Item	1970–1980	1980–1990	1990–2000
Lead	0.19	0.15	0.58
Zinc	0.07	0.10	0.11

policy items. For lead, considerable convergence in the 1970s is followed by less convergence in the 1980s and again followed by strong convergence in the 1990s. For zinc, we observe another pattern. Here delta-convergence is lower, but rather stable over time.

7.3.2 Aggregated results

Having established the policy gaps for all forty policy items and for all countries over time, the figures can now be aggregated. As set out in section 7.2, we will do so for two sub-sets which produce the most meaningful results, i.e., the sub-set of twenty-one settings items with metric data and the subset of all forty policy items reduced to nominal data, indicating 'presence-of-policy'. In addition, we have made calculations for two sets of sub-groups. On the one hand, a distinction is made between the regulation of products (P, eleven items), the regulation of production processes (PP, fifteen items) and policies that are not directly related to trade (i.e., regulation of neither products nor processes; NPP, fourteen items; see further chapter 4). On the other hand, policies that became subject to international harmonisation before or during the period 1970–2000 (or obligatory policies; O, nineteen items) and policies not subject to international harmonisation (non-obligatory policies; NO, twenty-one items) are distinguished. The results are shown in table 7.4.

Overall, delta-convergence exists and increases each decade. For settings, convergence amounts to 0.09 (1970s), 0.20 (1980s) and 0.21 (1990s) respectively; for presence-of-policy, these scores are 0.17, 0.19 and 0.33 respectively (minimum score = −1.00, maximum score = +1.00). This outcome once again strongly falsifies the 'race-to-the-bottom' thesis. Also, it confirms similar outcomes based

Table 7.4 *Aggregate and mean policy gaps and policy gap changes for policy settings, all policy items reduced to presence-of-policy and sub-groups*

	Mean policy gap						Mean gap change		
	1970 (SAPO 70s)	1980 (SAPO 70s)	1980 (SAPO 80s)	1990 (SAPO 80s)	1990 (SAPO 90s)	2000 (SAPO 90s)	1970–1980	1980–1990	1990–2000
Settings	**0.96**	**0.87**	**0.91**	**0.71**	**0.82**	**0.60**	**0.09**	**0.20**	**0.21**
Sub-groups:									
P	0.95	0.84	0.86	0.57	0.75	0.43	0.10	0.29	0.32
PP	0.97	0.86	0.95	0.84	0.91	0.74	0.11	0.12	0.18
NPP	0.96	0.90	0.91	0.75	0.77	0.63	0.06	0.17	0.15
O	0.96	0.87	0.91	0.72	0.83	0.58	0.09	0.20	0.25
NO	0.96	0.86	0.91	0.71	0.81	0.63	0.10	0.20	0.17
Presence-of-policy	**0.90**	**0.73**	**0.79**	**0.60**	**0.62**	**0.29**	**0.17**	**0.19**	**0.33**
Sub-groups:									
P	0.92	0.65	0.72	0.53	0.53	0.25	0.26	0.19	0.28
PP	0.94	0.82	0.83	0.60	0.66	0.30	0.12	0.23	0.35
NPP	0.93	0.81	0.87	0.68	0.68	0.32	0.12	0.18	0.37
O	0.87	0.66	0.71	0.51	0.51	0.22	0.21	0.20	0.29
NO	0.94	0.82	0.87	0.69	0.72	0.35	0.12	0.18	0.36

Note:
P = standards for product; PP = standards for production processes; NPP = policies not directly related to products or production processes; O = obligatory policies; NO = non-obligatory policies.

on different convergence assessment methodologies in chapters 5 and 6. Generally speaking (and notwithstanding the observation that the presence-of-policy sub-set exhibits a certain stabilisation in the 1970s and 1980s, whereas the settings sub-set does so in the 1980s and 1990s), delta-convergence is higher in the 1980s than in the 1970s and again higher in the 1990s.

Furthermore, convergence is definitely more pronounced for presence-of-policy than for settings (with the 1980s being an exception). This observation confirms the first hypothesis (H 1) in chapter 3, which states that the degree of policy convergence will be highest for policy presence and lowest for policy settings. Regarding the sub-groups, most figures are close to the overall picture. However, considering mean convergence scores over three decades and both data sets, product standards (P), process standards (PP) and obligatory policies (O) tend to converge most, and policies which are not related to trade (NPP) as well as non-obligatory policies (NO) tend to converge the least (although, admittedly, the differences are fairly marginal). This observation has to be related to hypothesis H 4.2 in chapter 3, which says that under a situation of regulatory competition, product standards will become stricter and process standards weaker. This hypothesis is not confirmed: both product and process standards do become stricter at about equal rate. It is interesting to note, however, that product standards exhibit relatively high rates throughout the three decades, whereas process standards converge most strongly in the 1990s. This may reflect the regulatory activity of international institutions such as the EU, which first focused on the elimination of barriers to trade, i.e., the harmonisation of standards for tradable products, and only later broadened their repertoire to process standards as well as policies not related to trade.

7.4 INDEPENDENT VARIABLES AND HYPOTHESES
In the descriptive part we have seen that environmental policies in our twenty-four countries exhibited clear trends developing towards the SAPOs over time. This was true both for the mere existence of policies

(presence-of-policy, assuming that having a policy regarding a given problem can be interpreted as 'stricter' than having no policy at all) and for the strictness of the policy settings. The remainder of this chapter is devoted to finding an explanation for this 'race-to-the-top'. In this section we will formulate a set of hypotheses, specifically adapted to the gap approach but based on the causal mechanisms and the general hypotheses set out in chapter 3 of this book. These mechanisms relate to international harmonisation, transnational communication, regulatory competition and a number of complementary other factors. The gap approach does not require as much adaptation to the independent variables as the pair approach, discussed in the previous chapter. Basically, we follow the operationalisation as set out in chapter 4. A few specific points will nevertheless be touched upon here. As in chapter 6, changes in the policy gap in a given period will be explained by variables referring to absolute figures at the beginning of that period, for instance EU membership or GDP per capita. As mentioned there, the independent variables are conceived as 'potentials' which are supposed to fuel processes actually taking place in the following years.

7.4.1 International harmonisation

As regards the direction of convergence, policy harmonisation in the EU may be expected to have two parallel effects. First, due to the EU's continuous efforts to harmonise policies, member states are obliged to adopt the same range of policies (presence-of-policy) and – at least to some extent – also the same range of instruments. In the gap approach, the mere adoption of policies and instruments in an increasing number of countries is conceptualised as a reduction of the average policy gap between the countries in the sample. The role played by EU harmonisation in disseminating policies and policy instruments among its member states across a wide range of environmental issues can thus be seen as one leading to convergence towards the SAPO, or upward convergence. Second, and more specifically, the EU may have an impact on the level of settings. Compared to other international institutions, the EU has strong mechanisms for reaching relatively high levels of harmonisation. Particularly important in this respect are the various opportunities for high-regulating member states to promote their policies at the European level, for instance by influencing processes of problem definition and agenda setting. In addition, individual countries usually have the right to maintain stricter standards unilaterally, which helps to keep up a dynamic towards higher levels of regulation (see further chapter 3). This leads to the following hypothesis:[4]

> (H 2.2.1): *EU membership at t_1 will lead to convergence towards the top in the period from t_1 to t_2.*

Moreover, new member states are forced to adopt the *acquis communautaire* within a relatively short period of time. In most cases, this will force countries to catch up with existing EU policies. Therefore:

> (H 2.2.2): *Accession to the EU from t_1 to t_2 will lead to convergence towards the top during the same period.*

As for the operationalisation of the EU variables, it must be noted that 'membership', as for most other variables, refers to the situation *at the beginning of* the period (t_1). The 'accession' variable departs from this practice: here it is decisive if accession talks started *during* the period under consideration (from t_1 to t_2) (see further chapter 4).

Other international institutions are supposed to have the same effect as the EU as regards the dissemination of policies and probably also instruments as such. At the moment a state joins an international treaty, it commits itself to implementing the measures prescribed by that treaty. However, these institutions have less powerful mechanisms at their disposal for reaching high levels of

---

[4] The numbering of hypotheses refers to the set of basic hypotheses developed in chapter 3 of this book.

harmonisation than the EU. As far as international treaties contain policy settings at all, these usually entail minimum harmonisation, i.e., countries are allowed to introduce and maintain stricter policies (see further chapter 3). Hence, accession to such institutions (i.e., all institutions in our sample minus the EU), weighed by their obligatory potential as set out in chapter 4, may be expected to lead to an upward shift of the mean, but to a lesser extent than accession to the EU.

> **(H 2.2.3)**: *Accession to international institutions (weighed by obligatory potential) from t_1 to t_2 will lead to convergence towards the top during that same period, however to a lesser extent than accession to the EU.*

7.4.2 Transnational communication

Generally speaking, enhanced transnational communication may be expected in the long term to contribute to the adoption of more similar ranges of policies and instruments. This effect, moreover, may be expected to be continuous, i.e., throughout membership of the institution. For presence-of-policy, therefore, institutional membership (weighed by communicative potential according to the procedure described in chapter 4) is hypothesised to lead to upward convergence. As regards the specific level of settings, lesson-drawing, transnational problem-solving and emulation may generally be expected to induce the adoption of stricter policies. Good examples, models and best practices, promoted either by individual 'pioneer' countries or by international institutions, play an important role in such processes (see further chapter 3).

> **(H 3.2)**: *High institutional membership at t_1 (weighed by communicative potential) will lead to convergence towards the top in the period from t_1 to t_2.*

7.4.3 Trade

As discussed in detail in chapter 3, trade is generally expected to have a downward effect on the direction of convergence. However, a distinction has to be made between process standards (P) and product standards (PP). According to the theory, countries are tempted to lower *process* standards in the face of competitive pressures, i.e., convergence to the bottom. In the case of standards for tradable *products*, a race-to-the-top is expected as countries are generally allowed to erect unilateral trade barriers for health and environmental reasons, for instance under EU and WTO rules (see further chapter 3).

(**H 4.2**): *For process standards, a high level of trade openness at t_1 will lead to a race-to-the-bottom in the period from t_1 to t_2, while for product standards a race-to-the-top is expected.*

7.4.4 Other variables

Whereas the main focus of the ENVIPOLCON project is on the influence of international institutions and international trade on environmental policy convergence, we also test a number of additional, mainly domestic variables which may be expected to be relevant. With one exception (see below), the set of other variables covered in the present chapter corresponds with that of chapter 6, i.e., environmental problem pressure, income, green party strength, cultural openness and time.

Environmental problem pressure is operationalised with the help of two indicators: industrial CO_2 emissions per square kilometre and population density. High environmental problem pressure is expected to lead to higher demand for environmental policies and thus to upward convergence.

(**H 5.2.1**): *High environmental problem pressure at t_1 (operationalised as industrial CO_2/km^2 and population density) will lead to convergence towards the top during the following period.*

Following the theory of the 'Environmental Kuznets Curve' a higher income (expressed as GDP per capita) is supposed to lead to upward convergence in two ways. First, higher income is generally associated with a higher degree of industrialisation, higher levels of environmental pollution and thus with higher demand for policy (see above). Second, political demand for the 'luxury good' of environmental policy may be assumed to be higher with increasing income (see further chapter 3).

(H 5.2.2): *High income at t_1 will lead to convergence towards the top during the following period.*

Similarly, the strength of green parties (operationalised with the help of three indicators: electoral success, membership in parliament and participation in government; cf. chapter 4) is expected to raise the public and political demand for environmental policies. Their increase is thus likely to lead to upward convergence.

(H 5.2.3): *High influence of green parties at t_1 will lead to convergence towards the top during the following period.*

Cultural openness replaces the variable of cultural similarity used in chapter 6. For this purpose, the pairwise data on which cultural similarity was based (common borders, common language, common historical and religious tradition) were reassigned to individual countries. The degree of cultural openness of a country, in other words, represents the accumulated cultural similarity with other countries in the sample. This variable may be expected to increase the receptiveness of countries for stimuli from outside.

(H 5.2.4): *High cultural openness at t_1 will lead to convergence towards the top during the following period.*

Furthermore, a time variable is included in the calculations of the present chapter. As in chapter 6, it controls for the time dependence of the models and covers a range of factors that may contribute to the development of environmental policy in general, but are not further specified in this project, such as increasing scientific knowledge, technological development or events like Seveso or Chernobyl.

In chapter 6, finally, the pairwise variable of pre-existing policy similarity was included. Its equivalent for the gap approach would have been the pre-existing gap: it might have been hypothesised that a low gap at t_1 (indicating a 'policy leader') would lead to low convergence during the following period. Or conversely: that a high gap at t_1 (indicating a 'policy laggard') would lead to high convergence during the following period. However, both effects cannot be considered particularly surprising. After all, convergence starting from a high policy gap will *always* lead to relatively high gap change when compared to convergence starting from a low policy gap, since the latter already is close to the SAPO (and hence, it simply *cannot* change much). Therefore, these effects are not further investigated here.

7.5 METHOD OF ANALYSIS

As outlined in the above, the dependent variable in the present analysis is *policy gap change* over time. To construct this dependent variable, we use two data sets. First, analyses are made with the entire set of forty policy items treated as 'presence-of-policy' (nominal scores). Second, the twenty-one settings (metric scores) are taken as the basis for the dependent variable. It has already been explained above why these two data sets were chosen for the analysis of delta-convergence. Analyses are then carried out for both data sets in their entirety as well as for the sub-groups mentioned above.

The methodology used is basically linear *regression* analysis with a *stepwise* approach. As such, it closely builds on chapter 6. Consequently, eight models are applied in which different (sets of) independent variables are isolated or combined to consider their effects on the dependent variable, i.e., policy gap change.[5] In our model 1, only the EU-related independent variables are included. In a next step, in model 2, the variables on 'access to institutions' and 'institutional membership' are added. In model 3, 'trade openness' is the only independent variable. In model 4, the EU-related

---

[5] In fact the main difference with chapter 6 is the absence of the variable of pre-existing policy similarity, resp. the pre-existing policy gap (see above). Hence, the equivalent of regression model 7 in chapter 6 is missing in the present chapter.

variables and the trade variable are combined, whereas all the institutional and trade variables are represented in model 5. In a next
step, only the other factors are included (model 6). Model 7 covers
all institutional, trade and other variables. Model 8, finally, adds the
time variable.

As it turned out, regressions for single decades (1970s, 1980s,
1990s) as well as for the entire period (1970–2000) did not provide
any significant outcomes, due to the relatively low number of
countries in the sample. For that reason, we pooled the data of the
three decades in our models. In doing so, we increased the number
of observations from $N = 24$ countries to $N = 72$. This led to more
valid outcomes, but the price paid for this, to be sure, was that no
conclusions with regard to single decades can be drawn.

All models were tested for multicollinearity. With one exception, the tests showed that the independent variables in our analysis
do not interfere to an unacceptable level (VIF-values between 1
and 4).[6] Therefore the additional analyses deployed in chapter 6 –
bivariate regressions and orthogonalisation – are absent in this
chapter. Unacceptably high VIF-values (>10) were found only for
institutional membership and the time variable in model 8.

7.6 FINDINGS

This section presents and discusses the results of the regression
analysis for pooled decades for, respectively, all forty policy items
reduced to presence-of-policy (table 7.5), twenty-one settings items
(table 7.6) and a number of sub-groups (table 7.7). The figures in the
tables are standardised coefficients, or beta-coefficients, conveying
the strength of the variables relative to each other.

With all forty items reduced to presence-of-policy, and limiting
ourselves to those models exhibiting an adjusted R^2 above 0.3
(i.e. models 2, 5 and 7), accession to institutions and institutional

---

[6] VIF (variance inflation factors) is a measure for multicollinearity. VIF-values are the
reverse of Tolerance values or Tol-values (VIF = 1/Tol).

Table 7.5 Regression results, policy gap change for all forty policy items reduced to presence-of-policy, pooled decades

	Models							
	1	2	3	4	5	6	7	8
Institutional variables								
EU membership	.337**	.083		.354**	.109		.094	.308*
EU accession	.429**	.145		.428**	.119		.078	.122
Accession to institutions		.386**			.411**		.388**	.298*
Institutional membership		.311**			.354**		.324*	−.502#
Trade openness			−.019	−.066	−.207*		−.219*	−.131
Other variables								
GDP per capita						.186	.051	.264
Green parties						.427**	.083	.019
Cultural openness						−.036	−.013	.038
Industrial CO_2 emissions						−.199	−.153	−.130
Population density						−.045	.032	−.041
Time (Decade 1980–1990)								.367*#
Time (Decade 1990–2000)								.906**#
Adjusted R^2	.170	.418	−.014	.163	.450	.193	.435	.505

Note:
N = 72, * = p<0.05; ** = p<0.01; # = VIF-value>10.

Table 7.6 Regression results, policy gap change for settings (21 settings items), pooled decades

	Models							
	1	2	3	4	5	6	7	8
Institutional variables								
EU membership	.325**	.060		.306*	.068		-.010	.030
EU accession	.217	-.026		.218	-.033		.013	.087
Accession to institutions		.265*			.272*		.259*	.231
Institutional membership		.413**			.425**		.366*	.287#
Trade openness			.130	.074	-.060		-.109	-.140
Other variables								
GDP per capita						.295*	.130	.172
Green parties						.273*	-.025	.046
Cultural openness						.185	.217	.213
Industrial CO_2 emissions						-.083	-.061	-.086
Population density						.015	.084	.079
Decade 1980–1990								.270#
Decade 1990–2000								.050#
Adjusted R^2	.076	.316	.003	.068	.309	.231	.337	.377

Note:
N = 72, * = p<0.05; ** = p<0.01; # = VIF-value>10.

Table 7.7 *Regression results, policy gap change for various sub-groups, pooled decades*

	All policy items reduced to presence of policy						Settings (21 settings items)					
	All	P	PP	NPP	O	NO	All	P	PP	NPP	O	NO
Institutional variables												
EU membership	.094	.397*	.045	-.144	.312*	-.113	-.010	.023	.062	-.151	.002	-.024
EU accession	.078	.041	.351**	-.202	.176	-.023	.013	-.043	.337*	-.353*	-.034	.077
Accession to institutions	.388**	.382*	.119	.426**	.421**	.272**	.259*	.189	-.021	.499**	.205	.275
Institutional membership	.324*	-.327	.432**	.568**	-.160	.664**	.366*	.368	.208	.219	.418*	.201
Trade openness	-.219*	-.060	-.081	-.331**	-.127	-.248**	-.109	-.009	.018	-.333**	-.049	-.169
Other variables												
GDP per capita	.051	.303	.039	-.159	.186	-.075	.130	.072	.297*	-.134	.174	.034
Green parties	.083	.124	.031	.052	.034	.105	-.025	-.064	.039	-.024	-.059	.032
Cultural openness	-.013	-.175	.034	.070	-.106	.068	.217	.060	.212	.259*	.152	.257*
Industrial CO_2 emissions	-.153	-.147	-.087	-.093	-.170	-.104	-.061	-.043	-.059	-.034	-.055	-.056
Population density	.032	-.094	.066	.092	-.007	.057	.084	.049	.023	.140	.044	.121
Adjusted R^2	.435	.119	.401	.457	.207	.587	.337	.135	.296	.244	.321	.211

Note:

P = standards for product; PP = standards for production processes; NPP = policies not directly related to products or production processes; O = obligatory policies; NO = non-obligatory policies; N=72, *p<0.05 **p<0.01.

membership show the strongest and most significant effects (table 7.5). It must be remembered here that *accession* to international institutions is modelled along the lines of a possible harmonisation effect (i.e., data on accession to international institutions are weighed according to their *obligatory* potential), whereas institutional *membership* refers to transnational communication (i.e., data on institutional membership are weighed according to their *communicative* potential, cf. chapter 4). This broadly confirms our theoretical expectations: both the harmonisation effect produced by accession to international institutions (except the EU) and the communication effect produced by membership in international institutions (including the EU) turn out to lead to gap change in an upward direction, or delta-convergence (hypotheses H 2.2.3 and H 3.2). As regards harmonisation, however, we expected the effect of EU accession and membership to be stronger than that of the other international institutions, covered by the variable of 'accession to institutions' (hypotheses H 2.2.1 and H 2.2.1 v. H 2.2.3). This turns out not to be the case. EU membership and EU accession have relatively strong and significant effects only in models 1 and 4, but both models show low values for the adjusted R^2. The EU effects vanish when institutional, trade and other variables are added (models 2, 5 and 7), suggesting that the latter have more explanatory power than EU accession and membership.

In models 5 and 7, moreover, trade openness has a notable and significant *negative* effect on gap change. This is not what we had anticipated. To be sure, the present finding cannot be interpreted by claiming that trade openness leads to a race-to-the-bottom. In the descriptive analysis in this chapter, after all, no race-to-the-bottom was found at all. The negative sign of the coefficient might rather be taken as an indication that countries that are less open to trade converge more to the top than countries that are more open to trade. This is of course still contrary to expectations and hard to explain.

As for the other variables, only green parties in model 6 shows a significant effect on gap change. However, the overall significance of this model is very low and the effect vanishes in model 7. None of the other domestic variables achieves any significant effect. Hence, international factors dominate the domestic ones in terms of explanation. This is in fact very much in line with the overall design of the explanatory model of this study, in which the domestic factors are considered control variables (chapters 3 and 4).

In sum, institutional variables seem to exhibit most explanatory power for delta-convergence with regard to presence-of-policy. Both membership of and accession to international institutions demonstrate the expected positive effect on gap change. Strikingly, however, the EU effect turns out to be more ephemeral than expected. Furthermore, trade openness is found to have a slightly negative effect on gap change.

Turning now to settings as dependent variable, most of the trends described above are replicated (table 7.6). Accession and institutional membership again show the strongest and most significant effects. Whereas for presence-of-policy the standardised coefficients for both variables were of approximately similar magnitude, however, institutional membership now consistently dominates over accession to institutions. Remembering again the fact that the accession variable reflects harmonisation potential of international institutions, whereas the membership variable refers to their communicative potential, this finding suggests the paramount importance of transnational communication in the upward convergence of settings. This effect as such is not unexpected (H 2.2.3 and H 3.2), but its relative size is. Processes such as lesson-drawing, transnational problem-solving and emulation, in other words, must to a considerable extent be held accountable not only for convergence in the adoption of policies as such (see above) but also for their increasing strictness. As for presence-of-policy, and just as surprisingly (cf. H 2.2.1 and H 2.2.2), the impact of the two EU variables on policy gap change for settings is low and mostly not significant.

In contrast with the calculations for presence-of-policy, trade openness does not produce any significant results for settings. This again, although less outspokenly than above, is in contrast with our theoretical expectations (H 4.2).

Also the other variables exhibit a similar pattern as for presence-of-policy. For settings, not only green parties but also GDP per capita have significant effects in model 6, but combined with international factors in model 7, these effects disappear.

To conclude, the predominance of institutional variables for the explanation of delta-convergence, observed for presence-of-policy, is confirmed by the models for settings. Within the institutional realm, it is once again striking that the specific EU effect, based on harmonisation with a high obligatory potential, turns out to be insignificant compared to that of harmonisation effects of accession to other international institutions and particularly transnational communication.

Table 7.7 presents the results of the regression analysis for a number of sub-groups of policy items. The left part of the table takes as the dependent variable all forty policy items, as well as the sub-group selections from these, reduced to presence-of-policy. The right part does the same for the settings items in the sample. The table summarises the results for the model in which all independent variables are included, except time (for reasons of multicollinearity, see above). Hence, the figures in the two columns entitled 'All' correspond with those listed under model 7 in tables 7.5 and 7.6 respectively. The other columns present figures for standards for the various sub-groups as introduced earlier.

Unfortunately, not too much additional information can be drawn from this exercise. First, it must be noted that only four out of ten sub-group models reach an acceptable level of overall model significance (adjusted $R^2 > 0.3$): PP, NPP and NO for presence-of-policy, as well as O for settings.[7] This is inevitably related to the low number of items in each sub-group. Second, as far as results are significant, they basically confirm the findings for the full sets of

---

[7] For the partial sub-group models (models 1–6, not presented in table 7.7), overall model performance is even lower.

presence-of-policy and settings, discussed above, without allowing for much further specification.

The sub-group analysis replicates the strong and significant positive effect of institutional membership on delta-convergence. It does so for all four sub-groups producing overall model significance. As far as the sub-group models with reasonable overall significance are concerned, the sub-groups NPP and NO regarding presence-of-policy confirm the lower but still notable effect of accession to international institutions. The latter finding may seem somewhat surprising. Remembering that accession to institutions is modelled according to their obligatory potential, one would expect an effect of this variable for obligatory (O), rather than for non-obligatory (NO) items. And indeed: for the obligatory presence-of-policy items, a considerably higher coefficient for accession to institutions is found than for the non-obligatory ones (0.421 v. 0.272). However, the 'O' model lacks overall significance.

The low effect of EU variables, discussed above, is also reflected in the sub-group calculations. The only significant results are produced by EU accession for the presence of production process standards (PP). This should not come as a surprise as such: the EU has issued many of those standards over the years and new member states entering the EU are supposed to catch up with them. If one for a moment brackets the low overall significance of the relevant models, a similar effect becomes visible for EU membership and product standards (P), a traditional key area in the EU's internal market policy. Furthermore, a stronger EU effect could have been expected for obligatory (O) than for non-obligatory (NO) items. However, this is hardly reflected in the figures. What remains as a basic conclusion is the overall low effect of the EU compared to harmonisation by other international institutions and particularly transnational communication.

For some of the presence-of-policy sub-groups (NPP and NO; as well as for NPP settings items, but within an overall non-significant model), the negative coefficient for trade openness is replicated. Most of the findings regarding the impact of trade, however, turn out to be insignificant. Again, however, the bigger surprise is in what turns out to be not significant. According to hypothesis H 4.2, we would have expected clear and distinct effects of trade openness on product (P) and production process (PP) standards, but here no significant results are available whatsoever. If anything, this once more confirms the marginal impact of trade on delta-convergence, compared to institutional factors.

With regard to other variables, apart from single factors incidentally flashing up in overall non-significant models, no notable effects can be reported. This reflects the low impact of other factors when compared to the international ones, as observed above.

7.7 CONCLUSION

This chapter investigated the question of delta-convergence, i.e., convergence towards an exemplary model or benchmark, with the help of the gap approach. In this particular analysis, the benchmark was the strictest available policy option (SAPO) found in the entire country sample in each decade under consideration. If the gap between a concrete policy or an aggregated set of policies and the SAPO decreases, this can be interpreted as delta-convergence and, thus, as a 'race' – or at least a movement – 'to the top'.

Although of course our attempt to explain the dynamic within our sample with the help of several international and domestic variables constitutes the ultimate goal of the exercise, the mere description of how the policy gaps of the twenty-four countries in the ENVIPOLCON database developed over time also raises some interesting observations.

First, there can be no doubt that delta-convergence has occurred over the entire period. Building upon chapters 5 and 6, we can now firmly claim that policies of our twenty-four countries have not only moved towards each other over time (sigma-convergence), but that they also did so in an upward direction (delta-convergence). This holds both for the sheer presence of policies and for the strictness of policy standards. Second, the analysis shows that – across the board – the strongest reduction of the policy gap took place in the 1990s. This is in line with the findings of chapter 5.

The explanatory analysis in the final sections of this chapter was carried out by pooling our data for the three decades. The findings thus achieved confirm several of the ones produced by the pair approach in chapter 6, but also give rise to some important qualifications.

First, as far as the key explanatory factors of the ENVIPOLCON project are concerned, the findings of the present chapter strongly confirm the prevalence of international institutions over regulatory competition. An effect of trade openness on delta-convergence was virtually absent for settings and even negative for presence-of-policy. In contrast, institutional factors could account for policy gap change almost throughout our pooled models.

Second, looking at institutional factors in more detail, our findings suggest a remarkably strong effect of transnational communication on policy gap change, especially when compared to that of international harmonisation. As pointed out in the conclusions to chapter 6, an effect of transnational communication as such was certainly hypothesised (cf. hypothesis H 3.2 in the present chapter), but intuitively one would have expected it to be smaller than that caused by international harmonisation. This expectation is refuted by the present analysis. Whereas the pair approach already somewhat surprisingly showed both effects to be of about equal size, the effect of transnational communication found in the gap approach even surpasses that of international harmonisation, notably in relation to settings, i.e., the level of standards, environmental levies, etc. This observation suggests that 'soft' mechanisms such as international problem-solving in epistemic communities (Haas 1992), lesson-drawing, emulation and benchmarking are at least as important as (binding) international rules in bringing about policy change at the domestic level. Further research (including the second, qualitative part of the ENVIPOLCON project) is no doubt necessary to test the robustness of this finding and to better understand its background and implications. In particular, it could shed light on the question whether transnational communication alone is indeed sufficient to bring about the observed effect on convergence, or if it occurs rather in anticipation of rules. In the latter case, we would be dealing here mainly with a temporal effect, with transnational communication in international institutions basically considered by the participating countries as preceding international harmonisation. The fact that the effect appears so striking here might then be linked to the phenomenon that transnational communication does not necessarily take place in the same institution as the eventual harmonisation, e.g., OECD recommendations preceding EU legislation, but already sparks off activities at the national level.

Third, the present analysis confirms the conclusion drawn on the basis of the pair approach that the effect of EU accession and membership is considerably more limited than expected. Although this may be partly explained by a numerical factor (i.e., the fact that the EU, particularly in the beginning of the period under consideration, covers only a small part of the country sample, cf. chapter 6), it is also very much in line with the apparent prevalence of transnational communication over harmonisation as a driving force behind convergence. Whereas the EU is the only international institution setting fully binding and enforceable rules, it is one among many institutions (although certainly an important one) facilitating transnational communication.

Finally, it must be noted that the other variables in the analysis (GDP per capita, green parties, cultural openness, industrial CO_2 emissions and population density) hardly explain anything. With a few exceptions, their effect appears to be statistically not significant. Obviously, when compared to the pair approach, these variables have suffered most from the small number of observations, even with N elevated to 72. Thus, without allowing for any specific inferences on this point, the only conclusion that may be justified here is that the effect of domestic factors indeed appears to fall back behind that of international ones, most notably transnational communication.

8 Conclusion

CHRISTOPH KNILL,
KATHARINA HOLZINGER AND BAS ARTS

8.1 INTRODUCTION

The central objective of this book was to advance our theoretical and empirical understanding of causes and conditions of cross-national policy convergence. In theoretical terms, we were especially interested in the extent to which growing economic and institutional interlinkages between nation states – developments that are usually associated with catchwords such as globalisation and Europeanisation – constitute major driving forces of cross-national policy convergence. In this regard, we studied the impact of three central convergence mechanisms, namely, international harmonisation, regulatory competition and transnational communication.

In empirical terms, we analysed the relevance of these factors for the area of environmental policy. More specifically, we were especially interested in two research questions. On the one hand, we studied the extent to which the policies of the countries under study actually became similar over time. On the other hand, we focused on the direction of convergence; i.e., the question whether potential similarity increases coincide with often-discussed races to the top or bottom of national environmental policies. To answer these questions, we analysed the development of forty different environmental policies of twenty-four countries over a period of thirty years (1970 until 2000).

In addressing these theoretical and empirical questions, our study not only indicates several new insights and innovations, but also points to new and interesting questions for future research. Both aspects, innovations and avenues for future research, will be presented in more detail in the following sections.

8.2 EMPIRICAL AND THEORETICAL FINDINGS

With regard to the first aspect – the new insights gained from our research – several innovations are worth mentioning. First, there is strong evidence for the fact that during the period of observation, the environmental policies of the countries under study indeed converged very strongly. Looking at changes in the policy similarity between the countries (sigma-convergence), policy similarity for the average country pair on all forty policies under investigation rose from 3.5 per cent in 1970 to 56.1 per cent in 2000.

Second, notwithstanding this overall pattern our results show that the degree of convergence varies with the type and dimension of the investigated policies. With regard to policy types, sigma-convergence is generally more pronounced for obligatory policies and trade-related policies than it is the case for non-obligatory or non-trade-related items. The degree of convergence also varies when different policy dimensions (policy presence, instruments, setting levels) are considered. More specifically, the convergence degree decreases with the level of specification of the different dimensions. It is least pronounced for setting levels and highest for the dimension of policy presence, with convergence on instruments remaining somewhere in between.

Third, our empirical findings provide no evidence for often-feared races to the bottom. Rather we observe a constant strengthening of environmental policies over time. This picture is confirmed not only by a merely descriptive analysis of aggregate data, but also when applying more sophisticated measurement approaches assessing the gaps between individual country policies and 'strictest available policy options' for each policy (delta-convergence). Our data reveal that average gaps strongly decreased over time, implying that policies converged in an 'upward' direction.

Fourth, both sigma- and delta-convergence are most pronounced towards the end of the observation period; i.e., the 1990s, indicating that policy similarity and tendencies towards stricter regulations not only increase, but also accelerate over time.

Fifth, turning to the theoretical findings of our study, we find that the above-mentioned developments of environmental policy convergence can basically be attributed to the effects of two causal mechanisms: international harmonisation and transnational communication. While the relevance of the first factor might hardly be considered a big surprise, the explanatory power of transnational communication is highly striking. Obviously, the mere fact that countries exchange information on each other's policy choices and discuss policy problems and potential solutions at the level of international institutions is equally important in driving cross-national policy convergence as the adoption of legally binding policy arrangements at the level of the EU or international regimes and institutions.

Sixth, similarly surprising as the high explanatory relevance of transnational communication is the negligible explanatory power of regulatory competition. We neither find evidence for the often-expected races to the bottom, nor is there an effect of regulatory competition that goes beyond the effects of harmonisation or communication. This statement holds even if we solely consider the sub-group of trade-related policies, although the latter should be particularly exposed to competitive pressures.

Finally, it should be emphasised that our analysis was based on two important methodological innovations that – compared to the state of the art – allowed for a more sophisticated measurement of policy convergence. On the one hand, the pair approach, which was used for measuring sigma-convergence, helped to overcome many problems associated with more traditional measurements relying on the variation coefficient. On the other hand, the gap approach – applied to assess delta-convergence – can be considered a highly valuable tool to account for an often-neglected dimension of convergence, namely the extent to which countries converge to an exemplary model or benchmark (see Heichel, Pape and Sommerer 2005).

8.3 IMPLICATIONS FOR FUTURE RESEARCH

From our research findings, important issues and implications emerge, that are of both scientific and political relevance. The first and most important insight in this respect is that globalisation drives environmental protection levels. In contrast to often-feared scenarios of environmental races to the bottom and in contrast to the anti-globalisation movement's rhetoric, the results show that growing similarity of environmental policies coincides with a constant strengthening of environmental standards over time. This development is essentially the result of growing international institutional interdependency between nation states. In other words, international institutions matter. And they do so not only as means of international harmonisation, but also as platforms for transnational communication.

Second, and related to this, the positive effect of globalisation and Europeanisation on environmental protection is to a considerable extent also triggered by the fact that nation states increasingly communicate with each other and exchange their perceptions and regulatory solutions with regard to environmental problems. Communication matters in particular by facilitating processes of cross-national policy-learning. Governments watch each other very closely, either because they want to avoid the impression of falling behind the others or because they seek to draw lessons from successful policies developed elsewhere.

Third, there is evidence that environmental leaders are able to pull along the laggards. This holds true, on the one hand, with regard to environmental standard-setting through international harmonisation. The establishment of legally binding agreements at the international level typically implies that low-regulating countries adjust their standards to the level of the environmental forerunner countries. In other words, the leaders are generally able to set the pace in international environmental harmonisation. On the other hand, this effect is also relevant in the absence of legally binding agreements. Mere communication and information exchange can induce laggard countries to raise their standards, as they seek to avoid the blame of being perceived as 'pollution havens'.

Fourth, our findings indicate the need for further research on the reasons for the rather weak effect of regulatory competition on cross-national policy convergence. In light of the parsimonious theory and its clear predictions, especially with regard to environmental process standards, the negligible explanatory power of regulatory competition is surprising. A factor that might help to resolve this puzzle refers to the fact that countries anticipate potential effects of regulatory competition by establishing a level playing field through international harmonisation. To avoid races to the bottom and inherent problems of collective action, countries engage in international cooperation. Viewed from this perspective, regulatory competition could be interpreted as driving international cooperation towards environmental protection. This hypothesis, however, can hardly be tested on the basis of our data, but needs further research, inquiry and testing.

Fifth, the high relevance of transnational communication indicates a further issue that deserves particular attention in future research. In this regard, the focus should be on a more detailed analysis of the concrete processes through which transnational communication unfolds its convergence effects. Our research design only allows for a profound statement on the relevance of transnational communication as such, rather than an in-depth analysis of the different communication mechanisms we have identified in the theoretical part of this book. Accordingly, future research should in particular investigate the extent to which communication effects are based on different and more or less demanding forms of learning. For instance, do countries adjust their policies primarily in light of a high number of other countries that have already adopted a similar policy? Do they take policy models or countries as reference points that they consider to be particularly successful? Or do they merely respond to benchmarking activities and policy discussions at the level of international institutions? Analysing these patterns and their causes would strongly enhance our understanding of the convergence effects of transnational communication.

Sixth, more detailed analysis of the factors enhancing or impeding cross-national policy convergence at the domestic level is desirable. In this study we tested a number of domestic factors as control variables. However, as this was not our main research interest, we did no in-depth analysis. In particular, we did not account for factors which might explain variation in the degree and direction of convergence over countries, such as the number of domestic veto players, the party in governance, or administrative fit or misfit with international regulation or policy models from abroad.

Finally, it is important for future research to watch the implementation of environmental standards and agreements. While laggards in the context of growing economic and institutional interdependencies have a strong interest in enhancing their international environmental reputation by adopting stricter environmental standards, they have at the same time an incentive to cheat with regard to the implementation of these standards. This is mainly due to reasons of economic competitiveness. Hence: although regulatory competition and a race to the bottom do not exist in terms of environmental protection levels, they may exist in terms of actual implementation of standards. Therefore it is advisable to combine future policy convergence studies with policy implementation studies.

Annex

Table A4.1 *Example from the questionnaire: lead emissions from vehicles*

2.1 In 2000, was there a policy to regulate lead emissions from vehicles?
○ no
○ yes

2.2 If yes, when was a policy in this field first adopted (year)? _____

2.3 Which type of instrument was the dominant one used to regulate lead emissions from vehicles?

	in 1970	in 1980	in 1990	in 2000
Obligatory standard, prohibition or ban	□	□	□	□
Technological prescription	□	□	□	□
Tax or levy	□	□	□	□
Subsidy or tax reduction	□	□	□	□
Liability scheme(s)	□	□	□	□
Planning instrument	□	□	□	□
Public investment	□	□	□	□
Data collection/monitoring programme(s)	□	□	□	□
Information based instrument	□	□	□	□
Voluntary instrument	□	□	□	□
Other	□	□	□	□

1970: name + short description of instrument

1980: name + short description of instrument

1990: name + short description of instrument

Table A4.1 (*cont.*)

2000: name + short description of instrument

2.4 If there was a limit value for lead content of petrol in force, at which level was it set?

	unit of limit value	no limit value
in 1970	_____	_____	☐ in 1970
in 1980	_____	_____	☐ in 1980
in 1990	_____	_____	☐ in 1990
in 2000	_____	_____	☐ in 2000

2.5 Remarks on lead emissions from vehicles policy, instruments and limit values

Table A4.2 *Example from the manual: lead emissions from vehicles*

In the past, lead was added to fuels to improve engine performance. Burning leaded fuels implied lead emissions from vehicles. There are two options to reduce lead emissions: a phase-out of leaded fuels and/or a reduction of the lead content in fuels and petrol. These measures would correspond to the category 'technical prescriptions' according to the instrument list used in this manual (see sub-section 3.1).

Most countries opted for a combination of both options in the past. However, lead in fuels is now banned in almost every EU country, which would correspond to the category 'obligatory standard, prohibition or ban' according to our instrument list.

Gasoline quality standards in the EU are regulated by Directive 85/210/EEC. A Technical Norm (EN 228) for unleaded gasoline with an octane number of 95 has been introduced by the European Committee for Standardisation (CEN), and is used by some EU countries as a basis for national standards.

In question 2.1–2.2, we ask for a policy to control lead emissions from vehicles and when such a policy was first adopted; please base your answer on explicit national regulation here.

In question 2.3, you are expected to name the dominant instrument used in national regulation to control lead emissions, its exact name and a short description for the respective time points. To define what a dominant instrument in this context is, please refer to the definition in sub-section 3.2.

Question 2.4 inquires about the limit value of lead in petrol; please give the existing limit value of lead in grams per litre of petrol (and not in grams per kilometre or mile driven) for each point in time. In any case, please indicate the unit of limit value next to the respective value for each year.

In section 2.5, please mention any details on lead emissions from vehicles policy, instruments and limit value, which are not covered by the questions above.

Table A4.3 *Indicators and index construction*

Indicator	Categories	Value	Scale	Aggregation Index // normalised	Cronbachs α
Institutional interlinkage					
Institutional membership	Membership in 35 international institutions	(0/1)	0–35	0–9 // 0–1	0.8
Encompassingness					
– Policy areas (1–14)	Almost all areas (>10)	3			
	Many areas (5–1)	2			
	One or few areas (<5)	1	0–3		
– Scope of environmental issues	All environmental issues	3			
	Various environmental issues	2			
	One environmental issue only	1	0–3		
– Importance of environmental issues	Environmental policy is important, but not the only issue	3			
	Environmental policy plays a dominant role	2			
	Environmental policy is not very important	1	0–3		
Obligatory potential					
– Type of law	Supranational law	3		0–10 // 0–1	0.6
	International hard law	2			
	International soft law	1	0–6		

– Monitoring	Monitoring by court	4	0–4		
	Specialised monitoring body	3			
	Reporting	2			
	Diplomacy	1			
Communicative potential				0–40 // 0–1	0.8
– Frequency of interaction	Number of annual meetings of national representatives	(0.33–150)	0–10		
– Number of organisational bodies	Organisational bodies where national representatives meet	(0–10)	0–10		
– Permanence of representation	Existence of permanent national representative	(0/1)	0–10		
– Size of staff	Number of permanent employees in environmental departments	(0–574)	0–10		
Economic interlinkage					
Trade openness	{[(Export of goods + import of goods) / 2] / total GDP} × 100	11–161			
Bilateral trade volume$_{ij}$	$(\text{Exports}_{i \rightarrow j} + \text{Exports}_{j \rightarrow i}) / \text{total } \text{GDP}_{i<j}\ \forall\, i,j \ni \{\text{WTO, market}\}$	0–40.964			
Other variables					
Cultural similarity	Existence of a common border	(0/1)	0–3		0.7
	Sharing of a common language	(0/1)			
	Common historical and religious tradition	(0/1)			
Level of income	GDP per capita in US $	1158–45.496			

Table A4.3 (cont.)

Indicator	Categories	Value	Scale	Aggregation Index // normalised	Cronbachs α
Political demand	Electoral success of green parties	(0/1)	0–3		0.8
	Membership in parliament	(0/1)			
	Participation in government	(0/1)			
Population density	capita/km^2	13–466			
CO_2 emission	Metric tons per capita	2–22			

Table A4.4 *List of international institutions*

Institution	ENC	CP	OP
(1) EU (EU)	1.00	1.00	1.00
European Economic Area (EEA)	0.88	1.00	0.50
Comecon	0.63	0.60	0.50
Organisation for Economic Cooperation and Development (OECD)	1.00	0.30	0.90
UN Economic Commission for Europe (UN-ECE)	0.88	0.20	0.45
(2) United Nations Environmental Programme (UNEP)	1.00	0.30	0.80
International Union on the Conservation of Nature (IUCN)	0.88	0.10	0.50
(3) European Free Trade Association (EFTA)	0.63	0.60	0.30
World Trade Organisation (WTO/GATT)	0.75	0.70	0.60
European Bank for Reconstruction and Development (EBRD)	0.63	0.20	0.55
World Health Organisation (WHO)	0.75	0.20	0.40
Food and Agriculture Organisation (FAO)	0.75	0.20	0.75
Council of Europe	0.75	0.40	0.25
(4) Convention on Environmental Impact Assessment in a Transboundary Context (Espoo Convention), Espoo	0.63	0.40	0.15
Convention on Long-Range Transboundary Air Pollution (LRTAP), Geneva	0.63	0.50	0.20
United Nations Framework Convention on Climate Change (UNFCCC), New York	0.63	0.50	0.30
Vienna Convention for the Protection of the Ozone Layer, Vienna, including the Montreal Protocol on Substances that Deplete the Ozone Layer, Montreal	0.63	0.60	0.30
Convention on the Control of Transboundary Movements of Hazardous Wastes and their Disposal (Basel Convention), Basel	0.63	0.50	0.25
Convention on the Transboundary Effects of Industrial Accidents, Helsinki	0.63	0.40	0.10
European Agreement concerning the International Carriage of Dangerous Goods by Road (ADR), Geneva	0.63	0.40	0.20

Table A4.4 (cont.)

Institution	ENC	CP	OP
Convention on Biological Diversity (CBD), Nairobi	0.63	0.40	0.30
Convention on the Conservation of Migratory Species of Wild Animals (CMS), Bonn	0.63	0.40	0.25
Convention on International Trade in Endangered Species of Wild Fauna and Flora (CITES), Washington, DC	0.63	0.50	0.25
Convention on Wetlands of International Importance especially as Waterfowl Habitat (Ramsar Convention), Ramsar	0.63	0.40	0.20
Bern Convention (The Convention on the Conservation of European Wildlife and Natural Habitats)	0.63	0.50	0.10
Convention on the Protection and Use of Transboundary Watercourses and International Lakes (ECE Water Convention), Helsinki	0.63	0.50	0.15
(5) Alpine Convention	0.75	0.40	0.25
Barcelona Convention (The Convention for the Protection of the Marine Environment and the Coastal Region of the Mediterranean)	0.63	0.50	0.10
International Commission for the Protection of the Rhine (ICPR)	0.63	0.40	0.30
International Commission for the Protection of the Danube River (ICPDR)	0.63	0.40	0.15
International Commission for the Protection of the Odra (IKSO)	0.63	0.40	0.15
Commission Internationale pour la Protection de la Meuse (CIM)	0.63	0.40	0.15
Commission Internationale pour la Protection de l'Escaut (CIPE)	0.63	0.40	0.15
Commission Internationale pour la Protection de la Moselle et de la Sarre (CIPMS)	0.63	0.40	0.15

Table A4.5 *Data sources for the other variables*

Variable	Indicator	Source
Cultural similarity	Common language	(common knowledge)
	Geographical proximity	(common knowledge)
	Religion	Vogel (2002) http://www.religioustolerance. org/rel_coun.htm http://www.nationmaster.com
Problem pressure	CO_2 emissions	World Bank (2002)
	Population density	World Bank (2002)
	Share of rural population	World Bank (2002)
Income	GDP per capita	World Bank (2002)
Political demand	Green parties	Armingeon and Careja (2004); Armingeon *et al.* (2005); EJPR (annually); Lawson (2004); Müller-Rommel (2002) http://cdp.binghamton.edu/era/ index.html http://www.ife.org.mx http://www.essex.ac.uk/elections

Table A6.1 Composition of dependent variables for the pair approach

	All policy items[a]	Presence of policies					Policy instruments					Policy settings				
Item name		All	Trade-related	Non-Trade-related	Obligatory (since)[b]	Non-Obligatory	All	Trade-related	Non-Trade-related	Obligatory (since)[b]	Non-Obligatory	All	Trade-related	Non-Trade-related	Obligatory (since)[b]	Non-Obligatory
1 Sulphur content in gas oil	○ ▲ ●	○			1980	(○)	▲	▲		1980	(▲)	●	●		1980	(●)
2 Lead in petrol	○ ▲ ●	○			1980	(○)	▲	▲		1980	(▲)	●	●		1980	(●)
3 Passenger cars NOx emissions	○ ▲ ●	○			1980	(○)	▲	▲		1980	(▲)	●	●		1980	(●)
4 Passenger cars CO emissions	○ ▲ ●	○			1970	(○)	▲	▲		1970	(▲)	●	●		1970	
5 Passenger cars HC emissions	○ ▲ ●	○			1970	(○)	▲	▲		1970	(▲)	●	●		1970	
6 Large combustion plants SO$_2$ emissions	○ ▲ ●	○			1990	(○)	▲	▲		1990	(▲)	●	●		1990	(●)
7 Large combustion plants NOx emissions	○ ▲ ●	○			1990	(○)	▲	▲		1990	(▲)	●	●		1990	(●)

No.	Indicator												
						1990			1990				1990
						1980			1980				1980
						1980			1980				
8	Large combustion plants dust emissions	○	◀	●	○	(○)	◀	◀	(◀)	●	●	●	(●)
9	Coliforms in bathing water	○	◀	●	○	(○)	◀	◀	(◀)	●	●	●	(●)
10	Hazardous substances in detergents	○	◀	●	○	(○)	◀	◀	(◀)	●	●	●	
11	Efficient use of water in industry	○		●	○	○	◀						
12	Industrial discharges in surface water — lead	○	◀	●	○	○	◀	◀	●	●	●		
13	Industrial discharges in surface water — zinc	○	◀	●	○	○	◀	◀	●	●	●		
14	Industrial discharges in surface water — copper	○	◀	●	○	○	◀	◀	●	●	●		
15	Industrial discharges in surface water — chromium	○	◀	●	○	○	◀	◀	●	●	●		

Table A6.1 (*cont.*)

Item name	All policy items[a]	Presence of policies					Policy instruments					Policy settings				
		All	Trade-related	Non-Trade related	Obligatory (since)[b]	Non-Obligatory	All	Trade-related	Non-Trade related	Obligatory (since)[b]	Non-Obligatory	All	Trade-related	Non-Trade related	Obligatory (since)[b]	Non-Obligatory
16 Industrial discharges in surface water BOD	▲ ●	○	○			○	▲	▲			▲	●	●			●
17 Soil protection		○		○		○										
18 Contaminated sites policy	▲	○		○		○	▲		▲		▲					
19 Waste recovery target		○		○	2000	(○)	▲									
20 Waste landfill target		○		○	2000	(○)	▲									
21 Glass reuse/ recycling target	▲ ●	○		○		○	▲		▲		▲	●		●		●
22 Paper reuse/ recycling target	▲ ●	○		○		○	▲		▲		▲	●		●		●
23 Promotion of refillable beverage containers	▲	○	○			○	▲	▲			▲					

#	Item												
24	Voluntary deposit system beverage containers			○	○		○						
25	Noise emissions standard from lorries	▲	●	○	○	1970	○	▲	1970	▲	●	●	1970 · ●
26	Motorway noise emissions	▲	●	○	○		○	▲			●	●	●
27	Noise level working environment	▲	●	○	(○)	1980	(○)	▲	1980	(▲)	●	●	1980 · (●)
28	Electricity from renewable sources	▲		○	○		○	▲		▲			
29	Recycling construction waste			○	○		○						
30	Energy efficiency of refrigerators	▲		○	○	2000	(○)	▲	2000	(▲)			
31	Electricity tax for households	▲	●	○	○		○	▲		▲	●	●	●

Table A6.1 (*cont.*)

Item name	All policy items[a]	Presence of policies					Policy instruments					Policy settings				
		All	Trade-related	Non-Trade-related	Obligatory (since)[b]	Non-Obligatory	All	Trade-related	Non-Trade-related	Obligatory (since)[b]	Non-Obligatory	All	Trade-related	Non-Trade-related	Obligatory (since)[b]	Non-Obligatory
32 Heavy fuel oil levy for industry	○ ▲ ●	○	○		2000	(○)	▲	▲		2000	(▲)	●	●		2000	(●)
33 CO_2 emissions from heavy industry	○ ▲	○	○	○		○	▲	▲			▲					
34 Forest protection	○ ▲	○		○		○	▲		▲		▲					
35 Eco-audit	○	○	○		2000	(○)										
36 Environmental impact assessment	○	○		○	1990	(○)										
37 Eco-labelling	○	○	○		2000	(○)										
38 Precautionary principle: reference in legislation	○	○		○		○										

	89	40	26	14	3/8/13/19	37/32/27/21	28	21	7	3/8/12/14	25/20/16/14	21	16	5	3/9/11/12	18/13/10/9
39 Sustainability: reference in legislation	o	o	o	o		o										
40 Environmental/ sustainable development plan	o	o	o	o		o										
N[c]	89	40	26	14	3/8/13/19	37/32/27/21	28	21	7	3/8/12/14	25/20/16/14	21	16	5	3/9/11/12	18/13/10/9

Note:

[a] o = Presence-of-Policy   ▲ = Policy Instrument   ● = Policy Setting

[b] Obligation changed over time

[c] Changing number of obligatory/non-obligatory items for 1970, 1980, 1990, 2000

Table A6.2 *Descriptive statistics of independent variables*

Mechanism	Variable	Model	Mean	Std. dev	Min	Max
International harmonisation	Common EU membership	1970	0.10	0.30	0.00	1.00
		1980	0.20	0.40	0.00	1.00
		1990	0.20	0.40	0.00	1.00
	Common EU accession	1970s	0.10	0.30	0.00	1.00
		1980s	0.00	0.00	0.00	0.00
		1990s	0.40	0.50	0.00	1.00
	Common accession to international institutions weighted by obligatory potential	1970s	9.93	4.56	0.00	25.43
		1980s	13.60	7.22	0.00	32.05
		1990s	21.82	9.87	2.25	41.65
Transnational communication	Common membership in international institutions weighted by communicative potential	1970	17.55	8.05	6.53	44.12
		1980	45.75	17.95	13.05	95.69
		1990	81.66	31.09	22.93	154.82
Regulatory competition	Bilateral trade data	1970	3.86	8.92	0.00	83.34
		1980	15.15	34.10	0.00	330.37
		1990	25.63	51.48	0.00	409.64
Economic development	Income difference* income level GDP/capita	1970	275148879.6	246356114.9	11681904	869445672
		1980	355293282.5	326151235.2	7850403	1203081248
		1990	414925592.2	397388057.8	1531	1439388053

Social emulation	Cultural similarity	1970s	0.64	0.76		3.00
		1980s	0.64	0.76		3.00
		1990s	0.64	0.76		3.00
Political demand	Influence of green parties, level * difference	1970	0.00	0.00	0.00	0.00
		1980	0.02	0.15	0.00	1.00
		1990	0.41	0.71	0.00	2.00
Problem pressure	CO_2 emissions per capita, level * difference	1970	5.93	2.67	2.00	13.00
		1980	7.42	2.51	3.00	20.00
		1990	7.00	1.76	4.00	12.00
	Population density, level * difference	1970	67.8	53.2	13.00	294.00
		1980	72.27	54.94	13.00	310.00
		1990	75.06	55.83	13.00	310.00
Pre-existing similarity	Policy similarity 40 policy items	1970	0.04	0.04	0.00	0.24
		1980	0.14	0.09	0.00	0.38
		1990	0.29	0.13	0.02	0.62

Table A6.3 *Bivariate analysis of policy convergence*

	All items				Policies					Instruments	Settings				
	Pooled	1970s	1980s	1990s	All	OB	NO	TR	NT	All	All	OB	NO	TR	NT
EU membership	.21	.29	.30	.09	.20	.37	.08	.21	.14	.12	.24	.30	.02	.23	.12
EU accession	.15	.19	-.01	.07	.16	.15	.13	.17	.14	.12	.11	.09	.09	.05	.25
Accession to institutions	.64	.41	.59	.40	.59	.48	.55	.60	.42	.52	.52	.32	.46	.52	.07
Institutional membership	.63	.39	.50	-.07	.77	.65	.68	.75	.69	.43	.36	.19	.29	.26	.44
Bilateral trade	.20	.34	.23	-.10	.26	.25	.24	.26	.23	.11	.15	.10	.10	.10	.23
Cultural similarity	.12	.27	.34	-.01	.09	.21	.05	.13	.01	.11	.20	.20	.13	.20	.06
GDP per capita * Diff	.23	.52	.37	-.16	.3	.36	.27	.33	.23	.12	.13	.15	.04	.06	.32
Existence of green parties * Diff	.31	–[a]	.18	.07	.37	.19	.41	.36	.33	.18	.19	.03	.28	.13	.24
CO2 *Diff	.00	.35	-.09	.17	-.01	.17	-.07	.01	-.03	-.01	.05	.13	-.08	.03	.06
Population density *Diff	.14	.11	.17	.01	.12	.14	.10	.12	.09	.07	.21	.11	.22	.22	.02
PSim	.55	.32	.09	-.12	.71	.62	.50	.60	.62	.24	.18	.04	-.02	.07	-.10
Time	.72	–	–	–	.82	.54	.78	.75	.78	.49	.41	.14	.43	.35	.34

Note:

[a] There are no green parties in 1970.

References

Abbott, Kenneth W. and Duncan Snidal (1998) 'Why states act through formal international organizations', *Journal of Conflict Resolution*, 42:1, 3–32.

(2000) 'Hard and soft law in international governance', *International Organization*, 54:3, 421–56.

Abbott, Kenneth W., Robert O. Keohane, Andrew Moravcsik, Anne-Marie Slaughter and Duncan Snidal (2000) 'The concept of legalization', *International Organization*, 54:3, 401–19.

Alcalá, Francisco and Antonio Ciccone (2004) 'Trade and productivity', *Quarterly Journal of Economics*, 119:2, 613–46.

Alesina, Alberto and Romain Wacziarg (1998) 'Openness, country size and government', *Journal of Public Economics*, 69:3, 305–21.

Andersen, Michael S. and Duncan Liefferink (eds.) (1997) *European Environmental Policy. The Pioneers*. Manchester: Manchester University Press.

Armingeon, Klaus and Romana Careja (2004) *Comparative Data Set for 28 Post-Communist Countries, 1989–2004*. Bern: Institute of Political Science, University of Bern.

Armingeon, Klaus, Philipp Leimgruber, Michelle Beyeler and Sarah Menegale (2005) *Comparative Political Data Set, 1960–2003*. Bern: Institute of Political Science, University of Bern.

Badaracco, Joseph L. (1985) *Loading the Dice. A Five-Country Study of Vinyl Chloride Regulation*. Boston: Harvard Business School Press.

Barrios, Salvador, Holger Görg and Eric Strobl (2003) 'Multinational enterprises and new trade theory: evidence for the convergence hypothesis', *Open Economies Review*, 14:4, 397–418.

Baum, Joel A. C. and Christine Oliver (1992) 'Institutional embeddedness and the dynamics of organizational populations', *American Sociological Review*, 57:4, 540–59.

Baumgartner, Frank R. and Beth L. Leech (1996) 'Good theories deserve good data', *American Journal of Political Science*, 40:2, 565–9.

Beckerman, Wilfred (1992) 'Economic growth and the environment. Whose growth? Whose environment?', *World Development*, 20:4, 481–96.

Bennett, Colin J. (1988) 'Different processes, one result. The convergence of data protection policy in Europe and the United States', *Governance*, 1:4, 162–83.

(1991) 'What is policy convergence and what causes it?', *British Journal of Political Science*, 21:2, 215–33.

Bernauer, Thomas and Christoph Achini (2000) 'From "real" to "virtual" states? Integration of the world economy and its effects on government activity', *European Journal of International Relations*, 6:2, 223–76.

Bernauer, Thomas and Vally Koubi (2004) 'On the political determinants of environmental quality'. Paper presented at the Annual Meeting of the American Political Science Association, Chicago, 2–5 September.

Berry, Frances S. and William D. Berry (1990) 'State lottery adoptions as policy innovations: an event history analysis', *American Political Science Review*, 84:2, 395–415.

Bikhchandani, Sushil, David Hirshleifer and Ivo Welch (1992) 'A theory of fads, fashion, custom, and cultural change as information cascades', *Journal of Political Economy*, 100:5, 992–1026.

Binder, Manfred (2002) *Umweltpolitische Basisinnovationen im Industrieländervergleich. Ein grafisch-statistischer Überblick*, FFU-report 02–06. Berlin: Centre for Environmental Policy Research.

(2005) 'Umweltpolitische Basisinnovationen im Industrieländervergleich. Ein grafisch-statistischer Überblick', in Kerstin Tews and Martin Jänicke (eds.), *Die Diffusion umweltpolitischer Innovationen im internationalen System*. Wiesbaden: VS Verlag, 195–232.

Binder, Seth and Eric Neumayer (2005) 'Environmental pressure groups, strength and air pollution: an empirical analysis', *Ecological Economics*, 55:4, 527–38.

Bogdandy, Amin von (1999) *Supranationaler Föderalismus als Wirklichkeit und Idee einer Herrschaftsform. Zur Gestalt der Europäischen Union nach Amsterdam*. Baden-Baden: Nomos.

Botcheva, Liliana and Lisa L. Martin (2001) 'Institutional effects on state behavior: convergence and divergence', *International Studies Quarterly*, 45:1, 1–26.

Boyce, James K. (2004) 'Green and brown? Globalization and the environment', *Oxford Review of Economic Policy*, 20:1, 105–28.

Boyle, Gerry E. and Tom G. McCarthy (1999) 'Simple measures of convergence in per capita GDP: a note on some further international evidence', *Applied Economics Letters*, 6:6, 343–7.

Braun, Dietmar and Fabrizio Gilardi (2006) 'Taking Galton's problem seriously. Towards a theory of policy diffusion', *Journal of Theoretical Politics*, 18:3, 298–322.

Bremer, Stuart A. (1992) 'Dangerous dyads: conditions affecting the likelihood of interstate war, 1816–1965', *Journal of Conflict Resolution*, 36:2, 309–41.

Brickman, Ronald, Sheila Jasanoff and Thomas Ilgen (1985) *Controlling Chemicals. The Politics of Regulation in Europe and the United States*. Ithaca: Cornell University Press.

Brune, Nancy and Geoffrey Garrett (2000) 'The diffusion of privatization in the developing world'. Paper presented at the Annual Meeting of the American Political Science Association, Washington D.C., 30 August–3 September.

Burke, B. (1999) 'Diffusion of regulatory and distributive innovations across the American states. Different paths?' Paper presented at the Annual Meeting of the American Political Science Association, Atlanta, 2–5 September.

Busch, Per-Olof and Helge Jörgens (2005a) 'International patterns of environmental policy change and convergence', *European Environment*, 15:2, 80–101.

(2005b) 'Globale Ausbreitungsmuster umweltpolitischer Institutionen', in Kerstin Tews and Martin Jänicke (eds.), *Die Diffusion umweltpolitischer Innovationen im internationalen System*. Wiesbaden: VS Verlag, 55–194.

(2005c) 'The international sources of policy convergence: explaining the spread of environmental policy innovations', *Journal of European Public Policy*, 12:5, 860–84.

Busch, Per-Olof, Helge Jörgens and Kerstin Tews (2005) 'The global diffusion of regulatory instruments: the making of a new international environmental regime', *The Annals of the American Academy of Political and Social Science*, 598:1, 146–67.

Castles, Frank G. and Peter Mair (1984) 'Left–right political scales: some "expert" judgments', *European Journal of Political Research*, 12:1, 73–88.

Cowles, Maria G., James A. Caporaso and Thomas Risse (eds.) (2001) *Transforming Europe. Europeanisation and Domestic Change*. Ithaca: Cornell University Press.

Crepaz, Markus M. L. (1995) 'Explaining national variations of air pollution levels: political institutions and their impact on environmental policy-making', *Environmental Politics*, 4:3, 391–414.

Daley, Dorothy M. and James C. Garand (2005) 'Horizontal diffusion, vertical diffusion, and internal pressure in state environmental policymaking', *American Politics Research*, 33:5, 615–44.

DiMaggio, Paul J. and Walter W. Powell (1991) 'The iron cage revisited. Institutionalized isomorphism and collective rationality in organizational fields', in Walter W. Powell and Paul J. DiMaggio (eds.), *The New Institutionalism in Organizational Analysis*. Chicago: Chicago University Press, 63–82.

Dimitrova, Antoaneta and Bernard Steunenberg (2000) 'The search for convergence of national policies in the European Union. An impossible quest?', *European Union Politics*, 1:2, 201–26.

Dobbin, Frank, Geoffrey Garrett and Beth Simmons (2003) 'The international diffusion of democracy and markets'. Paper presented at the conference 'Interdependence, Diffusion and Sovereignty', UCLA, 7–8 March.

Dollar, David (1992) 'Outward-oriented developing countries really do grow more rapidly: evidence from 95 LDC's 1976–85', *Economic Development and Cultural Change*, 40:3, 523–44.

Dolowitz, David P. and David Marsh (1996) 'Who learns what from whom? A review of the policy transfer literature', *Political Studies*, 44:3, 343–57.

(2000) 'Learning from abroad: the role of policy transfer in contemporary policy making', *Governance*, 13:1, 5–24.

Dowrick, Steve and Jane Golley (2004) 'Trade openness and growth: who benefits?', *Oxford Review of Economic Policy*, 20:1, 38–56.

Drezner, Daniel W. (2001) 'Globalization and policy convergence', *International Studies Review*, 3:1, 53–78.

Elkins, Zachary and Beth Simmons (2005) 'On waves, clusters, and diffusion: a conceptual framework', *The Annals of the American Academy of Political and Social Science*, 598:1, 33–51.

Eyestone, Robert (1977) 'Confusion, diffusion and innovation', *American Political Science Review*, 71:2, 441–7.

Finnemore, Martha (1996) *National Interests in International Society*. Ithaca: Cornell University Press.

Fisher, Dana R. and William R. Freudenburg (2004) 'Postindustrialization and environmental quality: an empirical analysis of the environmental states', *Social Forces*, 83:1, 157–88.

Frank, David J., Ann Hironaka and Evan Schofer (2000) 'The nation-state and the natural environment over the twentieth century', *American Sociological Review*, 65:1, 96–116.

Frankfort-Nachmias, Chava and David Nachmias (1996) *Research Methods in the Social Sciences*. London: Arnold.

Fredriksson, Per G. and Daniel L. Millimet (2004) 'Comparative politics and environmental taxation', *Journal of Environmental Economics and Management*, 48:1, 705–22.

Fredriksson, Per G., Eric Neumayer, Richard Damania and Scott Gates (2005) 'Environmentalism, democracy and pollution control', *Journal of Environmental Economics and Management*, 49:2, 343–65.

Fridtjof Nansen Institute (FNI) since 1992 (until 1997 as *Green Globe Yearbook*), *Yearbook of International Cooperation on Environment and Development*. London: Earthscan. See also: http://www.greenyearbook.org/.

Friedkin, Noah E. (1993) 'Structural bases of interpersonal influence in groups. A longitudinal case study', *American Sociological Review*, 58:6, 861–72.

Garrett, Geoffrey and Deborah Mitchell (2001) 'Globalization, government spending and taxation in the OECD', *European Journal of Political Research*, 39:2, 145–77.

Gilardi, Fabrizio (2005) 'The institutional foundations of regulatory capitalism: the diffusion of independent regulatory agencies in Western Europe', *The Annals of the American Academy of Political and Social Science*, 598:1, 84–101.

Gilardi, Fabrizio and Dietmar Braun (2005) 'Taking "Galton's Problem" seriously: towards a theory of policy diffusion'. Paper presented at the Convention of the International Studies Association, Honolulu, 1–5 March.

Gourevitch, Peter (2002) 'Domestic politics and international relations', in W. Carlsnaes, T. Risse and B. A. Simmons (eds.), *Handbook of International Relations*. London: Sage, 309–28.

Graesser, Art, Katja Wiemer-Hastings, Peter Wiemer-Hastings and Roger Kreuz (2000) 'The gold standard of question quality on surveys: experts, computer tools, versus statistical indices', *Proceedings of the Section on Survey Research Methods of the American Statistical Association*, 459–64.

Gray, Virginia (1973) 'Innovation in the states: a diffusion study', *American Political Science Review*, 67:4, 1174–85.

Guillén, Mauro F. (2001) 'Is globalization civilizing, destructive or feeble? A critique of five key debates in the social science literature', *Annual Review of Sociology*, 27, 235–60.

Haas, Peter M. (1992) 'Introduction: epistemic communities and international policy coordination', *International Organization*, 46:1, 1–36.

Hall, Peter A. (1993) 'Policy paradigms, social learning and the state. The case of economic policymaking in Britain', *Comparative Politics*, 25:3, 275–96.

Hallerberg, Mark and Scott Basinger (1998) 'Internationalization and changes in tax policy in OECD countries', *Comparative Political Studies*, 31:3, 321–52.

Heichel, Stephan, Jessica Pape and Thomas Sommerer (2005) 'Is there convergence in convergence research? An overview of empirical studies on policy convergence', *Journal of European Public Policy*, 12:5, 817–40.

Heidenheimer, Arnold J., Hugh Heclo and Carolyn T. Adams (1990) *Comparative Public Policy. The Politics of Social Choice in America, Europe, and Japan*. New York: St. Martin's Press.

Héritier, Adrienne and Christoph Knill (2001) 'Differential responses to European policies: a comparison', in Adrienne Héritier, Dieter Kerwer, Christoph Knill, Dirk Lehmkuhl, Michael Teutsch and Anne-Cécile Douillet (eds.), *Differential Europe. The European Union Impact on National Policymaking*. Lanham: Rowman and Littlefield, 257–94.

Héritier, Adrienne, Christoph Knill and Susanne Mingers (1996) *Ringing the Changes in Europe. Regulatory Competition and the Transformation of the State*. Berlin: De Gruyter.

Héritier, Adrienne, Dieter Kerwer, Christoph Knill, Dirk Lehmkuhl, Michael Teutsch and Anne-Cécile Douillet (eds.) (2001) *Differential Europe. The European Union Impact on National Policymaking*. Lanham: Rowman and Littlefield.

Hewitt, Joseph (2003) 'Dyadic processes and international crisis', *Journal of Conflict Resolution*, 47:5, 669–92.

Hironaka, Ann (2002) 'The globalization of environmental protection: the case of environmental impact assessment', *International Journal of Comparative Sociology*, 43:1, 65–78.

Hoberg, George (1991) 'Sleeping with an elephant: the American influence on Canadian environmental regulation', *Journal of Public Policy*, 11:1, 107–31.

(2001) 'Globalization and policy convergence: symposium overview', *Journal of Comparative Policy Analysis: Research and Practice*, 3:2, 127–32.

Hoberg, George, Keith Banting and Richard Simeon (1999) 'North American integration and the scope for domestic choice: Canada and policy sovereignty in a globalized world'. Paper presented at the Annual Meeting of the Canadian Political Science Association, Sherbrooke, Quebec, 6–8 June.

Holzer, Thomas and Gerald Schneider (2002) *Asylpolitik auf Abwegen. National-staatliche und europäische Reaktionen auf die Globalisierung der Flücht-lingsströme*. Opladen: Leske und Budrich.

Holzinger, Katharina (1994) *Politik des kleinsten gemeinsamen Nenners. Umweltpolitische Entscheidungsprozesse in der EG am Beispiel des Kataly-satorautos*. Berlin: Edition Sigma.

(2002) 'The provision of transnational common goods: regulatory competition for environmental standards', in Adrienne Héritier (ed.), *Common Goods: Reinventing European and International Governance*. Lanham: Rowman and Littlefield, 59–82.

(2003) 'Common goods, matrix games, and institutional solutions', *European Journal of International Relations*, 9:2, 173–212.

Holzinger, Katharina and Christoph Knill (2004) 'Regulatory competition and regulatory cooperation in environmental policy: individual and interaction effects', *Journal of Public Policy*, 24:1, 25–47.

(2005a) *Competition, Cooperation and Communication. A Theoretical Analysis of Different Sources of Environmental Policy Convergence and their Interaction.* Working Paper, Political Science Series 102. Vienna: Institute for Advanced Studies.

(2005b) 'Causes and conditions of cross-national policy convergence', *Journal of European Public Policy*, 12:5, 775–96.

Holzinger, Katharina, Christoph Knill and Ansgar Schäfer (2003) 'Steuerungswandel in der europäischen Umweltpolitik?', in Katharina Holzinger, Christoph Knill and Dirk Lehmkuhl (eds.), *Bedingungen und Muster politischer Steuerung im historischen Vergleich.* Opladen: Leske und Budrich, 57–85.

Howlett, Michael (2000) 'Beyond legalism? Policy ideas, implementation styles and emulation-based convergence in Canadian and US environmental policy', *Journal of Public Policy*, 20:3, 305–29.

Huber, John D. and Ronald Inglehart (1995) 'Expert interpretations of party space and party locations in 42 societies', *Party Politics* 1:1, 73–111.

Humphreys, Peter (2002) 'Europeanisation, globalisation and telecommunications governance: a neo-Gramscian analysis', *Convergence: The Journal of Research into New Media Technologies*, 8:2, 52–79.

Jahn, Detlef (1998) 'Environmental performance and policy regimes: explaining variations in 18 OECD countries', *Policy Sciences*, 31:2, 107–31.

(2000) 'Patterns and correlates of environmental politics in the Western democracies', in Stephen C. Young (ed.), *The Emergence of Ecological Modernization. Integrating the Environment and the Economy?* London and New York: Routledge, 153–70.

Jänicke, Martin (1992) 'Conditions for environmental policy success: an international comparison', *The Environmentalist*, 12:1, 47–58.

(1996) 'Erfolgsbedingungen von Umweltpolitik', in Martin Jänicke (ed.), *Umweltpolitik der Industrieländer. Entwicklung – Bilanz – Erfolgsbedingungen.* Berlin: Edition Sigma, 9–28.

(1998) 'Umweltpolitik. Global am Ende oder am Ende global?', in Ulrich Beck (ed.), *Perspektiven der Weltgesellschaft.* Frankfurt a. M.: Suhrkamp, 332–44.

Jänicke, Martin and Helge Jörgens (1998) 'National environmental policy planning in OECD countries: preliminary lessons from cross-national comparisons', *Environmental Politics*, 7:2, 27–54.

Jänicke, Martin and Helmut Weidner (eds.) (1997) *National Environmental Policies. A Comparative Study of Capacity-Building.* Berlin, Heidelberg and New York: Springer.

Jordan, Andrew and Duncan Liefferink (eds.) (2004) *Environmental Policy in Europe. The Europeanisation of National Environmental Policy.* London: Routledge.

Jordan, Andrew and Duncan Liefferink (2005) 'An "ever closer union" of national policy? The convergence of national environmental policy in the European Union', *European Environment*, 15:2, 102–13.

Jordan, Andrew, Rüdiger Wurzel and Anthony R. Zito (2000) 'Innovating with "new" environmental policy instruments: convergence or divergence in the European Union?' Paper presented at the Annual Meeting of the American Political Science Association, Washington, D.C., 31 August–3 September.

(2003) 'New instruments of environmental governance', *Environmental Politics*, 12:1, 1–224.

Jordan, Andrew, Rüdiger Wurzel, Anthony R. Zito and Lars Brückner (2002) 'The innovation and diffusion of "new" environmental policy instruments (NEPIs) in the European Union and its member states', in Frank Biermann, Rainer Brohm and Klaus Dingwerth (eds.), *Proceedings of the 2001 Berlin Conference on the Human Dimensions of Global Environmental Change 'Global Environmental Change and the Nation State'*. Potsdam: Potsdam Institute for Climate Impact Research, 151–60.

Jordana, Jacint and David Levi-Faur (2005) 'The diffusion of regulatory capitalism in Latin America: sectoral and national channels in the making of a new order', *The Annals of the American Academy of Political and Social Science*, 598:1, 102–24.

Jörgens, Helge (1996) 'Die Institutionalisierung von Umweltpolitik im internationalen Vergleich', in Martin Jänicke (ed.), *Umweltpolitik der Industrieländer. Entwicklung – Bilanz – Erfolgsbedingungen*. Berlin: Edition Sigma, 95–111.

(2004) 'Governance by diffusion – implementing global norms through cross-national imitation and learning', in William M. Lafferty (ed.), *Governance for Sustainable Development. The Challenge of Adapting Form to Function*. Cheltenham: Edward Elgar, 246–83.

Keck, Margaret E. and Kathryn Sikkink (1998) *Activists Beyond Borders. Advocacy Networks in International Politics*. Ithaca: Cornell University Press.

Kennedy, P. (2003) *A Guide to Econometrics*. Oxford: Blackwell Publishers.

Kern, Kristine (2000) *Die Diffusion von Politikinnovationen. Umweltpolitische Innovationen im Mehrebenensystem der USA*. Opladen: Leske und Budrich.

Kern, Kristine, Helge Jörgens and Martin Jänicke (2000) 'Die Diffusion umweltpolitischer Innovationen. Ein Beitrag zur Globalisierung von Umweltpolitik', *Zeitschrift für Umweltpolitik und Umweltrecht*, 23:4, 507–46.

(2001) 'The diffusion of environmental policy innovations: a contribution to the globalisation of environmental policy', Discussion Paper FS II 01–302, Berlin: WZB.

Kerr, Clark (1983) *The Future of Industrial Societies. Convergence or Continuing Diversity?* Cambridge: Cambridge University Press.

King, Ron F. and Alexandra Borchardt (1994) 'Red and green: air pollution levels and left party power in OECD countries', *Environment and Planning C: Government and Policy*, 12:22, 225–41.

Kinsella, David and Bruce Russett (2002) 'Conflict emergence and escalation in interactive international dyads', *Journal of Politics*, 64:4, 1045–68.

Kitschelt, Herbert (1983) *Politik und Energie. Energie-Technologiepolitiken in den USA, der Bundesrepublik Deutschland, Frankreich und Schweden*. Frankfurt a. M. and New York: Campus.

Knill, Christoph (2001) *The Europeanisation of National Administrations. Patterns of Institutional Change and Persistence*. Cambridge: Cambridge University Press.

(2003) *Europäische Umweltpolitik. Steuerungsprobleme und Regulierungsmuster im Mehrebenensystem*. Opladen: Leske und Budrich.

(2005) 'Introduction. Cross-national policy convergence: concepts, approaches and explanatory factors', *Journal of European Public Policy*, 12:5, 764–74.

Knill, Christoph and Andrea Lenschow (2005) 'Compliance, communication and competition: patterns of EU environmental policy making and their impact on policy convergence', *European Environment*, 15:2, 114–28.

Knoepfel, Peter, Lennart J. Lundqvist, Rémy Prud'homme and Peter Wagner (1987) 'Comparing environmental policies: different styles, similar content', in Meinolf Dierkes, Hans N. Weiler and Ariane Berthoin Antal (eds.), *Comparative Policy Research. Learning from Experience*. Aldershot: Gower, 171–87.

Knutsen, Oddbjørn (1998) 'Expert judgement of the left–right location of political parties: a comparative longitudinal study', *West European Politics* 21:2, 63–94.

Korpi, Walter and Joakim Palme (2003) 'New politics and class politics in the context of austerity and globalization: welfare state regress in 18 countries, 1975–95', *American Political Science Review*, 97:3, 435–46.

Kraemer, A. (1991) 'Muddy waters at the OECD: the data on water management', FFU-report 1991/1. Unpublished manuscript, University of Berlin, Centre for Environmental Studies.

Laver, Michael and Ben Hunt (1992) *Policy and Party Competition*. London: Routledge.

Lavigne, Marie (1999) *The Economics of Transition. From Socialist Economy to Market Economy*. Basingstoke: Macmillan.

Lawson, Chappell H. (2004) 'Fox's Mexico at midterm', *Journal of Democracy*, 15:1, 139–53.

Lenschow, Andrea, Duncan Liefferink and Sietske Veenman (2005) 'When the birds sing. A framework for analysing domestic factors behind policy convergence', *Journal of European Public Policy*, 12:5, 797–816.

Levi-Faur, David (2002) 'Herding towards a new convention. On herds, shepherds and lost sheep in the liberalization of the telecommunications and electricity industries'. Paper presented at the workshop 'Theories of Regulation', Nuffield College, University of Oxford, 25–26 May.

(2005) 'The global diffusion of regulatory capitalism', *The Annals of the American Academy of Political and Social Science*, 598:1, 12–32.

Li, Quan and Rafael Reuveny (2003) 'Economic globalization and democracy: an empirical analysis', *British Journal of Political Science*, 33:1, 29–54.

Liefferink, Duncan (1999) 'The Dutch national plan for sustainable society', in Norman J. Vig and Regina S. Axelrod (eds.), *The Global Environment. Institutions, Law and Policy*. Washington, D.C.: CQ Press, 256–78.

Lundqvist, Lennart J. (1974) 'Do political structures matter in environmental politics? The case of air pollution control in Canada, Sweden, and the United States', *Canadian Public Administration*, 17:1, 119–41.

(1980) *The Hare and the Tortoise. Clean Air Policies in the United States and Sweden*. Ann Arbor: University of Michigan Press.

Marcussen, Martin (2005) 'Central banks on the move', *Journal of European Public Policy*, 12:5, 903–23.

Martin, Lisa L. and Beth A. Simmons (1998) 'Theories and empirical studies of international institutions', *International Organization*, 52:4, 729–57.

Meseguer Yebra, Covadonga (2003) *Learning and Economic Policy Choices. A Bayesian Approach*. EUI Working Paper RSC No. 2003/5. San Domenico: European University Institute.

(2005) 'Policy learning, policy diffusion, and the making of a new order', *The Annals of the American Academy of Political and Social Science*, 598:1, 67–82.

Meyer, John W. and Brian Rowan (1977) 'Institutionalized organizations. Formal structure as myth and ceremony', *American Journal of Sociology*, 83:2, 340–63.

Meyer, John W., David J. Frank, Ann Hironaka, Evan Schofer and Nancy Brandon-Tuma (1997) 'The structuring of a world environmental regime, 1870–1990', *International Organization*, 51:4, 623–51.

Midlarsky, Manus I. (1998) 'Democracy and the environment: an empirical assessment', *Journal of Peace Research*, 35:3, 341–61.

Mintrom, Michael (1997) 'The state–local nexus in policy innovation diffusion: the case of school choice', *Publius – The Journal of Federalism*, 27:3, 41–59.

Mintrom, Michael and Sandra Vergari (1998) 'Policy networks and innovation diffusion: the case of state education reforms', *Journal of Politics*, 60:1, 126–48.

Müller-Rommel, Ferdinand (2002) 'The lifespan and the political performance of green parties in Western Europe', in Ferdinand Müller-Rommel and Thomas Poguntke (eds.), *Green Parties in National Governments*. London: Frank Cass, 1–16.

Murdoch, James C. and Todd Sandler (1997) 'The voluntary provision of a pure public good: the case of reduced CFC emissions and the Montreal Protocol', *Journal of Public Economics*, 63:3, 331–49.

Murdoch, James C., Todd Sandler and Keith Sargent (1997) 'A tale of two collectives: sulphur versus nitrogen oxides emission reduction in Europe', *Economica*, 64:254, 281–301.

Neumayer, Eric (2001) 'Improvements without convergence: pressure on the environment in EU countries', *Journal of Common Market Studies*, 39:5, 927–37.

(2003) 'Are left-wing strength and corporatism good for the environment? Evidence from panel analysis of air pollution in OECD countries', *Ecological Economics*, 45:2, 203–20.

Neyer, Jürgen (1999) 'Legitimes Recht oberhalb des demokratischen Rechtsstaates? Supranationalität als Herausforderung für die Politikwissenschaft', *Politische Vierteljahresschrift*, 40:3, 390–414.

OECD (no year) *International Trade by Commodities Statistics (ITCS)*, CD-ROM. Paris: OECD.

OECD (various years) *Environmental Data Compendium*. Paris: OECD.

Panayotou, Theodore (1993) *Empirical Tests and Policy Analysis of Environmental Degradation at Different Stages of Economic Development*. ILO Technology and Employment Programme Working Paper, WP 238. Geneva: ILO.

Potoski, Matthew (2001) 'Environmental clean air federalism: do states race to the bottom?', *Public Administration Review*, 61:3, 335–42.

Presser, Stanley (2004) 'Methods for testing and evaluating survey questions', *Public Opinion Quarterly*, 68:1, 109–30.

Radaelli, Claudio M. (2000) 'Policy transfer in the European Union: institutional isomorphism as a source of legitimacy', *Governance*, 13:1, 25–43.

(2005) 'Diffusion without convergence: how political context shapes the adoption of regulatory impact assessment', *Journal of European Public Policy*, 12:5, 924–43.

Ray, Leonard (1999) 'Measuring party orientations towards European integration: results from an expert survey', *European Journal of Political Research*, 36:6, 283–306.

Ricken, Christian (1995) 'Nationaler Politikstil, Netzwerkstrukturen sowie ökonomischer Entwicklungsstand als Determinanten einer effektiven Umweltpolitik: Ein empirischer Industrieländervergleich', *Zeitschrift für Umweltpolitik und Umweltrecht*, 18:4, 481–501.

(1997) *Determinanten der Effektivität der Umweltpolitik. Der nationale Politikstil im Spannungsfeld von Ökonomie, Politik und Kultur.* Frankfurt a. M.: Peter Lang.

Ringquist, Evan J. and Tatiana Kostadinova (2005) 'Assessing the effectiveness of international environmental agreements: the case of the 1985 Helsinki Protocol', *American Journal of Political Science*, 49:1, 86–102.

Rodrik, Dani, Arvind Subramanian and Francesco Trebbi (2002) *Institutions Rule. The Primacy of Institutions over Integration and Geography in Economic Development.* IMF Working Paper, 02/189.

Rogers, Everett M. (2003) *Diffusion of Innovations.* Fifth edition. New York: Free Press.

Rose, Richard (1991) 'What is lesson-drawing?', *Journal of Public Policy*, 11:3, 3–30.

(1993) *Lesson-Drawing in Public Policy. A Guide to Learning Across Time and Space.* Chatham: Chatham House.

Rudra, Nita (2004) 'Openness, welfare spending, and inequality in the developing world', *International Studies Quarterly*, 48:3, 683–709.

Sala-i-Martin, Xavier X. (1996) 'Regional cohesion: evidence and theories of regional growth and convergence', *European Economic Review*, 40:6, 1325–52.

Scharpf, Fritz W. (1997) 'Introduction. The problem-solving capacity of multi-level governance', *Journal of European Public Policy*, 4:4, 520–38.

Schimmelfennig, Frank and Ulrich Sedelmeier (2004) 'Governance by conditionality: EU rule transfer to the candidate countries of Central and Eastern Europe', *Journal of European Public Policy*, 11:4, 661–79.

Scruggs, Lyle (1999) 'Institutions and environmental performance in seventeen Western democracies', *British Journal of Political Science*, 29:1, 1–31.

(2001) 'Is there really a link between neo-corporatism and environmental performance? Updated evidence and new data for the 1980s and 1990s', *British Journal of Political Science*, 31:4, 686–92.

(2003) *Sustaining Abundance. Environmental Performance in Industrial Democracies.* Cambridge: Cambridge University Press.

Seeliger, Robert (1996) 'Conceptualizing and researching policy convergence', *Policy Studies Journal*, 24:2, 287–306.

Shandra, John M., Bruce London, Owen P. Whooley and John B. Williamson (2004) 'International nongovernmental organizations and carbon dioxide emissions in the developing world: a quantitative, cross-national analysis', *Sociological Inquiry*, 74:4, 520–45.

Simmons, Beth A. and Zachary Elkins (2004) 'The globalization of liberalization: policy diffusion in the international political economy', *American Political Science Review*, 98:1, 171–89.

Stern, David I. and Michael S. Common (2001) 'Is there an environmental Kuznets curve for sulfur?', *Journal of Environmental Economics and Management*, 41:2, 162–78.

Strang, David and John W. Meyer (1993) 'Institutional conditions for diffusion', *Theory and Society*, 22:4, 487–511.

Syrquin, Moshe (1988) 'Patterns of structural change', in Hollis Chenery and T. N. Srinivasan (eds.), *Handbook of Development Economics*. Amsterdam: North-Holland, 203–73.

Tews, Kerstin (2002) 'Politiktransfer: Phänomen zwischen Policy-Lernen und Oktroi. Überlegungen zu unfreiwilligen Umweltpolitikimporten am Beispiel der EU-Osterweiterung', *Zeitschrift für Umweltpolitik und Umweltrecht*, 25:2, 173–201.

(2005a) 'Die Diffusion umweltpolitischer Innovationen: Eckpunkte eines Analysemodells', in Kerstin Tews and Martin Jänicke (eds.), *Die Diffusion umweltpolitischer Innovationen im internationalen System*. Wiesbaden: VS Verlag, 25–54.

(2005b) 'The diffusion of environmental policy innovations. Cornerstones of an analytical framework', *European Environment*, 15:2, 63–79.

Tews, Kerstin, Per-Olof Busch and Helge Jörgens (2003) 'The diffusion of new environmental policy instruments', *European Journal of Political Research*, 42:3, 569–600.

Tsebelis, George (2002) *Veto Players. How Political Institutions Work*. Princeton: Princeton University Press.

Unger, Brigitte and Frans van Waarden (1995) 'Introduction: an interdisciplinary approach to convergence', in Brigitte Unger and Frans van Waarden (eds.), *Convergence or Diversity? Internationalization and Economic Policy Response*. Aldershot: Avebury, 1–35.

Vogel, David (1986) *National Styles of Regulation. Environmental Policy in Great Britain and the United States*. Ithaca: Cornell University Press.

(1995) *Trading Up: Consumer and Environmental Regulation in the Global Economy*. Cambridge, MA: Harvard University Press.

(1997) 'Trading up and governing across: transnational governance and environmental protection', *Journal of European Public Policy*, 4:4, 556–71.

(2002) 'The Protestant ethic and the spirit of environmentalism: exploring the cultural roots of contemporary green politics', *Zeitschrift für Umweltpolitik und Umweltrecht*, 25:3, 297–322.

(2003) 'The hare and the tortoise revisited: the new politics of consumer and environmental regulation in Europe', *British Journal of Political Science*, 33:4, 557–80.

Walker, Jack L. (1969) 'The diffusion of innovations among the American states', *American Political Science Review*, 63:3, 880–99.

Wallace, David (1995) *Environmental Policy and Industrial Innovation. Strategies in Europe, the US and Japan*. London: Earthscan.

Weidner, Helmut (2002) 'Capacity-building for ecological modernization: lessons from cross-national research', *American Behavioral Scientist*, 45:9, 1340–68.

Weidner, Helmut and Martin Jänicke (eds.) (2002) *Capacity Building in National Environmental Policy. A Comparative Study of 17 Countries*. Berlin, Heidelberg and New York: Springer.

World Bank (2002) *World Development Indicators*. Washington, D.C.: World Bank (CD-ROM).

Zürn, Michael (2000) 'Democratic governance beyond the nation-state: the EU and other international institutions', *European Journal of International Relations*, 6:2, 183–221.

Zürn, Michael and Christian Joerges (eds.) (2005) *Law and Governance in Postnational Europe*. Cambridge: Cambridge University Press.

Index

Page number followed by 'g', 'n' or 't' indicates 'figure', 'note' or 'table' respectively.